湖南工学院校本级规划教材

湖南工学院校本级双语教学示范课程教材

战略管理

Strategic Management

康健 张平 唐欣 编著

Written and Edited by Kang Jian Zhang Ping Tang Xin

浙江工商大学出版社

ZHEJIANG GONGSHANG UNIVERSITY PRESS

图书在版编目(CIP)数据

战略管理 = Strategic Management / 康健，张平，唐欣编著. —杭州：浙江工商大学出版社，2016.2
ISBN 978-7-5178-1533-4

Ⅰ. ①战… Ⅱ. ①康… ②张… ③唐… Ⅲ. ①企业战略—战略管理 Ⅳ. ①F272

中国版本图书馆 CIP 数据核字(2016)第 008670 号

战略管理 Strategic Management

康健　张平　唐欣　编著

责任编辑　沈　娴　吴岳婷
封面设计　林朦朦
责任印制　包建辉
出版发行　浙江工商大学出版社
(杭州市教工路 198 号　邮政编码 310012)
(E-mail:zjgsupress@163.com)
(网址:http://www.zjgsupress.com)
电话:0571-88904980,88831806(传真)
排　　版　杭州朝曦图文设计有限公司
印　　刷　虎彩印艺股份有限公司
开　　本　787mm×1092mm　1/16
印　　张　11.75
字　　数　306 千
版 印 次　2016 年 2 月第 1 版　2016 年 2 月第 1 次印刷
书　　号　ISBN 978-7-5178-1533-4
定　　价　52.00 元

浙江工商大学出版社营销部邮购电话　0571-88904970

CONTENTS

Chapter 1 Introduction to Strategic Management ········ 1

1.1 Strategic Competitiveness ········ 1
1.2 The Global Economy ········ 3
1.3 Vision ········ 4
1.4 Mission ········ 4
1.5 Strategic Management Process ········ 5
1.6 Developing a Strategic Vision and Mission ········ 8
1.7 Setting Objectives ········ 10
1.8 Crafting a Strategy ········ 10
1.9 Implementing and Executing a Strategy ········ 12
1.10 Approaches to Performing the Strategy-Making Task ········ 13
1.11 Strategic Management Principle ········ 14

Chapter 2 The External Environment ········ 22

2.1 The General, Industry, and Competitor Environments ········ 24
2.2 External Environmental Analysis ········ 27
2.3 Scanning ········ 29
2.4 Monitoring ········ 30
2.5 Industry Environment Analysis ········ 30
2.6 Threat of New Entrants ········ 32
2.7 Bargaining Power of Buyers ········ 33

2.8 Threat of Substitute Products ······ 34
2.9 Strategic Groups ······ 35
2.10 Ethical Considerations ······ 36
2.11 Rivalry Among Competing Sellers ······ 38

Chapter 3 The Internal Environment ······ 42

3.1 Analyzing the Internal Organization ······ 42
3.2 Creating Value ······ 42
3.3 Resources, Capabilities, and Core Competencies ······ 44
3.4 Resources ······ 45
3.5 Tangible Resources ······ 45
3.6 Intangible Resources ······ 46
3.7 Capabilities ······ 48
3.8 Core Competencies ······ 49
3.9 The Four Criteria of Sustainable Competitive Advantage ······ 49
3.10 Value Chain Analysis ······ 50
3.11 Outsourcing ······ 58
3.12 Analyzing Driving Forces ······ 59

Chapter 4 Evaluating Resources and Competitive Capabilities ······ 64

4.1 A Model of Competitive Rivalry ······ 64
4.2 Competitor Analysis ······ 65
4.3 Resource Similarity ······ 66
4.4 Competitive Rivalry ······ 66
4.5 Strategic and Tactical Actions ······ 67
4.6 Competitive Dynamics ······ 68
4.7 Slow-Cycle Markets ······ 69
4.8 Fast-Cycle Markets ······ 69
4.9 Company Situation Analysis ······ 70
4.10 Typical Company Value Chain ······ 74

4.11 How Strong the Company's Competitive Position Is ······ 76

Chapter 5 Business-Level Strategies ······ 78

5.1 Customers: Their Relationship with Business-Level Strategies ······ 78
5.2 The Purpose of Business-Level Strategies ······ 78
5.3 Types of Business-Level Strategies ······ 81
5.4 Cost Leadership Strategies ······ 82
5.5 Differentiation Strategies ······ 84
5.6 Focus Strategies ······ 87
5.7 Focused Cost Leadership Strategies ······ 88
5.8 Competitive Risks of Focus Strategies ······ 89
5.9 Integrated Cost Leadership/Differentiation Strategies ······ 89
5.10 Levels of Diversification ······ 93
5.11 Low Levels of Diversification ······ 94
5.12 Reasons for Diversification ······ 94
5.13 Value-Creating Diversification: Related Constrained and Related Linked Diversification ······ 95

Chapter 6 Functional Strategies and Strategic Choices ······ 98

6.1 Operational Relatedness: Sharing Activities ······ 98
6.2 Market Power ······ 99
6.3 Simultaneous Operational Relatedness and Corporate Relatedness ······ 100
6.4 Value-Neutral Diversification: Incentives and Resources ······ 101
6.5 Resources and Diversification ······ 101
6.6 Value-Reducing Diversification: Managerial Motives to Diversify ······ 102
6.7 The Popularity of Merger and Acquisition Strategies ······ 103
6.8 Increased Market Power ······ 104
6.9 Cost of New Product Development and Increased Speed to Market ······ 104
6.10 Learning and Developing New Capabilities ······ 105
6.11 Managers Overly Focused on Acquisitions ······ 106

6.12 Three Basic Benefits of International Strategies …… 107
6.13 International Strategies …… 108
6.14 International Business-Level Strategies …… 108
6.15 Global Strategy …… 109
6.16 Acquisitions …… 109
6.17 Risk of Best-Cost Provider Strategies …… 113
6.18 Merger and Acquisition Strategies …… 115
6.19 Unbundling and Outsourcing Strategies …… 117
6.20 Offensive Strategies and Competitive Advantage …… 119
6.21 First-Mover Advantages …… 119

Chapter 7 Strategy Implementation …… 121

7.1 Implementing Internal Innovations …… 121
7.2 Facilitating Integration and Innovation …… 122
7.3 Innovation Through Cooperative Strategies …… 122
7.4 Organizational Structure and Controls …… 124
7.5 Functional Structure …… 126
7.6 The Role of Top-Level Managers …… 128
7.7 Top Management Teams …… 129
7.8 Managerial Succession …… 130
7.9 Sustaining an Effective Organizational Culture …… 130
7.10 Establishing Balanced Organizational Controls …… 131
7.11 Entrepreneurship and Entrepreneurial Opportunities …… 132
7.12 Innovation …… 133
7.13 Internal Innovation …… 134
7.14 Incremental and Radical Innovation …… 135
7.15 Autonomous Strategic Behavior …… 136
7.16 Why the World Economy Is Globalizing …… 137
7.17 Multi-domestic Strategy Maximizes Local Responsiveness …… 138
7.18 Locating Activities to Build a Global Competitive Advantage …… 140
7.19 What Profit Sanctuaries Are …… 141

7.20 Advantages and Disadvantages of the Four Strategies ······ 142
7.21 New Business Model for the Internet Economy ······ 142
7.22 Internet Strategies for Traditional Businesses ······ 145
7.23 Tailoring Strategy to Fit Specific Industry Situations ······ 146
7.24 Competitive Advantage in Diversified Companies ······ 153
7.25 Sales and Marketing Fits ······ 156
7.26 What Unrelated Diversification Is ······ 157
7.27 How Broadly a Company Should Diversify ······ 158
7.28 Turnaround Strategies ······ 161

Chapter 8 Strategic Evaluation and Control ······ 162

8.1 Product Diversification as an Example of an Agency Problem ······ 162
8.2 Ownership Concentration ······ 162
8.3 Enhancing the Effectiveness of the Board of Directors ······ 163
8.4 Evaluating the Strategy of Diversified Companies ······ 164
8.5 How Corporate Strategies Form ······ 168
8.6 Building Core Competencies and Competitive Capabilities ······ 169
8.7 What the Goals of the Strategy Implementing-Executing Process Are ······ 170
8.8 Key Traits to Building Core Competencies ······ 172
8.9 Instituting Best Practices and Installing Support Systems ······ 176
8.10 What Total Quality Management Is ······ 177
8.11 What Areas Information Systems Should Address ······ 179
8.12 Guidelines for Designing an Effective Compensation System ······ 180

后 记 ······ 182

Chapter 1 Introduction to Strategic Management

1.1 Strategic Competitiveness

A strategy of a corporation is a comprehensive plan stating how the corporation will achieve its mission and objectives. 战略是表明一个公司将如何实现使命和目标的综合性计划。

The study of strategic management therefore emphasizes the monitoring and evaluating of external opportunities and threats in light of a corporation's strengths and weaknesses in order to generate and implement a new strategic direction for an organization.

Strategic management is that set of managerial decisions and actions that determines the long-run performance of a corporation. It includes environmental scanning (both external and internal), strategy formulation (strategic planning), strategy implementation, and evaluation and control. 战略管理是决定公司长期绩效的一系列管理决策和行动。包括环境扫描(外部和内部)、战略制定(战略计划)、战略实施,以及评价和控制。

Strategic competitiveness is achieved when a firm successfully formulates and implements a value-creating strategy. A strategy is an integrated and coordinated set of commitments and actions designed to exploit core competencies and gain a competitive advantage. When choosing a strategy, firms make choice among competing alternatives as the pathway for deciding how they will pursue strategic competitiveness. In this sense, the chosen strategy indicates what the firm will do as well as what the firm will not do.

A firm has a competitive advantage when it implements a strategy that creates superior value for customers and that its competitors are unable to duplicate or find too costly to imitate. An organization can be confident that its strategy has resulted in one or more useful competitive advantages only after competitors' efforts to duplicate its strategy have ceased or failed. In addition, firms must understand that no competitive advantage is permanent. The speed with which competitors are able to acquire the skills needed to duplicate the benefits of a firm's value-creating strategy determines how long the competitive advantage will last.

Corporate strategy describe a company's overall direction in terms of its general attitude toward growth and the management of its various businesses and product lines. 企业战略描述了公司的总体方向,对其成长和管理的各种业务和产品线的总体方向。

Above-average returns are returns in excess of what an investor expects to earn from other investments with a similar amount of risk. Risk is an investor's uncertainty about the economic gains or losses that will result from a particular investor's uncertainty about the economic gains or losses that will result from a particular investment. The most successful companies learn how to effectively manage risk. Effectively managing risks reduces investors' uncertainty about the results of their investment. Returns are often measured in terms of accounting Figures, such as return on assets, return on equity, or return on sales. Alternatively, returns can be measured on the basis of stock market returns, such as monthly returns (the end-of-the-period stock price minus the beginning stock price, divided by the beginning stock price, yielding a percentage return). In smaller, new venture firms, returns are sometimes measured in terms of the amount and speed of growth rather than more traditional profitability measures because new ventures require time to earn acceptable returns (in the from of return on assets and so forth) on investors' investments.

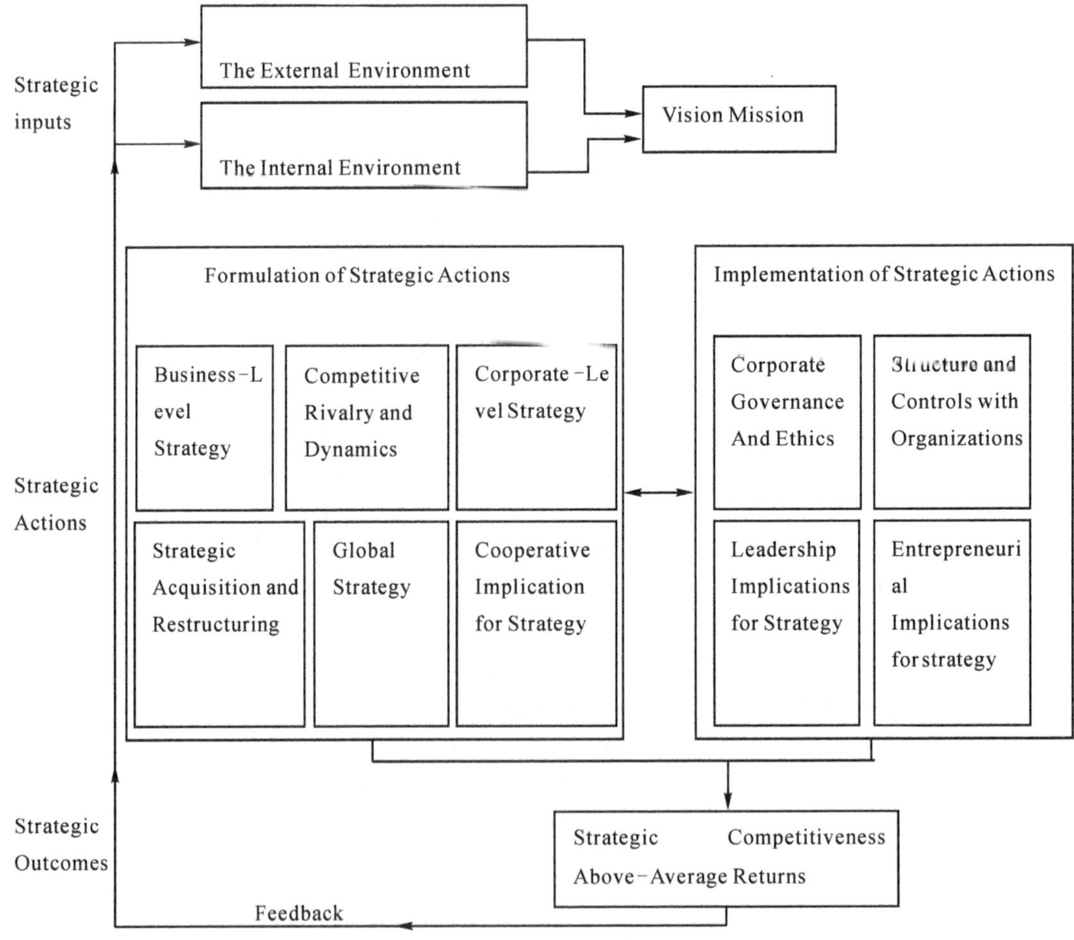

Figure 1.1

The typical business firm usually considers three types of strategy: corporate, business, and functional. 有代表性的公司经常把战略分为三种类型:公司战略、业务战略和职能战略。

Business strategy usually occurs at the business unit or product level, and it emphasizes improvement of the competitive position of a corporation's products or services in the specific industry or market segment served by that business unit. 业务战略经常发生在业务部门或产品层面,它强调的是一个公司在特定产业或细分市场中通过业务部门提供的服务带来的公司产品或服务中的竞争地位的提升。

Function strategy is the approach taken by a functional area, such as marketing or research and development, to achieve corporate and business unit objectives and strategies by maximizing resource productivity. 职能战略是为了公司和业务单位目标及战略,最大限度地提高资源生产率被企业功能领域,比如市场营销或研开和发展等划分的方法。

A hierarchy of strategy is the grouping of strategy types by level in the organization. 战略的层级是指根据组织的层级对战略类型进行的分组。

1.2 The Global Economy

A global economy is one in which goods, service, people, skills, and ideas move freely move freely across geographic borders. Relatively unfettered by artificial constraints, such as tariffs, the global economy significantly expands and complicates a firm's competitive environment.

1. Study the external environment, especially the industry environment.	**The External Environment** • The general environment • The industry environment • The competitor environment
	↓
2. Locate an industry with high potential for above average returns.	**An Attractive Industry** • An industry whose structural Characteristics suggest above-average returns
	↓
3. Identify the strategy called for by the attractive industry to earn above average return	**Strategy Formulation** • Selection of a strategy linked with above-average returns in a particular industry
	↓

4. Develop or acquire assets and skills needed to implement the strategy.

5. Use the firm's strengths(its developed or acquired assets and skills) to implement the strategy.

Assets and Skills
- Assets and skills required to implement a chosen strategy

↓

Strategy Implementation
- Selection of strategic actions linked with effective implementation of the chosen strategy

↓

Superior Returns
- Earning of above-average returns

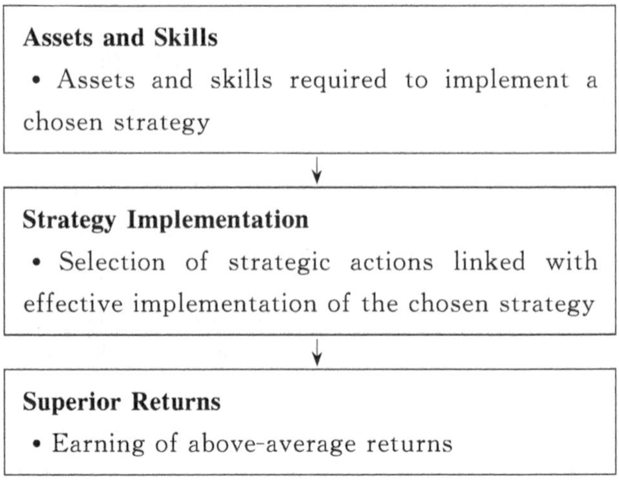

Figure 1.2

The strategic management model includes a feedback /learning process in which information from each element of the process is used to make possible adjustments to each of the previous elements of the process. 战略管理模型包括一个反馈/学习过程。在这个过程中,来自各个组成部分的信息对前一个过程中的组成部分进行调整。

1.3 Vision

Vision is a picture of what the firm wants to be and, in broad terms, what it wants to ultimately achieve. Thus, a vision statement articulates the ideal description of an organization and gives shape to its intended future. In other words, a vision statement points the firm in the direction of where it would like to be in the years to come. An effective vision stretches and challengers people as well. In her book about Steve Jobs, Apple's phenomenally successful CEO, Carmine Gallo argues that one of the reasons that Apple is so innovative was Jobs' vision for the company. She suggests that he thought bigger and differently than most people-She describes it as "putting a dent in the universe."To be innovative, she explains that one has differently about their products and customers-"sell dreams not products"-and differently about the story to "create great expectations." Steve Jobs passed away in October 2011. Apple will be challenged to remain highly innovative without him. Interestingly, many new entrepreneurs are highly optimistic when they develop their ventures.

1.4 Mission

The vision is the foundation for the firm's mission. A mission specifies the business or businesses in which the firm intends to compete and the customers it intends to serve. The firm's mission is more concrete than its vision. However, similar to the vision, a mission should establish a firm's individuality and should be inspiring and relevant to all stakeholders. Together, the vision and mission provide the foundation that the firm needs to choose and implement one or more strategies. The probability of forming an effective mission increases when employees have a strong sense of the ethical standards that guide their behaviors as they work to help the firm reach its vision. Thus, business ethics are a vital part of the firm's discussions to decide what it wants to become (its vision) as well as who it intends to serve and how it desires to serve those individuals and groups (its mission).

Examples: Mission and Vision Statements

Otis Elevator

Our mission: To provide any customer a means of moving people and things up, down, and sideways over short distances with higher reliability than any similar enterprise in the world.

Avis Rent-a-Car

Our business is renting cars. Our mission is total customer satisfaction.

Examples: Mission and Vision Statements (a unique grocery store chain)

Our mission: To give our customers the best food and beverage values that they can find anywhere and to provide them with their formation required for informed buying decisions. We provide these with a dedication to the highest quality of customer satisfaction delivered with a sense of warmth, friendliness, fun, individual pride, and company spirit.

An organization's mission is its purpose or the reason for its existence. It tells what the company is providing to society, such as housecleaning or manufacturing automobiles. A well-conceived mission statement defines the fundamental, unique purpose that sets a company apart from other firms of its type and identifies the scope of the company's operations in terms of products offered and markets served. 使命是组织的目的或存在的理由。一份完美构建的使命陈述诠释了根本而独特的目的,将企业与其他相同类型的公司区别开来,明确了公司产品(包括服务)的经营范围以及所面对的市场。

1.5 Strategic Management Process

The strategic management process is a rational approach firms use to achieve strategic competitiveness and earn above-average returns. Figure 1.1 also features the topics we examine in this book present the strategic management process to you.

This book is divided into three parts. We describe what firms do to analyze their external environment and internal organization. These analyses are completed to identify marketplace opportunities and threats in the external environment and to decide how to use the resources, capabilities, core competencies, and competitive advantages in the firm's internal organization to pursue opportunities and overcome threats. The analyses explained in compose the well-known SWOT analyses (strengths, weaknesses, opportunities, threats). With knowledge about its external environment and internal organization, the firm forms its strategy taking into account the firm's vision and mission.

The firm's strategic inputs provide the foundation for choosing one or more strategies and deciding how to implement them. As suggested in Figure1. 1 by the horizontal arrow linking the two types of implement them. As suggested in Figure 1. 1 by the horizontal arrow linking the two types of strategic actions, formulation and implementation must be simultaneously integrated to successfully use the strategic management process. Integration happens as decision makers think about implementation issues when choosing strategies and as they think about possible changes to the firm's strategies while implementing a currently chosen strategy.

We discuss the different strategies firms may choose to use. First, we examine business-level strategies. A business-level strategy describes the actions a firm takes to exploit its competitive advantage over rivals. A company competing in a single product market (e. g. , a locally owned grocery store operating in only one location) has but one business-level strategy while a diversified firm competing in only one location) has but one business-level strategy while a diversified firm competing in multiple product markets (e. g. , General Electric) forms a business-level strategy for each of its businesses. Then we describe the actions and reactions that occur among firms in marketplace competition. Competitors typically respond to and try to anticipate each other's actions. The dynamics of competition affect the strategies firms choose as well as how they try to implement the chosen strategic.

For the diversified firm, corporate-level strategy is concerned with determining the businesses. Other topics vital to strategy formulation, particularly in the diversified company, include acquiring other businesses and, as appropriate, restructuring the firm's portfolio of businesses and selecting an international strategy. With cooperative strategies, firms form a partnership to share their resources and capabilities in order to develop a competitive advantage. Cooperative strategies are becoming increasingly important as firms seek ways to compete in the global economy's array of different markets.

To examine actions taken to implement strategies, we consider several topics in the book. First, we examine the different mechanisms used to govern firms. With demands for improved corporate governance being voiced by many stake-holders in the current business environment, organizations are challenged to learn how to simultaneously satisfy their stakeholders' different interests. Finally, the organizational structure and actions needed to control a firm's operations, the patterns of strategic leadership appropriate for today's firms and competitive environments, and strategic entrepreneurship as a path to continuous innovation are addressed.

It is important to emphasize that primarily because they are related to how a firm interacts with its stakeholders, almost all strategic management process decisions have ethical dimensions. Organizational ethics are revealed by an organization's culture; that is to say, a firm's decisions are a product of the core values that are shared by most or all of a company's managers and employees. Especially in the turbulent and often ambiguous competitive landscape of the twenty-first century, those making decisions as a part of the strategic management process are challenged to recognize that their decisions affect capital market, product market, and organizational stakeholders differently and to regularly evaluate the ethical implications of their decisions. Decision makers failing to recognize these realities accept the risk of placing their firm at a competitive disadvantage with regard to ethical business practices.

As you will discover, the strategic management process examined in this book calls for disciplined approaches to serve as the foundation for developing a competitive advantage. These approaches provide the pathway through which firms will be able to achieve strategic competitiveness and earn above-average returns. Mastery of this strategic management process will effectively serve you, our readers, and the organizations for which you will choose to work.

Strategic management within a firm generally evolves through four sequential phases of development: 战略管理过程在公司内部的演变分为四个连续阶段:

Phase 1. Basic financial planning: Seeking better operational control by trying to meet annual budgets. 第 1 阶段 基本财务规划:寻求更好的操作控制以满足年度预算。

Phase 2. Forecast-based planning: Seeking more effective planning for growth by trying to predict the future beyond the next year. 第 2 阶段 以预测为基础的规划:寻求更有效的增长计划,试图预测未来。

Phase 3. Externally oriented strategic planning: Seeking increased responsiveness to markets and competition by trying to think strategically. 第 3 阶段 外部导向型战略规划:寻求增加对市场和竞争的反应,试图认为战略。

Phase 4. Strategic management: Seeking a competitive advantage by considering implementation and evaluation and control when formulating a strategy. 第 4 阶段 战略管理:在制定战略时,考虑实施、评估和控制,寻求竞争优势。

Strategic management consists of four basic elements: (1) environmental scanning,

(2) strategy formulation, (3) strategy implementation, and (4) evaluation and control. 战略管理包括四个基本组成部分:(1)环境扫描;(2)战略制定;(3)战略实施;(4)评价和控制。

1.6 Developing a Strategic Vision and Mission

Corrective Adjustments. Why Strategic Management Is a Process. Who Performs the Tasks of Strategy? Benefits of "Thinking and Managing Strategically".

Thinking Strategically. The Three Big Strategic Questions: 1. Where are we now? 2. Where do we want to go? (Business to be in and market positions to stake out? Buyer needs and groups to serve? Outcomes to achieve?) 3. How do we get there?

What is Strategy? A company's strategy consists of the set of competitive moves and business approaches that management is employing to run the company Strategy is management's "game plan" to Attract and please customers Stake out a market position Conduct operations Compete successfully Achieve organizational objectives.

What is a Business Model? A company's business model addresses "How do we make money in this business? "Is the strategy that management is pursuing capable of delivering good bottom-line results? Do the revenue-cost-profit economics of the company's strategy make good business sense? Look at the revenue streams the strategy is expected to produce Look at the associated cost structure and potential profit margins Do the resulting earnings streams and ROI indicate the strategy makes sense and that the company has a viable business model?

Strategy vs. Business Model: What is the Difference? Strategy—Deals with a company's competitive initiative sand business approaches Business Model—Concerns whether the revenues and costs flowing from the strategy demonstrate that the business can be amply profitable and viable Strategy Business Model.

Microsoft's Business Model Employ a cadre of highly skilled programmers to develop proprietary code; keep source code hidden from users Employ a cadre of highly skilled programmers to develop proprietary code; keep source code hidden from users Sell resulting operating system and software packages to PC makers and users at relatively attractive prices and achieve large unit sales Sell resulting operating system and software packages to PC makers and users at relatively attractive prices and achieve large unit sales Most costs arise in developing the software; variable costs are small—once breakeven volume is reached, revenues from additional sales are almost pure profit. Most costs arise in developing the software; variable costs are small—once breakeven volume is reached, revenues from additional sales are almost pure profit.

Redhat Linux's Business Model Use volunteer programmers to create the software; make source code open and available to all users Use volunteer programmers to create the software; make source code open and available to all users Give Linux operating system away free of charge to those who download it(charge a small fee to users who want a copy on CD)Give Linux operating system away free of charge to those who download it(charge a small fee to users who want a copy on CD)Make money by employing a cadre of technical support personnel who provide technical support to users for a fee Make money by employing a cadre of technical support personnel who provide technical support to users for a fee.

Why Are Strategies Needed? To proactively shape how a company's business will be conducted To mold their dependent actions and decisions of managers and employees into coordinated, company-wide game plan.

Strategic Management Concept Competent execution of a well-conceived strategy is the best test of managerial excellence and a proven recipe for organizational success! Good Strategy +Good Strategy Execution=Good Management.

Developing a Strategic Vision First Task of Strategic Management Involves thinking strategically about Firm's future business plans Where to "go" Tasks include Creating a roadmap of the future Deciding future business position to stake out Providing long-term direction Giving firm a strong identity

Characteristics of a Strategic Vision A roadmap of a company's future Future technology-product-customer focus Geographic and product markets to pursue Capabilities to be developed Kind of company management is trying to create.

Missions vs. Strategic Visions A strategic vision concerns a firm's future business path—"where we are going" Markets to be pursued Future technology -product-customer focus Kind of company that management is trying to create A mission statement focuses on current business activities—"who we are and what we do" Current product and service offerings Customer needs being served Technological and business capabilities.

Why is a Strategic Vision Important? A managerial imperative exists to look beyond today and think strategically about Impact of new technologies How customer needs and expectations are changing What it will take to outrun competitors Which promising market opportunities ought to be aggressively pursued External and internal factors driving what accompany needs to do to prepare for the future?

A policy is a broad guideline for decision making that links the formulation of strategy with its implementation. Companies use policies to make sure that employees throughout the firm make decisions and take actions that support the corporation's mission, objectives, and strategies. 政策是连接战略制定和实施的决策的广泛纲要。公司利用政策确保全体员工所做出的决策以及采取的行动支持公司的使命、目标和战略。

1.7 Setting Objectives

Types of Objectives Required Financial Objectives Strategic Objectives Outcomes focused on improving financial performance Outcomes focused on improving long-term, competitive business position.

Examples of Financial Objectives Grow earnings per share 15% annually Boost annual return on investment (or EVA) from 15% to 20% within three years Increase annual dividends per share to stockholders by 5% each year Strive for stock price appreciation equal to or above the S&P 500 average Maintain a positive cash flow every year Achieve and maintain a AA bond rating

Examples of Strategic Objectives Increase firm's market share Overtake key rivals on quality or customer service or product performance Attain lower overall costs than rivals Boost firm's reputation with customers Attain stronger foothold in international markets Achieve technological superiority Become leader in new product introductions Capture attractive growth opportunities

Examples: Strategic Objectives Banc One Corporation To be one of the top three banking companies in terms of market share in all significant markets we serve. Domino's Pizza To safely deliver a hot, quality pizza in 30 minutes or less at a fair price and a reasonable profit.

Objectives are the end results of planned activity. They state what is to be accomplished by when and should be quantified if possible. 短期目标是计划活动的最终结果。短期目标通常明确了各项任务完成的时间和结果，如果可能的话，一般采取量化的形式。

The term goal is often confused with objective. In contrast to an objective, a goal is an open-ended statement of what one wishes to accomplish with no quantification of what is to be achieved and no time frame for completion. 长期目标经常与短期目标混淆。与短期目标相比，长期目标是一种开放式的目标，它没有量化和完成时间的限制。

1.8 Crafting a Strategy

Strategy involves determining whether to Concentrate on a single business or several businesses (diversification) Cater to a broad range of customers or focus on a particular niche Develop a wide or narrow product line Pursue a competitive advantage based on Low cost or Product superiority or Unique organizational capabilities.

Crafting a Strategy Involves deciding how to Respond to changing buyer preferences Respond to new market conditions Grow the business over the long-term The How's That

Define a Firm's Strategy. How to grow the business How to please customers How to outcompete rivals. How to respond to changing market conditions. How to manage each functional piece of the business and develop needed organizational capabilities.

Strategic Priorities of McDonald's Continued growth Providing exceptional customer care. Remaining an efficient and quality producer. Developing people at every organizational level. Sharing best practices among all units. Reinventing the fast food concept by fostering innovation in the menu, facilities, marketing, operation and technology.

Core Elements of McDonald's Strategy. Add 1750 restaurants annually Promote frequent customer visits via attractive menu items, low-price specials, and Extra Value Meals. Be highly selective in granting franchises. Locate on sites offering convenience to customers and profitable growth potential. Focus on limited menu and consistent quality. Careful attention to store efficiency. Extensive advertising and use of Mc prefix. Hire courteous personnel pay an equitable wage provide good training.

Crafting Strategy is an Exercise in Entrepreneurship. Strategy-making is a market-driven and customer-driven activity that involves Keen eye for spotting emerging market opportunities. Keen observation of customer needs. Innovation and creativity Prudent risk-taking Strong sense of how to grow and strengthen business

Characteristics of Managers with Good Entrepreneurial Skills Boldly pursue new strategic opportunities. Emphasize out-innovating the competition Lead the way to improve firm performance Willing to be a first-mover and take risks Respond quickly and opportunistically to new developments Devise trail blazing strategies

Why Do Strategies Evolve? There is always an ongoing need to react to Shifting market conditions Fresh moves of competitors. New technologies Evolving customer preferences Political and regulatory changes New windows of opportunity Crisis situations.

Strategic flexibility demands a long-term commitment to the development and nurturing of critical resources. It also demands that the company becomes a learning organization: an organization skilled at creating, acquiring, and transferring knowledge and at modifying its behavior to reflect new knowledge and insights. 战略灵活性需要公司长期努力开发和培育关键性资源，还需要公司成为一个学习型组织——善于创造、获取和转换知识，并不断根据新知识和新见解调整自身行为。

Strategy formulation is the development of long-range plans for the effective management of environmental opportunities and threats, in light of corporate strengths and weaknesses. 战略制定是指基于公司自身的优势和劣势，为有效管理环境中存在的机会和威胁制定企业的长期计划。

1.9 Implementing and Executing a Strategy

What is a Strategic Plan? Where firm is headed—Strategic vision and business mission. Action approaches to achieve targeted results—A comprehensive strategy Short and long term performance targets—Strategic and financial objectives

Strategy Implementation and Execution Strategy implementation and execution is an action-oriented, "make-it-happen" process involving people management, developing competencies and capabilities, budgeting, policy-making, motivating, culture-building and leadership.

What Does Strategy Implementation and Execution Include? Building a capable organization. Allocating resources to strategy-critical activities Establishing strategy-supportive policies Motivating people to pursue the target objectives Tying rewards to achievement of results Creating a strategy-supportive corporate culture Installing needed information, communication, and operating systems. Instituting best practices and programs for continuous improvement. Exerting the leadership necessary to drive the process forward and keep improving.

Strategy implementation is the process by which strategies and policies are put into action through the development of programs, budgets, and procedures. 战略实施是通过开发各种方案、预算和流程,将战略和政策付诸行动的过程。

Sometimes referred to as operational planning, strategy implementation often involves day-to-day decisions in resource allocation. 战略实施有时称为运营计划,通常涉及资源分配的日常决策。

Monitoring, Evaluating and Taking Corrective Actions as Needed. The tasks of crafting, implementing, and executing a strategy are not a one-time exercise Customer needs and competitive conditions change. New opportunities appear; technology advances; any number of other outside developments occur. One or more aspects of executing the strategy may not be going well New managers with different ideas take over Organizational learning occurs All these trigger the need for corrective actions and adjustments Fifth Task of Strategic Management

Characteristics of the Strategic Management Process. Need to do the five tasks never goes away Boundaries among the five tasks are blurry Strategizing is not isolated from other managerial activities Time required comes in lumps and spurts. The big challenge : To get the best strategy-supportive performance from employees, perfect current strategy, and improve strategy execution.

A program is a statement of the activities or steps needed to accomplish a single-use plan. It makes the strategy action oriented. 方案是完成某个单一用途计划所必需的各种活

动或步骤的详细说明，有助于使战略以行动为导向。

Research has revealed that organizations that engage in strategic management generally outperform those that do not. The attainment of an appropriate match or "fit" between an organization's environment and its strategy, structure, and processes has positive effects on the organization's performance. 研究表明，进行战略管理的组织，其绩效通常优于那些没有进行战略管理的组织。组织的战略、结构和流程与环境之间的匹配或"适合"，对于实现预期绩效有积极的影响。

1.10 Approaches to Performing the Strategy-Making Task

Chief Architect Manager personally functions as chief strategist Delegate-It -to-Down-the-Line Managers Manager delegates some strategy-making responsibility to subordinates in charge of key organizational units. Collaborative Team Manager enlists assistance and advice of key subordinates in hammering out a consensus strategy Corporate Entrepreneur Manager encourages subordinates to develop and champion proposals for new ventures

Strategic Role of a Board of Directors Critically appraise and ultimately approve strategic action plans. Evaluate strategic leadership skills of the CEO and candidates to succeed the CEO,

Strategic Management Principle. A board of director's role in the strategic management process is to critically appraise and ultimately approve strategic action plans and to evaluate the strategic leadership skills of the CEO and others in line to succeed the incumbent CEO.

Benefits of "Strategic Thinking" and a" Strategic Approach" to Managing Guides entire firm regarding "what it is we are trying to do and to achieve" Makes managers more alert to "winds of change, new opportunities, and threatening developments Unifies numerous strategy-related decisions and organizational efforts. Creates a proactive atmosphere. Promotes development of an evolving business model focused on bottom-line success Provides basis for evaluating competing budget requests.

Environmental scanning is the monitoring, evaluating, and disseminating of information from the external and internal environments to key people within the corporation. 环境扫描是指监测和评估公司内外部环境，并向内部重要成员传递信息的过程。

A budget is a statement of a corporation's programs in dollar terms. Used in planning and control, it lists the detailed cost of each program. 预算是以货币计量的财务报表形式阐述公司的方案。预算应用于计划和控制领域，罗列出每个项目的详细成本。

According to Henry Mintzberg, the most typical strategic decision making modes are entrepreneurial, adaptive, and planning. 根据亨利·明茨伯格的研究，最典型的战略决策

模式包括企业家模式、适应性模式和规划模式。

Entrepreneurial mode: In this mode of strategic decision making, the strategy is developed by one powerful individual. 企业家模式：在这种战略决策模式中，战略是被一种强有力的个体所推动的。

Adaptive mode: Sometimes referred to as "muddling through," this decision making mode is characterized by reactive solutions to existing problems, rather than a proactive search for new opportunities. 适应性模式：有时被称为"得过且过"，这种决策模式以反应存在的问题为解决方案为特征，而不是对新的机会做积极研究。

Planning mode: This decision-making mode involves the systematic gathering of appropriate information for situation analysis, the generation of feasible alternative strategies, and the rational selection of the most appropriate strategy. 规划模式：这一决策模式包括对形势分析的系统收集、可行的替代战略的产生以及对最合适战略的合理选择。

Good arguments can be made for using either the entrepreneurial or adaptive modes or planning mode in certain situations. 在某些特定情况下，无论使用企业家模式还是适应性模式或规划模式，都有很好的理由。

The planning mode includes the basic elements of the strategic management process, is a more rational and thus better way of making strategic decisions. 规划模式包括战略管理过程的基本组成部分，是更加理性，也是更好的战略决策方式。

1.11 Strategic Management Principle

Effective strategy-making begins with a vision of where the organization needs to head! Example: John Deere's Strategic Vision Who Are We? John Deere has grown and prospered through a long-standing partnership with the world's most productive farmers. Today, John Deere is a global company with several equipment operations and complementary service businesses. These businesses are closely interrelated, providing the company with significant growth opportunities and other synergistic benefits.

Procedures, sometimes termed standard operating procedures, are a system of sequential steps or techniques that describe in detail how a particular task or job is to be done. They typically detail the various activities that must be carried out for completion of a corporation's program. 流程有时称为标准作业流程，是一个连续的步骤或技术的系统，详细描述了如何完成一项特定任务或工作。流程通常必须详细描述完成公司方案所必需的各种活动。

Evaluation and control is the process by which corporate activities and performance results are monitored so that actual performance can be compared with desired performance. 评价和控制是指监控公司各种活动和绩效的结果，从而保证实际绩效与期望绩效之间具有可比性的过程。

Example: John Deere's Strategic Vision Where Are We Going? Deere is committed to providing genuine evaluate to the company's stakeholders. In support of that commitment, Deere aspires to: Grow and pursue leadership positions in each of our businesses. Extend our preeminent leadership position in the agricultural equipment market worldwide. Create new opportunities to leverage the John Deere brand globally.

Example: John Deere's Strategic Vision How Will We Get There? By pursuing the broader corporate goals of profitable growth and continuous improvement, each of the company's businesses is expected to: Achieve world-class performance by attaining a strong competitive position in target markets. Exceed customer expectations for quality and value. Earn in excess of the cost of capital over a business cycle.

Example: John Deere's Strategic Vision How Will We Get There? By growing profitably and continuously improving, each of the company's businesses will benefit from and contribute to Deere's unique intangible assets: Our distinguished brand. Our heritage of integrity and team work. Our advanced skills. The special relationships that have long existed between the company and our employees, customers, dealers and other business partners around the world.

Example: John Deere's Strategic Vision. How Will We Measure Our Performance? Each business will make a positive contribution to the corporation's objectives in the pursuit of creating genuine value for our stakeholders. Our "scorecard" includes: Human Resources—employee satisfaction, training Customer Focus—loyalty, market leadership Business Processes—productivity, quality, cost, environment Business Results—return on assets, sales growth.

Characteristics of a Mission Statement. Defines current business activities Highlights boundaries of current business Conveys Who we are, What we do, and Where we are now Company specific, not generic—so as to give a company its own identity. A company's mission is not to make a profit! The real mission is always—"What will we do to make a profit? "

Defining a Company's Business. A good business definition incorporates three factors Customer needs—What is being satisfied Customer groups—Who is being satisfied Technologies and competencies employed—How value is delivered to customers to satisfy their needs.

The distinguishing characteristic of strategic management is its emphasis on strategic decision making. 战略管理的显著特征是强调战略决策。

Unlike many other decisions, strategic decision deal with the long-run future of the entire organization and have three characteristics: Rare, Consequential, Directive. 不同于其他决策,战略决策面对的是整个组织的未来,主要有三个特征:稀缺性、重要性、指导性。

Business Mission: Cardinal Health Cardinal Health is a leading provider of services supporting health care worldwide. The company offers a broad array of services for health-care providers and manufacturers to help them improve the efficiency and quality of health care. These services include pharmaceutical distribution, health-care product manufacturing and distribution, drug delivery systems development... retail pharmacy franchising, and health-care information systems development.

Business Mission: JDS Uniphase is the leading provider of advanced fiber optic components and modules. These products are sold to the world's leading telecommunications and cable television system providers... Our products perform both optical-only functions and optoelectronic functions within fiber option networks. Our products include semiconductor lasers, and isolators for fiber optic applications. In addition, we design, manufacture, and market laser subsystems for a broad range of OEM applications.

Business Mission: Russell Corp. Russell Corporation is a vertically integrated international designer, manufacturer, and marketer of athletic uniforms,..., and a comprehensive line of light weight, yarn-dyed woven fabrics. The Company's manufacturing operations include the entire process of converting raw fibers into finished apparel and fabrics. Products are marketed to sporting goods dealers, department and specialty stores, mass merchandisers, ..., and other apparel manufacturers.

Broad or Narrow Mission Statements? Narrow enough to specify real arena of interest Serve as Boundary for what to do and not do Beacon of where top management intends to take firm Diversified companies have broader business definitions than single-business enterprises.

Definitions: Broad vs. Narrow Scope Broad Definition Furniture Telecommunications Beverages Global mail delivery Travel &tourism Narrow Definition Wrought-iron lawn furniture. Long-distance telephone service. Soft drinks Overnight package delivery Caribbean cruises

Business Mission: The McGraw Hill Companies (a diversified firm) The McGraw-Hill Companies is a global publishing, financial, information and media services company with such renowned brands as Standard&Poor's, Business Week, and McGraw-Hill educational and professional materials. The Company provides information via various media platforms: books, magazines and newsletters; on-line; via television, satellite and FM sideband broadcast; and software, videotape, facsimile and CD-ROM products. The Company now creates more than 90% of its information on digital platforms and its business units are represented on more than 75 Web sites.

Business Mission: FDX Corporation(a diversified firm)FDX is composed of a powerful family of companies: FedEx, RPS, Viking Freight, FDX Global Logistics and Roberts Express. These companies offer logistics and distribution solutions on a regional, national and global scale: fast, reliable, time-definite express delivery; ... expedited same-day delivery; ... ; and integrated information and logistics solutions With all this expertise under one umbrella, the FDX companies can provide businesses with the competitive advantage they need by providing streamlined solutions that are on the cutting edge of technology.

Example: Mission Statement The Gillette Company Our mission is to achieve or enhance clear leadership, worldwide, in the existing or new core consumer product categories in which we choose to compete. Current core categories are: Male grooming products-blades and razors, electric shavers, shaving preparations and deodorants... Female grooming products-wet shaving products, hair removal and hair care appliances and deodorants... Alkaline and specialty batteries and cells. Writing instruments and correction products. Certain areas of the oral care market- toothbrushes... Selected areas of the high-quality small household appliance business-coffeemakers.

Mission Statements for Functional Departments Spotlights department's Role and scope of activities Direction which department needs to pursue Contribution to firm's overall mission.

Mission Statements of Functional Departments HUMAN RESOURCES To contribute to organizational success by developing effective leaders, high performance teams, and maximizing the potential of individuals. CORPORATE SECURITY to provide services for the protection of corporate personnel and assets through preventive measures and investigations.

Questions to Address in Developing a Strategic Vision1. What changes are occurring in the market arena(s) where we operate and what implications do these changes have for our future direction? 2. What new or different customer needs should we be moving to satisfy? 3. What new or different buyer segments should we be concentrating on? 4. What new geographic or product markets should we be pursuing? 5. What should the company's business makeup look like in 5 years? 6. What kind of company should we be trying to become?

Entrepreneurial Challenges in Forming a Strategic Vision How to creatively prepare a company for the future How to keep the company responsive to Evolving customer needs Competitive pressures. New technologies New market opportunities Growing or shrinking opportunities.

Intel's "Strategic Inflection points" prior to mid-1980s focused on memory chips. It abandoned memory chip business and became a preeminent supplier of microprocessors to PC industry. Thus, it made PC a central appliance in workplace and home and became the undisputed leader in driving PC technology forward. In 1998, it shifted focus from PC technology to becoming the preeminent building block supplier to the Internet economy.

Communicating the Vision. An exciting, inspirational vision Challenges and motivates workforce Arouses strong sense of organizational purpose Induces employee buy-in Galvanizes people to live the business

Managerial Value of a Well-Conceived Strategic Vision and Mission Crystallizes long-term direction. Reduces risk of rudderless decision-making Conveys organizational purpose and identity Keeps direction-related actions of lower-level managers on common path Helps organization prepare for the future.

Establishing Objectives Second Direction-Setting Task Represent commitment to achieve specific performance targets by a certain time Should be stated in quantifiable terms and contain a deadline for achievement Spell-out how much of what kind of performance by when.

Purpose of Objective-Setting Substitutes results-oriented decision-making for aimlessness over what to accomplish. Provides a set of benchmarks for judging organizational performance.

Two Types of Objectives Are Required Financial Objectives Strategic Objectives Outcomes that improve firm's financial performance. Outcomes that strengthen a firm's competitiveness and long-term market position.

Example: Corporate Objectives To make all our companies leaders in their industries in quality while exceeding customer expectations. To achieve a 50% share of the U. S. beer market. To establish and maintain a dominant leadership position in the international beer market. To provide all our employees with challenging and rewarding work, ..., and opportunities for personal development, advancement, and competitive compensation. To provide our shareholders with superior returns by achieving double-digit annual earnings per share growth, Anheuser-Busch(strategic &financial objectives).

Example: Corporate Objectives Exodus Communications (strategic objectives) Extend our market leadership and position Exodus as the leading brand name in the category. Enhance our systems and network management and Internet technology services. Accelerate our domestic and international growth. Leverage our technical expertise to address new market opportunities in e-commerce.

Strategic or Financial Objectives—Which Take Precedence? Pressures for better short-term financial performance become pronounced when Firm is struggling financially Resource commitments for new strategic initiatives may hurt bottom-line for several years. Proposed strategic moves are risky. Otherwise strategic objectives merit top priority—a firm that consistently passes up opportunities to strengthen its long-term competitive position. Risks diluting its competitiveness Risks losing momentum in its markets. Hurts its ability to fend off rivals' challenges.

Strategic Management Principle. Building a stronger long-term competitive position benefits shareholders more lastingly than improving short-term profitability!

Concept of Strategic Intent. A company exhibits strategic intent when it relentlessly pursues an ambitious strategic objective and concentrates its competitive actions and energies on achieving that objective!

Characteristics of Strategic Intent Indicates firm's intent to stake out a particular position over the long-term. Involves establishing a BHAG-"big, hairy, audacious goal" Signals relentless commitment to winning.

Short-Range Versus Long-Range Objectives Short-Range objectives. Targets to be achieved soon. Serve as stair steps for reaching long-range performance. Long-Range objectives Targets to be achieved within3 to 5 years Prompt actions now that wil permit reaching targeted long-range performance later.

Objectives Are Needed at All Levels Objective-setting process is top-down, not bottom-up! 1. First, establish organization-wide objectives and performance targets. Next, set business and product line objectives. Then, establish functional and departmental objectives4. Individual objectives are established last.

Strategic Management Principle Objective-setting needs to be more of atop-down than a bottom-up process in order to guide lower-level managers and organizational units toward outcomes that support the achievement of overall business and company objectives.

Crafting a Strategy Third Direction-Setting Task An organization's strategy deals with How to make the strategic vision a reality and achieve target objectives. The game plan for Pleasing customers Conducting operations Building a sustainable competitive advantage. Strategy constitutes management's business model for producing good profitability.

Strategizing Involves HOW to... Achieve performance targets Out-compete rivals and achieve a sustainable competitive advantage Respond to changing market conditions and new customer requirements. Make the strategic vision a reality Our game plan for running the company will be. Characteristics of Strategy-Making Strategy is action-oriented Strategy evolves over time Strategy-making is an ever-ending, ongoing task.

Rule-Breaking Strategies Challenge fundamental conventions by Reconceiving a product or service(Creating a single-use disposable camera) Redefining the marketplace (Detouring retailers by selling online at the company's website) Redrawing industry boundaries(Getting credit cards from Shell Oil or General Motors or AOL).

Tasks of Corporate Strategy Moves to achieve diversification. Actions to boost performance of individual businesses Capturing valuable cross-business strategic fits that result in 1 + 1 = 3 effects! Establishing investment priorities and steering corporate resources into the most attractive businesses

What Business Strategy Involves Forming responses to changes in industry and competitive conditions, buyer needs and preferences, economy, regulations, etc. Crafting competitive moves to produce sustainable competitive advantage. Building competitively valuable competencies and capabilities. Uniting strategic initiatives of functional areas Addressing strategic issues facing the company.

Functional Strategies Game plan for a strategically-relevant function activity, or business process. Details how key activities will be managed Provide support for business strategy Specify how functional objectives are to be achieved.

Operating Strategies Concern narrower strategies for managing grassroots activities and strategically-relevant operating units. Add detail to business and functional strategies.

Example: Operating Strategy Improving Delivery &Order-Filling Manufacturer of plumbing equipment emphasizes quick delivery and accurate order-filling ask its customer service approach. Warehouse manager took following approaches: Inventory stocking strategy allowing 99%of all orders to be completely filled without backordering any item Staffing strategy of maintaining workforce capability to ship any order within 24 hours.

Example: Operating Strategy Boosting Worker Productivity. To boost productivity by 10%, managers of firm with low-price, high-volume strategy take following actions: Recruitment manager develops selection process designed to weed out all but best-qualified candidates. Information systems manager devises way to use technology to boost productivity of office workers. Compensation manager devises improved incentive compensation plan Purchasing manager obtains new efficiency -increasing tools and equipment.

Uniting the Company's Strategy-Making Effort. A company's strategy is a collection of strategies and initiatives being acted on by managers at various organizational levels. Separate levels of strategy must be unified into a cohesive, company-wide action plan Pieces of strategy should fit together like the pieces of a puzzle.

What Do We Mean by "Corporate Social Responsibility? " Conducting company activities within bounds of what is considered ethical and in public interest. Responding positively to emerging societal priorities and expectations. Demonstrating willingness to take need education ahead of regulatory confrontation. Balancing stockholder interests against larger interest of society as a whole Being a"good citizen" in community.

Competitive Conditions and Industry Attractiveness. A company's strategy has to be responsive to Fresh moves of rival competitors Changes in industry' spruce-cost-profit economics. Shifting buyer needs and expectations. New technological developments Pace of market growth.

Strategic Management Principle. A company's strategy can't produce real market success unless it is well-matched to industry and competitive conditions! Company Opportunities and Threats For strategy to be successful, it has to Be well matched to capturing a company's best opportunities. And help counteract threats to the company's well-being.

Company Strengths, Competencies, and Competitive Capabilities A company must have or be able to acquire the resources, competencies, and competitive capabilities needed to execute the chosen strategy. Resource deficiencies, gaps in skills, and weaknesses in competitive position make pursuit of certain strategies risky or altogether unwise.

Strategic Management Principle A company's strategy ought to be grounded in its resource strengths and in what it is good at doing (its competencies and competitive capabilities); it is perilous to discount the competitive liabilities of company's resource deficiencies and skills gaps.

Ambitions, Philosophies, and Ethics of Key Executives Managers generally stamp strategies they craft with their own personal. Ambitions Values Business philosophies Attitudes toward risk Ethical belief.

Shared Values and Company Culture Values and culture often shape the strategic moves a company will Consider Reject. It is generally unwise for a company to undertake strategic moves which conflict with Its culture Values widely shared by managers and employees.

Hewlett-Packard's Basic Values: "The HP Way" Sharing firm's success with employees Showing trust and respect for employees. Providing customers with products or services of the greatest value. Being genuinely interested in providing customers with effective solutions to their problems. Making profit a high stockholder priority. Avoiding use of long-term debt to finance growth Individual initiative, creativity, &teamwork Being a good corporate citizen

Linking Strategy With Ethics Ethical and moral standards go beyond Prohibitions of law and Language of "thou shaft not" Ethical and moral standards involve Issues of duty and Language of "should and should not do".

A Firm's Ethical Responsibilities to Its Stakeholders Owners/ shareholders - Rightfully expect some form of return on their investment. Owners/ shareholders - Rightfully expect some form of return on their investment Employees-Rightfully expect respect for their worth and devoting their energies to firm Employees-Rightfully expect respect for their worth and devoting their energies to firm Customers-Rightfully expect a seller to provide them with a reliable, safe product or service. Customers-Rightfully expect a seller to provide them with a reliable, safe product or service. Suppliers-Rightfully expect to have an equitable relationship with firms they supply. Community-Rightfully expect businesses to be good citizens in their community.

Chapter 2 The External Environment

Things are always different—the art is figuring out which differences matter.

What Is Situation Analysis? Two considerations Company's external or macro-environment Industry and competitive conditions Company's internal or micro-environment Competencies, capabilities, resource strengths and weaknesses, and competitiveness

Environmental scanning is the monitoring, evaluating, and disseminating of information from the external and internal environments to key people within the corporation. 环境扫描是监测、评估内外部环境，并将这些信息传达给公司内部关键人物的过程。

Strategic Thinking and Analysis Leads to Good Strategic Choices1. Industry's dominant economic traits. Nature of competition & strength of competitive forces. Drivers of industry change. Competitive position of rivals. Strategic moves of rivals. Key success factors. Conclusions about industry attractiveness. Assess Industry &Competitive Conditions. Assessment of company's present strategy. Resource strengths and weaknesses, market opportunities, and external threats. Company's costs compared to rivals. Strength of company's competitive position. Strategic issues that need to be addressed. Assess Company Situation Identify Strategic Options for the Company Select the Best Strategy for the Company.

A corporation's scanning of the environment should include analyses of all the relevant elements in the task environment. 扫描一个公司的环境应该包括分析任务环境中的所有相关要素。

This is known as strategic myopia: the willingness to reject unfamiliar as well as negative information. 战略性近视是指乐于拒绝陌生以及负面的信息。

Key Considerations Regarding the Industry and Competitive Environment Industry's dominate economic traits Competitive forces and strength of each force Drivers of change in their industry Competitor analysis Key success factors Conclusions : Industry attractiveness.

What are the Industry's Dominant Economic Traits? Market size and growth rate Scope of competitive rivalry Number of competitors and their relative sizes Prevalence of backward/forward integration Entry/exit barriers Nature and pace of technological change. Product and customer characteristics Scale economies and experience curve effects. Capacity utilization and resource requirements Industry profitability.

The Experience Curve Effect An experience curve exists when a company's unit costs decline as its cumulative production volume increases because of accumulating production know-how. Growing mastery of the technology. The bigger the experience curve effect, the bigger the cost advantage of the firm with the largest cumulative production volume

Relevance of Key Economic Features Economic Feature Market Size Market growth rate Capacity surpluses/shortages Industry profitability Entry/exit barriers. Product is big-ticket item for buyers. Standard products Rapid technological change. Capital requirements Vertical integration Economies of scale Rapid product innovation. Strategic Importance Small markets don't tend to attract new firms; large markets attract firms looking to acquire rivals with established positions in attractive industries. Fast growth breeds new entry; slow growth spawns increased rivalry& shake-out of weak rivals. Surpluses push prices& profit margins down; shortages pull them up High-profit industries attract new entrants; depressed conditions lead to exit. High barriers protect positions and profits of existing firms; low barriers make existing firms vulnerable to entry. More buyers will shop for lowest price Buyers have more power because it's easier to switch from seller to seller Raises risk; investments in technology facilities/equipment may become obsolete before they wear out. Big requirements make investment decisions critical; timing becomes important; creates a barrier to entry and exit. Raises capital requirements; often creates competitive &cost differences among fully vs. partially vs. non-integrated firms. Increases volume& market share needed to be cost competitive Shortens product life cycle; increases risk because of opportunities for leapfrogging.

Analyzing the Five Competitive Forces: How to Do It Assess strength of each of the five competitive forces (Strong? Moderate? Weak?) Rivalry among competitors Competition from substitute products Competitive threat from potential entrants. Bargaining power of suppliers and supplier-seller collaboration. Bargaining power of buyers and buyer-seller collaboration. Explain how each force acts to create competitive pressure—What are the factors that cause each force to be strong or weak? Decide whether overall competition(the combined effect of all five competitive forces)is brutal, fierce, strong, normal/moderate, or weak.

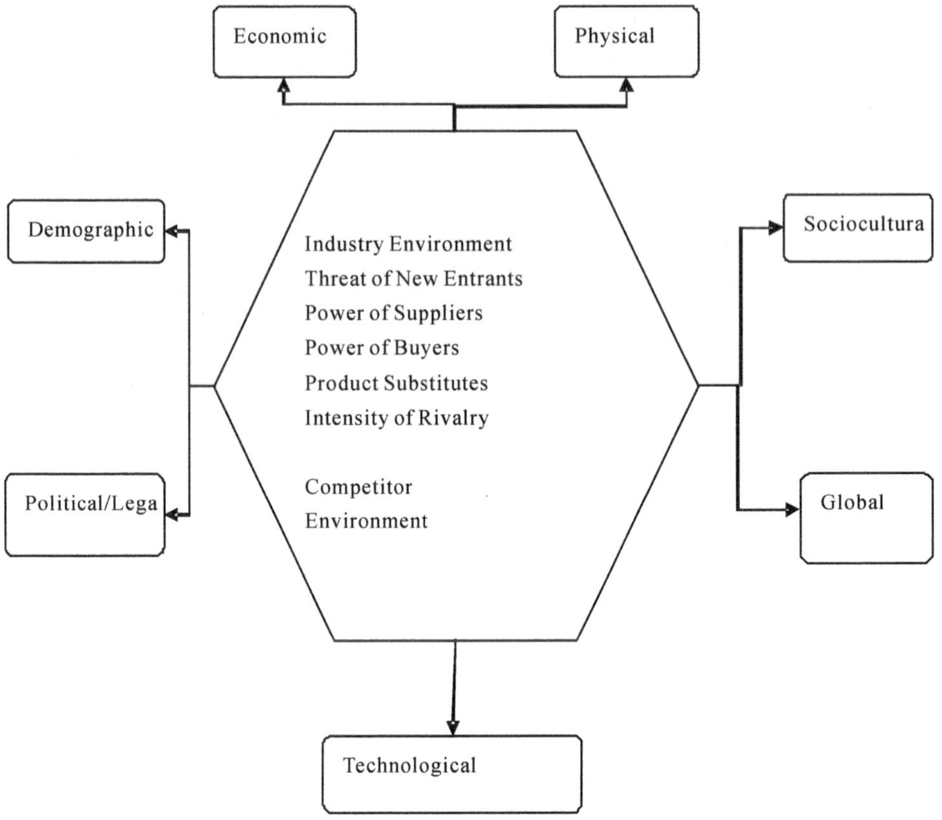

Figure 2. 1 The External Environment

2. 1 The General, Industry, and Competitor Environments

The general environment is composed of dimensions in the broader society that influence an industry and the firms within it. We group these dimensions into seven environmental segment: demographic, economic, political/legal, socio-cultural, technological, global, and physical. Examples of elements analyzed in each of these segments are shown in Table 2. 1.

Table 2. 1 The General Environment: Segments and Elements

Demographic segment	• Population size • Age structure • Geographic distribution	• Ethnic mix • Income distribution

Economic segment	• Inflation rates • Interest rates • Trade deficits or surpluses • Budget deficits or surpluses	• Personal savings rate • Business savings rates • Gross domestic product
Political/Legal segment	• Antitrust laws • Taxation laws • Deregulation philosophies	• Labor training laws • Educational philosophies and policies
Sociocultural segment	• Women in the workforce • Workforce diversity • Attitude about the quality of work life	• Shift in work and career preferences • Shift in preferences regarding product and service characteristics
Technological segment	• Product innovations • Applications of knowledge	• Focus of private and government-supported R&D expenditures • New communication technologies
Global segment	• Important political events • Critical global markets	• Newly industrialized countries • Different cultural and institutional attributes
Physical environment segment	• Energy consumption • Practices used to develop energy sources • Renewable energy efforts • Minimizing a firm's environmental footprint	• Availability of water as a resource • Producing environmentally friendly products • Reacting to natural or man-made disasters

Industry environment analysis refers to an in-depth examination of key factors within a corporation's task environment. 行业环境分析是指全面深入地检验公司任务环境中的关键驱动力量。

The natural environment, the societal environment, the task environment should be analyzed in external environment. 自然环境、社会环境、任务环境应该在企业外部环境中被分析。

The natural environment includes physical resources, wildlife, and climate that are an inherent part of existence on Earth. These factors form an ecological system of interrelated life. 自然环境包括物理资源、野生生物和气候，是地球上的固有存在。这些因素构成具有内在关联的生态系统。

The societal environment is mankind's social system that includes general forces that do not directly touch on the short-run activities of the organization that can, and often do, influence its long-run decisions. These forces involve economic forces, technological forces, political-legal forces, sociocultural forces. 社会环境是人类的社会制度，包括各种

一般驱动力量。这些驱动力量不会直接触及组织的短期活动,但往往会影响组织的长期决策。这些驱动力量包括经济驱动力量、技术驱动力量、政治(法律)驱动力量、社会文化驱动力量。

The task environment includes those elements or groups that directly affect the corporation and, in turn, are affected by it. 任务环境包括那些直接影响公司,反过来又被公司影响的驱动力量或群体。

Firms cannot directly control the general environment's segments. The recent bankruptcy filings by General Motors and Chrysler Corporation highlight this fact. These firms could not directly control various parts of their external environment, including the economic and political/legal segments; however, these segments are influencing the actions the firms are taking, including Chrysler's alliance with Fiat. Because firms cannot directly control the segments of their external environment, successful ones learn how to gather the information needed to understand all segments and their implications for selecting and implementing the firm's strategies.

The industry environment is the set of factors that directly influences a firm and its competitive actions and responses: the threat of new entrants, the power of suppliers, the power of buyers, the threat of product substitutes, and the intensity of rivalry among competitors. In total, the interactions among these five factors determine an industry's profit potential; in turn, the industry's profit potential influences the choices each firm makes about its strategic actions. The challenge for a firm is to locate a position within an industry where it can favorably influence the five factors or where it can successfully defend against their influence. The greater a firm's capacity to favorably influence its industry environment, the greater the likelihood that the firm will earn above-average returns.

How companies gather and interpret information about their competitors is called competitor analysis. Understanding the firm's competitor environment complements the insights provided by studying the general and industry environments. This means, for example, that BP wants to learn as much as it can about its major competitors-such as Exxon-Mobil and Royal Dutch Shell plc-while also learning about its general and industry environments.

Analysis of the general environment is focused on environmental trends while an analysis of the industry environment is focused on the factors and conditions influencing an industry's profitability potential and an analysis of competitors is focused on predicting competitors' actions, responses, and intentions. In combination, the results of these three analyses influence the firm's vision, mission, and strategic actions. Although we discuss each analyses of the general environment, the industry environment, and the competitor environment.

An industry is a group of firms producing a similar product or service, such as financial services or soft drinks. 行业是指生产类似产品或服务的公司集群，如金融服务或软饮料。

Michael Porter, an authority on competitive strategy, contends that a corporation is most concerned with the intensity of competition within its Industry. 竞争战略的学术权威迈克尔·波特认为，公司最关心的是所处行业内的竞争强度。

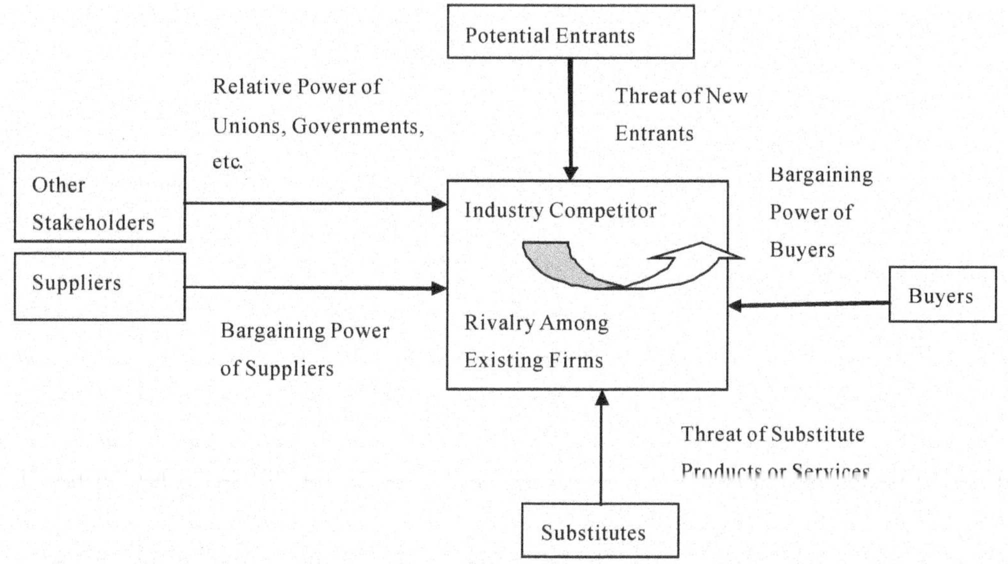

Figure 2.2

In carefully scanning its industry, the corporation must assess the importance to its success of each of the following six forces: threat of new entrants, rivalry among existing firms, threat of substitute products, bargaining power of buyers, bargaining power of suppliers, and relative power of other stakeholders. 在认真扫描行业的过程中，公司必须评估以下六个因素对于成功的重要性：新进入者的威胁、现有企业之间的竞争对抗性、替代产品的威胁、购买者的议价能力、供应商的议价能力、其他利益相关者的相对力量。

2.2 External Environmental Analysis

Most firms face external environments that are highly turbulent, complex, and global-conditions that make interpreting those environments difficult. To cope with often ambiguous and incomplete environmental data and to increase understanding of the general environment, firms engage in external environmental analysis. This analysis has four parts: scanning, monitoring, forecasting, and assessing. Analyzing the external environment is a difficult, yet significant, activity.

Identifying opportunities and threats is an important objective of studying the general environment. An opportunity is a condition in the general environment that, if exploited effectively, helps a company achieve strategic competitiveness. For example, recent market research results suggested to Procter & Gamble (P&G) after its acquisition of Gillette, a shaving products company, that an increasing number of men across the globe are interested in fragrances and skin care products. To take advantage of this opportunity, P&G is reorienting toward beauty products to better serve both men and women. The change constitutes an organization change focused on combining product categories rather than its typical organization around a specific branded product.

Environmental scanning provides reasonably hard data on the present situation and current trends, but intuition and luck are needed to accurately predict if these trends will continue. The resulting forecasts are, however, usually based on a set of assumptions that may or may not be valid. 环境扫描理性地提供了有关目前情况和当前趋势的坚实数据，但是还需要依靠直觉和运气以预测这些趋势是否会继续下去。

Various techniques are used to forecast future situations, and each has its proponents and critics. The most popular forecasting technique is extrapolation—the extension of present trends into the future. Trend extrapolation rests on the assumption that the world is reasonably consistent and changes slowly in the short run. Approaches of this type include time-series methods, which attempt to carry a series of historical events forward into the future. 最流行的预测方法是外推法——将目前的趋势扩展到未来。趋势外推法的假设是世界是同质的，并且在短期内变化缓慢。时间序列方法试图将一系列历史事件带入未来。

Scenarios are focused descriptions of different likely futures presented in a narrative fashion. 情境分析以叙事的方式重点描述各种不同的、可能的未来。

An industry scenario is a forecasted description of a particular industry's likely future. It is a scenario that is developed by analyzing the probable impact of future societal forces on key groups in a particular industry. 行业情境分析是预测特定行业未来可能性的文字描述。通过分析某个特定行业中未来各种社会驱动力量对关键群体可能产生的影响，撰写出行业情境分析报告。

A threat is a condition in the general environment that may hinder a company's efforts to achieve strategic competitiveness. Microsoft is currently experiencing a severe external threat as smartphones are expected to surpass personal computer (PC) sales in the near future. Although Microsoft has a smartphone operating system, Apple, Google, and Research in Motion (BlackBerry phones) have operating system, Apple, Google, and Research in motion (BlackBerry phones) have operating platforms that are much more popular than those using Microsoft's platform. Although PC growth will continue to expand, it is not growing at the rate that smartphones are, and possible substitution may happen between PCs, smartphones, and additional devices, such as Apple's iPad and similar devices. The main software platform is needed to assure other software producers will develop applications for the platform. Apple has large numbers of applications being developed, and Google's Android system software applications are rapidly increasing as well. As such, Microsoft is in a severe catch-up position relative to its competition. It recently formed a joint venture with Nokia Corporation to establish a firmer platform for its existing software using Nokia Corporation to establish a firmer platform for its existing software using Nokia's large potential smartphone base. However, this threat remains until this opportunity is realized.

Firms use several sources to analyze the general environment, including a wide variety of printed materials (such as trade publications, newspapers, business publications, and the results of academic research and public polls), trade shows and suppliers, customers, and employees of public-sector organizations. People in boundary-spanning positions can obtain a great deal of this type of information. Salespersons, purchasing managers, public relations directors, and customer service representatives, each of whom interacts with external constituents, are examples of boundary-spanning positions.

2.3 Scanning

Scanning entails the study of all segments in the general environment. Through scanning firms identify early signals of potential changes in the general environment and detect changes that are already under way. Scanning often reveals ambiguous, incomplete, or unconnected data and information. Thus, environmental scanning is challenging but critically important for firms, especially those competing in highly volatile environments. In addition, scanning activities must be aligned with the organizational context; a scanning system designed for a volatile environment is inappropriate for a firm in a stable environment.

Many firms use special software to help them identify events that are taking place in the environment and that are announced in public sources. For example, news event detection uses information-based systems to categorize text and reduce the trade-off between an important missed event and false alarm rates. The Internet provides significant opportunities for scanning. Amazon. com, for example, records significant information about individuals visiting its Web site, particularly if a purchase is made. Amazon then welcome these customers by name when they visit the Web site again. The firm sends messages to customers about specials and new products similar to those they purchased in previous visits. A number of other companies such as Netflix also collect demographic data about their customers in an attempt to identify their unique preferences(demographics is one of the segments in the general environment).

Philip Morris International continuously scans segments of its external environment to detect current conditions and to anticipate changes that might take place in different segments. For example, PMI always studies various nations' tax policies on cigarettes (these policies are part of the political/legal segment). The reason for this is that raising cigarette taxes might reduce sales while lowering these taxes might increase sales.

2.4 Monitoring

When monitoring, analysts observe environmental changes to see if an important trend is emerging from among those spotted through scanning. Critical to successful monitoring is the firm's ability to detect meaning in environmental events and trends. For example, Tesco, the United Kingdom's largest retailer, plans to add Turkish, Sri Lankan, Latin, Filipino, African, and South African cuisine to its food offerings. One analyst noted, " Britain has become one of the most ethnically diverse nations on earth, and there is a very strong, growing by those who have settled here to buy food from their homelands. Tesco already sells Asian, Oriental, Afro-caribbean, Kosher, Polish, and Halal foods. Continual monitoring of these trends is necessary for a large retailer such as Tesco to maintain the right balance among its products.

Effective monitoring requires the firm to identify important stakeholders and understand its reputation among these stakeholders as the foundation for serving their unique needs. Scanning and monitoring are particularly important when a firm competes in an industry with high technological uncertainty. Scanning and monitoring can provide the firm with information; they also serve as a means of importing knowledge about markets and about how to successfully commercialize new technologies the firm has developed.

2.5 Industry Environment Analysis

An industry is a group of firms producing products that are close substitutes. In the course of competition, these firms influence one another. Typically, industries include a rich mixture of competitive strategies that companies use in pursuing above-average returns, In part, these strategies are chosen because of the influence of an industry's characteristics.

Compared with the general environment, the industry environment has a more direct effect on the firm's strategic competitiveness and ability to earn above-average returns. An industry's profit potential is a function of five forces of competition: the threats posed by new entrants, the power of suppliers, the power of buyers, product substitutes, and the intensity of rivalry among competitors(see Table 2.2).

Table 2.2 The Five Forces of Competition Model

Threat of new entrants
Bargaining power of suppliers
Bargaining power of buyers
Threat of substitute products
Rivalry among competing firms

The five forces model of competition expands the arena for competitive analysis. Historically, when studying the competitive environment, firms concentrated on companies with which they competed directly. However, firms must search more broadly to recognize current and potential competitors by identifying potential customers as well as the firms serving them. For example, the communications industry is now broadly defined as encompassing media companies, telecos, entertainment companies, and companies producing devices such as smartphones. In such an environment, firms must study many other industries to identify firms with capabilities (especially technology-based capabilities) that might be the foundation for producing a good or a service that can compete against what they are producing. Using this perspective finds firms focusing on customers and their needs rather than on specific industry boundaries to define markets.

When studying the industry environment, firms must also recognize that suppliers can become a firm's competitors (by integrating forward) as can buyers (by integrating backward). For example, several firms have integrated forward in the pharmaceutical industry by acquiring distributors or wholesalers. In addition, firms choosing to enter a new market and those producing products that are adequate substitutes for existing products can become a company's competitors. Next, we examine the five force the firm analyzes to understand the profitability potential within the industry (or a segment of an industry) in which it competes or may choose to compete.

Industry analysis refers to an in-depth examination of key factors within a corporation's task environment. 行业分析是指全面深入地检验公司任务环境中的关键驱动力量。

Rivalry is the amount of direct competition in an industry. 竞争对抗性是一个行业内直接竞争者的数量。

According to Porter, intensive rival is related to the presence of the following factors: number of competitors, rate of industry growth, product or service characteristics, amount of fixed costs, capacity, height of exit barriers, diversity of rivals. 根据波特理论，竞争的激烈程度与以下因素相关:竞争者的数量、行业的增长率、产品或服务特征、固定成本的多少、产能、退出壁垒的高度、竞争对手的多样性。

Suppliers can affect an industry through their ability to raise prices or reduce the quality of purchased goods and services. 供应商影响行业的能力可以通过提高价格或降低产品和服务的质量来实现。

2.6 Threat of New Entrants

Identifying new entrants is important because they can threaten the market share of existing competitors. One reason new entrants pose such a threat is that they bring additional production capacity. Unless the demand for a good or service is increasing, additional capacity holds consumers' costs down, resulting in less revenue and lower returns for competing firms. Often, new entrants have a keen interest in gaining a large market share. As a result, new competitors may force existing firms to be more efficient and to learn how to compete on new dimensions (e. g. , sing an Internet-based distribution channel).

New entrants are newcomers to an existing industry. They typically bring new capacity, a desire to gain market share, and substantial resources. 新进入者是指现有行业的新参与者。它们通常带来新的产能、获得市场份额的渴望以及充足的资源。

An entry barrier is an obstruction that makes it difficult for a company to enter an industry. 进入壁垒是提高公司进入一个行业的困难程度的障碍。

Some of the possible barriers to entry involve economic of scale, product differentiation, capital requirements, switching costs, access to distribution channels, cost disadvantages independent of size, government policy and so on. 一些可能的进入壁垒包括规模经济、产品差异化、资本要求、转换成本、进入销售渠道、与成本无关的劣势、政府政策等。

The likelihood that firms will enter an industry is a function of two factors :barriers to entry and the retaliation expected from current industry is a function of two factors: barriers to entry and the retaliation expected from current industry participants. Entry barriers make it difficult for new firms to enter an industry and often place them at a competitive disadvantage even when they are able to enter. As such, high entry barriers tend to increase the returns for existing firms in the industry and may allow some firms to dominate the industry. Thus, firms competing successfully in an industry want to maintain high entry barriers in order to discourage potential competitors from deciding to enter the industry.

Bargaining Power of Suppliers

Increasing prices and reducing the quality of their products are potential means suppliers use to exert power over firms competing within an industry. If a firm is unable to recover cost increases by its suppliers through its own pricing structure, its profitability is reduced by its supplier's actions. A supplier group is powerful when

It is dominated by a few large companies and is more concentrated than the industry to which it sells.

Satisfactory substitute products are not available to industry firms.

Industry firms are not a significant customer for the supplier group.

Suppliers' goods are critical to buyers' marketplace success.

The effectiveness of suppliers' products has created high switching costs for industry firms.

It poses a credible threat to integrate forward into the buyers' industry. Credibility is enhanced when suppliers have substantial resources and provide a highly differentiated product.

The airline industry is one in which suppliers' bargaining power is changing. Though the number of suppliers is low, the demand for major aircraft is also relatively low. Boeing and Airbus aggressively compete for orders of major aircraft, creating more power for buyers in the process. When a large airline signals that it might place a "significant" order for wide-body airliners which either Airbus or Boeing might produce, both companies are likely to battle for the business and include a financing arrangement, highlighting the buyer's power in the potential transaction.

2.7 Bargaining Power of Buyers

Firms seek to maximize the return on their invested capital. Alternatively, buyers(customers of an industry or a firm) want to buy products at the lowest possible price-the point at which the industry earns the lowest acceptable rate of return on its invested capital. To reduce their costs, buyers bargain for higher quality, greater levels of service, and lower prices. These outcomes are achieved by encouraging competitive battles among the industry's firms. Customers(buyer groups)are powerful when

They purchase a large portion of an industry's total output.

The sales of the product being purchased account for a significant portion of the seller's annual revenues.

They could switch to another product at little, if any, cost.

The industry's products are undifferentiated or standardized, and the buyers pose a credible threat if they were to integrate backward into the sellers' industry.

Consumers armed with greater amounts of information about the manufacturer's costs and the power of the Internet as a shopping and distribution alternative have increased bargaining power in many industries. One reason for this shift is that individual buyers incur virtually zero switching costs when they decide to purchase from one manufacturer rather than another or from one dealer as opposed to any other.

Buyers affect an industry through their ability to force down prices, bargain for higher quality or more services, and play competitors against each other. 购买者影响行业的能力通过以下几个方面实现:强迫降价,对交易提供更高的质量或更多的服务讨价还价,以及发挥竞争者的作用。

2.8 Threat of Substitute Products

Substitute products are goods or service from outside a given industry that perform similar or the same functions as a product that the industry produces. For example, as a sugar substitute, NutraSweet (and other sugar substitutes) place an upper limit on sugar manufacturers' prices—NutraSweet and sugar perform the same function, though with different characteristics. Other product substitutes include e-mail and fax machines instead of overnight deliveries, plastic containers rather than glass jars, and tea instead of coffee. Newspaper firms have experienced significant circulation declines over the past decade or more. The declines are due to substitute outlets for news including Internet sources, cable television news channels, and e-mail and cell phone alerts. Likewise, satellite TV and cable and telecommunication companies provide substitute services for basic media services such as television, Internet, and phone. However, as illustrated in the Strategic Focus, the possible switching is becoming more complicated as consumer demand for content changes through increasing use of mobile devices such as tablets and smartphones. Tablets such as the iPad are reducing the number of PCs sold and this is curtailing the growth of PC producers such as China Taiwan's Acer Computers, at least until they can come out with their own successful tablet product. These products are increasingly popular, especially among younger and technologically savvy people, and as product substitutes they have significant potential to continue to reduce traditional media sources such as newspaper circulation sales.

In general, product substitutes present a strong threat to a firm when customers face few, if any, switching costs and when the substitute product's price is lower or its quality and performance capabilities are equal to or greater than those of the competing product. Differentiating a product along dimensions that customers value (such as quality, service after the sale, and location) reduces a substitute's attractiveness.

Substitute products are those products that appear to be different but can satisfy the same need as another product. 替代品是指那些看似不同但能满足相同需要的其他产品。

According to Porter, "substitutes limit the potential returns of industry by placing a ceiling on the prices firms in the industry can profitably charge."根据波特理论,一个产业的潜在收益之所以是有限的是由于替代品为这个行业设置了价格上限。

A sixth force should be added to Porter's list to include a variety of stakeholder groups from the task environment. 应该加入波特五力清单的第六种力量，包括来自任务环境的各种利益相关者群体。

A complementor is a company (e. g. , Microsoft) or an industry whose product works well with a firm's (e. g. , Intel's) product and without which the product would lose much of its value. 互补者是指一个公司(如微软)或行业的产品与其他公司(如英特尔)的产品结合将发挥更大的作用，否则产品将失去很多优良价值。

2.9 Strategic Groups

A set of firms that emphasize similar strategic dimensions and use a similar strategy is called a strategic group. The competition between firms within a strategic group is greater than the competition between a member of a strategic group and companies outside that strategic group. Therefore, intrastrategic group competition is more intense than is interstragegic group competition. In fact, more heterogeneity is evident in the performance of firms within strategic groups than across the groups. The performance leaders within groups are able to follow strategies similar to those of other firms in the group and yet maintain strategic distinctiveness to gain and sustain a competitive advantage.

The extent of technological leadership, product quality, pricing policies, distribution channels, and customer service are examples of strategic dimensions that firms in a strategic group may treat similarly. Thus, membership in a particular strategic group defines the essential characteristics of the firm's strategy.

The notion of strategic groups can be useful for analyzing an industry's competitive structure. Such analyses can be helpful in diagnosing competition, positioning, and the profitability of firms within an industry. High mobility barriers, high rivalry, and low resources among the firms within an industry limit the formation of strategic groups. However, research suggests that after strategic groups are formed, their membership remains relatively stable over time, although recent research does examine how change occurs. Using strategic groups to understand an industry's competitive structure requires the firm to plot companies' competitive actions and competitive responses along strategic dimensions such as pricing decisions, product quality, distribution channels, and so forth. This type of analysis shows the firm how certain companies are competing similarly in terms of how they use similar strategic dimensions.

Multinational corporation (MNC) is a company having significant manufacturing and marketing operations in multiple countries. 跨国公司是指在多个国家从事大量生产和营销业务的公司。

Before a company plans its strategy for a particular international location, it must scan the particular country's societal environment in question for opportunities and threats and compare them to its own organizational strengths and weaknesses. 一个公司在为特定国际市场制定战略计划之前，必须认真扫描特定国家的社会环境，发现机会和威胁，并与组织自身的优势和劣势相比较。

Strategic groups have several implications. First, because firms within a group offer similar products to the same customers, the competitive rivalry among them can be intense. The more intense the rivalry, the greater the threat to each firm's profitability. Second, the strengths of the ve industry forces differ across strategic groups. Third, the closer the strategic groups are in terms of their strategies, the greater is the likelihood of rivalry between the groups.

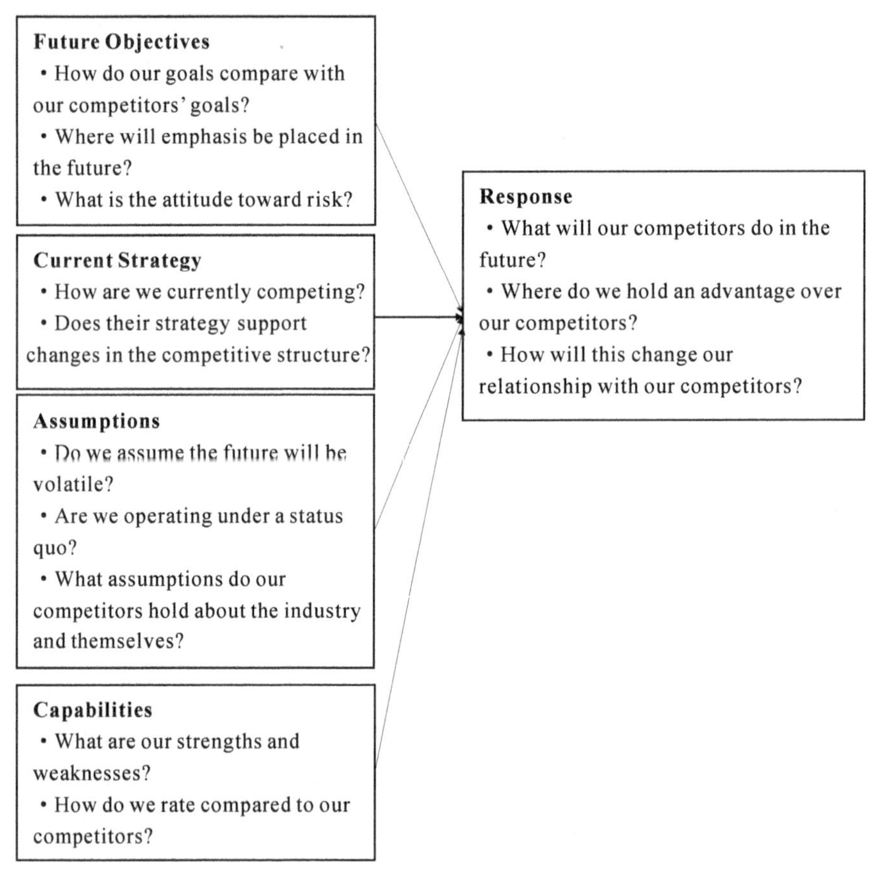

Figure 2.3 Competitor Analysis Components

2.10 Ethical Considerations

Firms must follow relevant laws and regulations as well as carefully articulated ethical guidelines when gathering competitor intelligence. Industry associations often develop lists of these practices that firms can adopt. Practices considered both legal and ethical include (1) obtaining publicly available information (e. g., court records, competitors' help-wanted advertisements, annual reports of publicly held corporations, and Uniform Commercial Code filings), and(2) attending trade fairs and shows to obtain competitors' brochures, view their exhibits, and listen to discussions about their products. In contrast, certain practices(including blackmail, trespassing, eavesdropping, and stealing drawings, samples, or documents) are widely viewed as unethical and often are illegal.

The industry life cycle is useful for explaining and predicting trends among the six forces that drive industry competition. 行业生命周期可以用来解释和预测驱动行业竞争的六种驱动力量的趋势。

By the time an industry enters maturity, products tend to become more like commodities. This is now a consolidated industry—dominated by a few large firms, each of which struggles to differentiate its products from the competitors. 当一个行业进入成熟期,产品出现变为普通商品的趋势。如今行业已经成熟——几家大公司主导行业,彼此通过产品差异化相互竞争。

No firm has large market share and each firm serves only a small piece of the total market in competition with others in a fragmented industry. 在分散行业中,没有任何企业占有较高的市场份额,每个企业在总的市场竞争中只占据很小一部分。

As an industry moves through maturity toward possible decline, the growth rate of its products' sales slows and may even begin to decrease. 当行业从成熟阶段转向衰退阶段,产品销售的增长速度减缓,甚至可能开始下降。

A global industry, in contrast, operates world-side, with MNCs making only small adjustments for country-specific circumstances. 全球性行业在世界各地经营运作,跨国公司根据特定国家的具体情况所做出的调整非常小。

Some competitor intelligence practices may be legal, but a firm must decide whether they are also ethical, given the image it desires as a corporate citizen. Especially with electronic transmissions, the line between legal and ethical practices can be difficult to determine. For example, a firm may develop Web site addresses that are similar to those of its competitors and thus occasionally receive e-mail transmissions that were intended for those competitors. The practice is an example of the challenges companies face in deciding how to gather intelligence about competitors while simultaneously determining how to prevent competitors from learning too much about them. To deal with these challengers, firms should establish principles and take actions that are consistent with them. Many firms follow the Strategy and Competitive Intelligence Professionals, a professional association, code of professional practice and ethics dealing with this issue.

Open discussions of intelligence-gathering techniques can help a firm ensure that employees, customers, suppliers, and even potential competitors understand its convictions to follow ethical practices for gathering competitor intelligence. An appropriate guideline for competitor intelligence practices is to respect the principles of common morality and the right of competitors not to reveal certain information about their products, operations, and strategic intentions.

Using an EFAS (External Factors Analysis Summary) Table is one way to organize the external factors into the generally accepted categories of opportunities and threats as well as to analyze how we a particular company's management(rating) is responding to these specific factors in light of the perceived importance(weight) these factors the company.

Table 2.3 External Factor Analysis Summary Table for Maytag

External Factors	Weight	Rating	Weighted Score	Comments
Opportunities				
• Economic integration of European Union	0.20	4	0.80	Acquisition of Hoover
• Demoqraphics favor quality appliances	0.10	5	0.50	Maytag quality
• Economic development of Asia	0.05	1	0.05	Low Maytag presence
• Opening of Eastern Europe	0.05	2	0.10	Will take time
• Trend to superstores	0.10	2	0.20	Maytag weak in this channel
Threats				
• Increasing government regulations	0.10	4	0.40	Well positioned
• Strong U.S. competition	0.10	4	0.40	Well positioned
• Whirlpool and Electrolux strong globally	0.15	3	0.45	Hoover weak globally
• New product advances	0.05	1	0.05	Questionable
• Japanese appliance companies	0.10	2	0.20	Only Asian presence is Australia
Totals	1.00		3.15	

2.11 Rivalry Among Competing Sellers

Usually the most powerful of the five forces. The big factor determining the strength of rivalry is how actively and aggressively are rivals employing the various weapons of competition in jockeying for a stronger market position and seeking bigger sales Is price competition vigorous? Active efforts to improve quality? Are rivals racing to offer better performance features? Are rivals racing to offer better customer service? Lots of advertising/sales promotions? Active efforts to build a stronger dealer network? Active product innovation? Active use of other weapons of rivalry?

What Causes Rivalry to be Stronger? Active jockeying for position among rivals and frequent launches of new offensives to gain sales and market share. One or more firms initiates moves to bolster their standing at expense of rivals. Lots of firms that are relatively equal in size and capability. Slow market growth Industry conditions tempt some firms to go on the offensive to boost volume and market share. Customers have low costs in switching to rival brands. A successful strategic move carries a big payoff Costs more to get out of business than to stay in Firms have diverse strategies, corporate priorities, resources, and countries of origin.

Principle of Competitive Markets Competitive jockeying among rival firms is dynamic and ever-changing. As industry members initiate new offensive and defensive moves. As emphasis swings from one mix of competitive weapons to another.

Competitive Force of Potential Entry Seriousness of threat depends on. Barriers to entry. Reaction of existing firms to entry. Barriers exist when Newcomers confront obstacles Economic factors put potential entrant at a disadvantage relative to incumbent firms.

Common Barriers to Entry Sizable economies of scale In ability to gain access to specialized technology Existence of strong learning/experience curve effects. Strong brand preferences and customer loyalty. Large capital requirements and/or other specialized resource requirements. Cost disadvantages independent of size Difficulties in gaining access to distribution channels Regulatory policies, tariffs, trade restrictions.

Principle of Competitive Markets Threat of entry is stronger when: Entry barriers are low Sizable pool of entry candidates exists Incumbents are unwilling or unable to contest a newcomer's entry efforts. Newcomers can expect to earn attractive profits.

Competitive Force of Substitute Products Concept Substitutes matter when customers are attracted to the products of firms in other industries Eyeglasses vs. Contact Lens Sugar vs. Artificial Sweeteners Newspapers vs. TV vs. Internet E-mail vs. Overnight Delivery Examples.

How to Tell Whether Substitute Products are a Strong Force Sales of substitutes are growing rapidly Producers of substitutes plan to add new capacity Profits of producers of substitutes are up.

Principle of Competitive Markets Competitive threat of substitutes is stronger when they are: Readily available Attractively priced Believed to have comparable or better performance features Customer switching costs are low.

A strategic group is a set of business units or firms that "pursue similar strategies with similar resources.”战略集团是以“类似资源寻求类似战略”的一系列业务单位或企业。

In analyzing the level of competitive intensity within a particular industry or strategic group, it is useful to characterize the various competitors for predictive purposes. A strategic type is category of firms based on a common strategic orientation and a combination of structure, culture, and processes consistent with that strategy. According to Miles and Snow, competing firms within a single industry can be categorized on the basis of their general strategic orientation into one of four basic types: defenders, prospectors, analyzers, and reactors. 战略类型是基于共同的战略导向,并综合考虑结构、文化和流程与战略的一致性,对企业进行分类的方法。根据迈尔斯和斯诺的研究,单个行业内的竞争性公司可以基于总体战略导向分为四种基本类型:防御者、探索者、分析者和反应者。

Defenders are companies with a limited product line that focus on improving the efficiency of their existing operations. 防御者是那些在有限的产品线中关注于提高目前的运行效率的公司。

Prospectors are companies with fairly broad product lines that focus on product innovation and market opportunities. 探索者是指有相当广泛的产品线,专注于产品创新和市场机会的公司。

Analyzers are companies that operate in at least two different product-market areas, one stable and one variable. 分析者是指那些至少在两个不同的产品市场领域运作,一个是稳定的市场,另一个是多样化的市场。

Reactors are companies that lack a consistent strategy-structure relationship. 反应者是指那些与战略、结构、文化缺乏一致联系的公司。

Competitive Pressures From Suppliers and Supplier-Seller Collaboration. Whether supplier-seller relationships represent a weak or strong competitive force depends on Whether suppliers can exercise sufficient bargaining leverage to influence terms of supply in their favor Extent and competitive importance of collaborative partnerships between one or more sellers and their suppliers.

Competitive Force of suppliers are a strong competitive force when: Item makes up large portion of product costs, is crucial to production process, and/or significantly affects product quality. It is costly for buyers to switch suppliers. They have good reputations and growing demand. They can supply a component cheaper than industry members can make it themselves. They do not have to contend with substitutes Buying firms are not important customers.

Competitive Pressures: Collaboration Between Sellers and Suppliers Rival sellers are forming long-term strategic partnerships with select suppliers to Promote just-in-time deliveries and reduced inventory and logistic costs. Speed availability of next-generation components. Enhance quality of parts being supplied Reduce suppliers' costs which paves way for lower prices on items supplied. Competitive advantage potential may accrue to industry rivals doing the best job of managing supply-chain relationships.

Principle of Competitive Markets Suppliers are a stronger force the more they can exercise power over: Prices charged Quality and performance of items supplied Reliability of deliveries.

Competitive Pressures From Buyers and Seller-Buyer Collaboration. Whether seller-buyer relationships represent a weak or strong competitive force depends on. Whether buyers have sufficient bargaining leverage to influence terms of sale in their favor Extent and competitive importance of collaborative partnerships between one or more sellers and their customers.

Hypercompetition describes an industry undergoing an ever-increasing level of environmental uncertainty in which competitive advantage is only temporary. 超级竞争描述了一个行业正在经历环境不确定程度不断提高的形势。

Competitive intelligence is a formal program of gathering information on a company's competitors. Sometimes called business intelligence, this is one of the fastest growing fields in strategic management. 竞争情报是一个收集公司竞争对手信息的正式项目。有时也称为商业情报,是战略管理增长最快的领域之一。

Chapter 3 The Internal Environment

3.1 Analyzing the Internal Organization

One of the conditions associated with analyzing a firm's internal organization is the reality that in today's global economy, some of the resources that were traditionally critical to firm's efforts to produce, sell, and distribute their goods or services such as labor costs, access to financial resources and raw materials, and protected or regulated markets are still important; but, it is now less likely that these resources will become core competencies and possibly competitive advantages. An important reason for this is that an increasing number of firms are using their resources to form core competencies through which they successfully implement an international strategy as a means of overcoming the advantages created by these more traditional resources.

The Volkswagen Group has established "Strategy 2018" as its international strategy. The firm, which sells its products in over 150 countries, employs 400, 000 people to operate its 62 production plants located in 15 European countries. By using its resources to form technological and innovation capabilities, Volkswagen intends to create superior customer service and quality as core competencies on which it will rely to implement its international strategy.

Organizational analysis is concerned with identifying and developing an organization's resources. 内部扫描通常称为组织分析,主要考虑识别和开发组织资源的有关问题。

Resources are organization's assets and are thus its basic building blocks. They include tangible assets such as plant, equipment, finances, and location; human assets, in terms of the number of employees and their skills; and intangible assets, such as technology, culture, and reputation. 资源是一个组织的资产,因而属于基本必备条件。有形资源如厂房、设备、资金和位置;人力资源是指一定数量的员工及其技能;无形资源包括技术、文化和声誉。

3.2 Creating Value

Firm use their resources as the foundation for producing goods or services that will create value for customers. Value is measured by a product's performance characteristics and by its attributes for which customers are willing to pay. Firms create value by innovatively bundling and leveraging their resources to form capabilities and core competencies. Firms with a competitive advantage create more value for customers than do competitors. Walmart uses its "every day low price" approach to doing business (an approach that is grounded in the firm's core competencies, such as information technology and distribution channels) to create value for those seeking to buy products at a low price compared to competitors' price for those seeking to buy products at a low price compared to competitors' price for those products. Mattress manufacture E. S. Kluft. (The firm's upper-end mattress sells for \$50000 per unit.) The stronger these firms' core competencies, the grater the amount of value they're able to create for their customers.

Ultimately, creating value for customers is the source of above-average returns for a firm. What the firm intends regarding value creation affects its choice of business-level strategy and its organizational structure. In discussion of business-level strategies, we note that value is created by a product's low cost, by its highly differentiated features, or by a combination of low cost and high differentiation, compared with competitors' offerings. A business-level strategy is effective only when it is grounded in exploiting the firm's capabilities and core competencies. Thus, the successful firm continuously examines the effectiveness of current capabilities and core competencies while thinking about the capabilities and competencies it will require for future success.

Capabilities refer to a corporation's ability to exploit its resources. 能力是指一个公司运用资源的能力。

A competency is the cross-functional integration and coordination of capabilities. 竞争力是指跨职能部门进行整合和协调的能力。

A core competency is a collection of competencies that cross divisional boundaries, is widespread within the corporation, and is something that a corporation can do exceedingly well. 核心竞争力是公司内部普遍存在的各种跨部门边界竞争力的集合,也是一些企业表现出色的原因所在。

A core rigidity is a strength that over time matures and becomes a weakness. 所谓核心刚性是指某种优势随着时间的推移逐渐成熟并成为劣势。

When core competencies are superior to those of the competition, they are called distinctive competencies. 当某种核心竞争力优于竞争对手相应的能力时,则称为独特竞争力。

At one time, the firm's efforts to create value were largely oriented to understanding the characteristics of the industry in which it competed and, in light of those characteristics, determining how it should be positioned relative to competitors. This emphasis on industry characteristics and competitive strategy underestimated the role of the firms' resources and capabilities in developing core competencies as the source of competitive advantages. In fact, core competencies, in combination with product-market positions, are the firm's most important sources of competitive advantage. A firm's core competencies, integrated with an understanding of the results of studying the conditions in the external environment, should drive the selection of strategies. As Clayton Christensen noted," Successful strategists need to cultivate a deep understanding of the processes of competition and progress and of the factors that undergird each advantage. Only thus will they be able to see when old advantages are poised to disappear and how new advantages can be built in their stead." By emphasizing learn to competencies when selecting and implementing strategies, companies learn to compete primarily on the basis of firm-specific differences. However, while doing so they must be simultaneously aware of how things are changing in the external environment.

Table 3.1 Conditions Affecting Managerial Decisions about Resources, Capabilities and Core Competencies

Conditions	Uncertainty	Uncertainty exists about the characteristics of the firm's general and industry environments and customers' needs
	Complexity	Complexity results from the interrelationships among conditions shaping a firm.
	Intra-organizational Conflicts	Intra-organizational conflicts may exist among managers making decisions as well as among those affected by the decisions.

3.3 Resources, Capabilities, and Core Competencies

Resources, capabilities, and core competencies are the foundation of competitive advantage. Resources are bundled to created organizational capabilities. In turn, capabilities are the source of a firm's core competencies, which are the basis of establishing competitive advantages. We show these relationships in Figure 3.2. Here, we define and provide examples of these building blocks of competitive advantage.

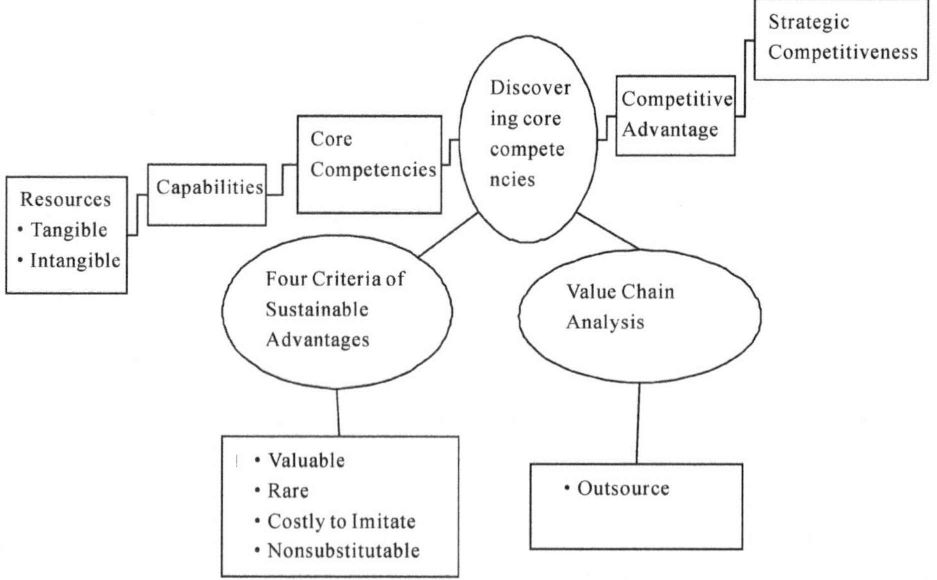

Figure 3.1 Components of an Internal Analysis

3.4 Resources

Broad in scope, resources over a spectrum of individual, social, and organizational phenomena. By themselves, resources do not allow firms to create value for customers as the foundation for earning above-average returns. Indeed, resources are combined to form capabilities. Subway links its fresh ingredients with several other resources including the continuous training it provides to those running the firm's units as the foundation for customer service as a capability; as explained in the Opening Case, customer service is also a core competence for Subway. As its sole distribution channel, the Internet is a resource for Amazon. com. The firm uses the Internet to sell goods at prices that typically are lower than those offered by competitors selling the same goods through what are more costly brick-and-mortar storefronts. By combining other resources (such as access to a wide product inventory), Amazon has developed a reputation for excellent customer service. Amazon's capability in terms of customer service is a core competence as well in that the firm creates unique value for customers through the services it provides to them. Amazon also uses its technological core competence to offer AWS (Amazon Web Services), services through which businesses can rent computing power from Amazon at a cost of pennies per hour. In the words of the leader of this effort, "AWS makes it possible for anyone with an Internet connection and a credit card to access the same kind of world-class computing systems that Amazon uses to run its $34 billion-a - year retail operation."

Proposing that a company's sustained competitive advantage is primarily determined by its resource endowments, Grant presents a five-step, resource-based approach to strategy analysis. 格兰特认为，公司可持续的竞争优势主要取决于自身的资源禀赋，并提出了以资源为基础的战略分析的五个步骤。

The sustainability of an advantage determines that durability and imitability. 优势的可持续性取决于持久性和模仿性。

Durability is the rate at which a firm's underlying resources, capabilities, or core competencies depreciate or become obsolete. 持久性是指公司的基础性资源、能力和核心竞争力贬值或过时的速度。

Imitability is the rate at which a firm's underlying resources, capabilities, or core competencies can be duplicated by others. 模仿性是指公司的基础性资源、能力和核心竞争力可以被别人复制的速度。

3.5 Tangible Resources

As tangible resources, a firm's borrowing capacity and the status of its physical facilities are visible. The value of many tangible resources can be established through financial statements, but these statements do not account for the value of all the firm's assets, because they disregard some intangible resources. The value of tangible resources is also constrained because they are hard to leverage-it is difficult to derive additional business or value from a tangible resource. For example, an airplane is a tangible resource, but "You can't use the same airplane on five different routes at the same time. You can't put the same crew on five different routes at the same time. And the same goes for the financial investment you've made in the airplane.

Table 3.2 Tangible Resources

Financial Resources	• The firm's capacity to borrow • The firm's ability to generate funds through internal operations
Organizational Resources	• Formal reporting structures
Physical Resources	• The sophistication of a firm's plant and equipment and the attractiveness of its location • Distribution facilities • Product inventory
Technological Resources	• Availability of technology-related resources such as copyrights, patents, trademarks, and trade secrets

Table 3.3 Intangible Resources

Human Resources	• Knowledge • Trust • Skills • Abilities to collaborate with others
Innovation Resources	• Ideas • Scientific capabilities • Capacity to innovate
Reputational Resources	• Brand name • Perceptions of product quality, durability, and reliability • Positive reputation with stakeholders such as suppliers and customers

3.6 Intangible Resources

Compared to tangible resources, intangible resources are a superior source of capabilities and subsequently, core competencies. In fact, in the global economy, "the success of a corporation lies more in its intellectual and systems capabilities than in its physical assets. Moreover, the capacity to manage human intellect-and to convert it into useful products and services-is fast becoming the critical executive skill of the age".

Because intangible resources are less visible and more difficult for competitors to understand, purchase, imitate, or substitute for, firms prefer to rely on them rather than on tangible resources as the foundation for their capabilities. In fact, the more unobservable (i. e., intangible) a resource is, the more valuable that resource is to create capabilities. Another benefit of intangible resources is that, unlike most tangible resources, their use can be lever-aged. For instance, sharing knowledge among employees does not diminish its value for any one person. To the contrary, two people sharing their individualized knowledge sets often can be leveraged to create additional knowledge that, although new to each individual, contributes to performance improvements for the firm.

Reputational resources are important sources of a firm's capabilities and core competencies. Indeed, some argue that a positive reputation can even be a source of competitive advantage. Earned through the firm's actions as well as its words, a value-creating reputation is a product of years of superior marketplace competence as perceived by stakeholders. A reputation indicates the level of awareness a firm has been able to develop among stakeholders and the degree to which they hold the firm in high esteem.

A well-known and highly valued brand name is a specific reputational resource. A continuing commitment to innovation and aggressive advertising facilitates firms' efforts to take advantage of the reputation associated with their brands. Harley-Davidson has a reputation for producing and servicing high-quality motorcycles with unique designs. Because of the desirability of its reputation, the company also produces a wide range of accessory items that it sells on the basis of its reputation for offering unique products with high quality. Sunglasses, jewelry, belts, wallets, shirts, slacks, belts, and hats are just a few of the large variety of accessories customers can purchase from a Harley-Davidson dealer or from its online store.

Generally speaking, each organization structure tend to support some corporate strategies over others. 一般来说，每一种组织结构都会倾向于支持某些企业战略。

The typical organization structure involves that simple structure, functional structure and divisional structure. 典型的组织结构包括简单结构、职能结构、分部结构。

Corporate culture is the collection of beliefs, expectations, and values learned and shared by a corporation's members and transmitted from one generation of employees to another. 企业文化是公司成员学习、共享并且代代相传的信念、期望和价值观的集合。

Cultural intensity (or depth) is the degree to which members of a unit accept the norms, values, or other culture content associated with the unit. 文化的强度或深度是指全体成员作为一个整体接受各种规范、价值观或其他相关文化内涵的程度。

Cultural integration (or breadth) is the extent to which units throughout an organization share a common culture. 文化的集成度或宽度是整个组织的各个单位共享文

化的程度。

3.7 Capabilities

The firm combines individual tangible and intangible resources to create capabilities. In turn, capabilities are used to complete the organizational tasks required to produce, distribute, and service the goods or services the firm provides to customers for the purpose of creating value for them. As a foundation for building core competencies and hopefully competitive advantages, capabilities are often based on developing, carrying, and exchanging information and knowledge through the firm's human capital. Hence, the value of human capital in developing and using capabilities and, ultimately, core competencies cannot be overstated. At IBM, for example, human capital is critical to forming and using the firm's capabilities for long-term customer relationships and deep scientific and research skills, and the breadth of the firm's technical skills, and the breadth of the firm's technical skills in hardware software, and services.

As illustrated in Table 3.3, capabilities are often developed in specific functional areas (such as manufacturing, R&D, and marketing) or in a part of a functional area(e.g., advertising). Table 3.3 shows a grouping of organizational functions and the capabilities that some companies are thought to possess in terms of all or parts of those functions.

Table 3.4 example of Firms' Capabilities

Functional Areas	Capabilities	Examples of Firms
Distribution	• Effective use of logistics management techniques	• Walmart
Human Resources	• Motivating, empowering, and retaining employees	• Microsoft
Management Information Systems	• Effective and efficient control of inventories through point-of-purchase data collection methods	• Walmart
Marketing	• Effective promotion of brand-name products • Effective customer service • Innovative merchandising	• Procter & Gamble • Ralph Lauren Corp. • Mckinsey & Co. • Nordstrom Inc. • Crate & Barrel
Management	• Ability to envision the future of clothing	• Hugo Boss • Zara

Manufacturing	• Design and production skills yielding reliable products • Product and design quality • Miniaturization of components and products	• Komatsu • Witt Gas Technology • Sony
Research & Development	• Innovative technology • Development of sophisticated elevator control solutions • Rapid transformation of technology into new products and processes • Digital technology	• Caterpillar • Otis Elevator Co. • Chaparral Steel • Thomson Consumer Electronics

3.8 Core Competencies

Defined in chapter, core competencies are capabilities that serve as a source of competitive advantage for a firm over its rivals. Core competencies distinguish a company competitively and reflect its personality. Core competencies emerge over time through an organizational process of accumulating and learning how to deploy different resources and capabilities. As the capacity to take action, core competencies are "crown jewels of a company," the activities the company performs especially well compared to competitors and through which the firm adds unique value to the goods or services it sells to customers.

Two tools help firms identify their core competencies. The first consists of four specific criteria of sustainable competitive advantage that can be used to determine which capabilities are core competencies. Because the capabilities shown in Table 3. 3 have satisfied these four criteria, they are core competencies. The second tool is the value chain analysis. Firms use this tool to select the value-creating competencies that should be maintained, upgraded, or developed and those that should be outsourced.

3.9 The Four Criteria of Sustainable Competitive Advantage

Capabilities that are valuable, rare, costly to imitate, and nonsubstitutable are core competencies (see Table 3. 4). In turn, core competencies can lead to competitive advantages for the firm over its rivals. Capabilities failing to satisfy the four criteria are not core competencies, meaning that although every core competence is a capability, not every capability is a core competence. In slightly different words, for a capability to be a core competence, it must be valuable and unique from a customer's point of view. For a core competence to be a potential source of competitive advantage, it must be inimitable and nonsubstitutable by competitors.

Table 3. 5 The Four Criteria of Sustainable Competitive Advantage

Valuable Capabilities	• Help a firm neutralize threats of exploit opportunities
Rare Capabilities	• Are not possessed by many others
Costly-to Imitate Capabilities	• Historical: A unique and a valuable organizational culture or brand name • Ambiguous cause: The causes and uses of a competence are unclear • Social complexity: Interpersonal relationships, trust, and friendship among managers, suppliers, and customers
Nonsubstituable Capabilities	• No strategic equivalent

A sustainable competitive advantage exists only when competitors cannot duplicate the benefits of a firm's strategy or when they lack the resources to attempt imitation. For some period of time, the firm may have a core competence by using capabilities that are valuable and rare, but imitable. For example, some firms are trying to develop a core competence and potentially a competitive advantage by out-greening their competitors. Since 2005, Walmart has used its resources in ways that have allowed it to reduce its stores' carbon footprint by more than 10 percent and the carbon footprint of its trucking fleet by several times this percentage. Additionally, progress is being made toward the firm's goal of zero waste going to landfills from its operations. A reduction of its waste by 81 percent in California suggests that this goal may be attainable. Competitor Target is also using its resources and capabilities for the purpose of forming a "green" core competence. "Environmental sustainability is integrated throughout our businesses-from the way we build our stores to the products on our shelves," the store says. Packaging its Archer Farms Balanced Potato Crisps in bags that are manufactured with 25 percent renewable plant-based plastic is one example of actions Target is taking to be environmentally sustainable.

The length of time a firm can expect to create value by using its core competencies is a function of how quickly competitors can successfully imitate a good, service, or process. Value-creating core competencies may last for a relatively long period of time only when all four of the criteria we discuss next are satisfied. Thus, either Walmart or Target would know that it has a core competence and possibly a competitive advantage in terms of green practices if the way the firm uses its resources to complete these practices satisfies the four criteria.

3. 10 Value Chain Analysis

Value chain analysis allows the firm to understand the parts of its operations that create value and those that do not. Understanding these issues is important because the firm earns above-average returns only when the value it creates is greater than the costs incurred to create that value.

The value chain is a template that firms use to analyze their cost position and to identify the multiple means that can be used to facilitate implementation of a chosen strategy. Today's competitive landscape demands that firms examine their value chains in a global rather than a domestic-only contest. In particular, activities associated with supply chains should be studied within a global context. 、

A value chain is a linked set of value-creating activities beginning with basic raw materials coming from suppliers, to a series of value-added activities involved in producing and marketing a product or service, and ending with distributors getting the final goods into the hands of the ultimate consumer. 价值链是指一系列具有内在联系的价值创造活动,开始于供应商提供的基本原材料,经过涉及产品或服务的生产和销售的一系列增值活动的转换,结束于将最终产品提供给最终消费者的经销商。

The value chains of most industries can be split into two segments: upstream and downstream halves. 大多数行业的价值链可以分为两个部分:上游部分和下游部分。

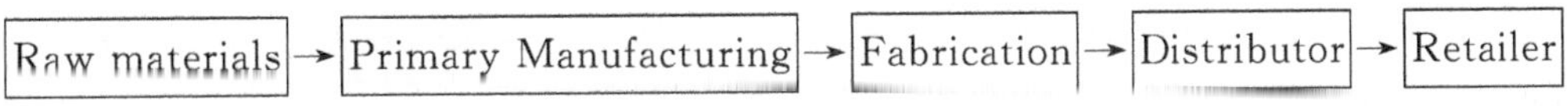

Raw materials → Primary Manufacturing → Fabrication → Distributor → Retailer

Figure 3.2 Typical Value Chain For a Manufactured Product

Table 3.6 Inter Factor Analysis Summary (IFAS) Table for Maytag

Internal factors	Weight	Rating	Weighted Score	Weighted Comments
Strengths				
• Quality Maytag Culture	0.15	5	0.75	Quality key to success
• Experienced top management	0.05	4	0.20	Know appliances
• Vertical integrations	0.10	4	0.40	Dedicated factories
• Employee relations	0.05	3	0.15	Goods, but deteriorating
• Hoover's international orientation	0.15	3	0.45	Hoover name in cleaners
Weaknesses				
• Process-oriented R&D	0.05	2	0.10	Slow on new products
• Distribution channels	0.05	2	0.10	Superstores replacing small dealers
• Financial position	0.15	2	0.30	High debt load
• Global positioning	0.20	2	0.40	Hoover weak outside the New Zealand, U.K., and Australia
• Manufacturing facilities	0.05	4	0.20	Investing now
Totals	1.00		3.05	

Each corporation has its internal value chain of activities. Porter proposes that a manufacturing firm's primary activities usually begin with inbound logistics(raw materials handling and warehousing), go through an operations process in which a product is manufactured, and continue to outbound logistics (warehousing and distribution), marketing and sales and finally to service(installation, repair, and sale of parts). 每家公司都有内部价值链活动。波特认为一家制造型企业的基础活动贯穿于产品制造的运行过程,经常开始于采购物流(原材料处理和仓储),继续于出境物流(仓储和分销),并最终服务于市场和销售(安装、维修和销售的部分)

Several support activities, such as procurement(purchasing), technology development (R&D), human resource management, and firm infrastructure(accounting, finance, and strategic planning), ensure that the primary value-chain activities operate effectively and efficiently. 几种辅助活动可保证公司价值链活动有效运行,比如采购、技术研发、人力资源管理和公司日常活动(会计,财务和战略计划)。

Corporate value-chain analysis involves the following steps: 公司价值链分析包括以下步骤:

Examine each product line's value chain in terms of the various activities involved in producing that product or service. 根据生产产品或服务所涉及的各种活动检查每条产品线的价值链。

Examine the "linkages" within each product line's value chain. Linkage are the connections between the way one value activity (e. g. , marketing) is performed and the cost of performance of another activity(e. g. , quality control). 检验每条产品线的价值链的内在联系。联系是指执行某个价值活动的方式(例如营销)与其他活动(如质量控制)的绩效成本之间的关系。

Examine the potential synergies among the value chains of different product lines of business units. 检验不同产品线或业务单位价值链之间的潜在协同作用。

We show a model of the value chain in Figure 3. 2. As depicted in the model, a firm's value chain is segmented into value chain activities and support functions. Value chain activities are activities of tasks the firm completes in order to produce products and then sell, distribute, and service those products in ways that create value for customers. Support functions include the activities or tasks the firm completes in order to support the work being done to produce, sell, distribute, and service the products the firm is producing. A firm can develop a capability and/or a core competence in any of the value chain activities and in any of the support functions. When it does so, it has established an ability to create value for customers. In fact, as shown in Figure 3. 2, customers are the one firms seek to serve when using value chain analysis to identify their capabilities and core competencies. When using their unique core competencies to create unique value for customers that competitors cannot duplicate, firms have established one or more competitive advantages. This appears to be the case for P&G as it relies on the five core competencies described earlier in a Strategic Focus to produce unique, high-quality branded products that are sold to customers throughout the world.

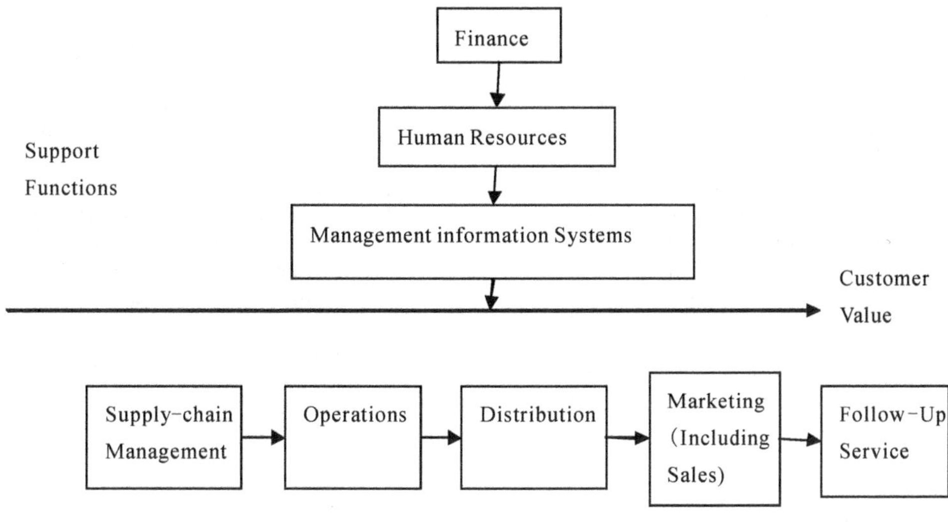

Figure 3.3 A Model of the Value Chain

The activities associated with each part of the value chain are shown in Figure 3. 4while the activities that are part of the tasks firms complete when dealing with support functions appear in Figure 3. 5. All items in both Figures should be evaluated relative to competitors' capabilities and core competencies. To become a core competence and a source of competitive advantage, a capability must allow the firm(1) to perform an activity in a manner that provides value superior to that provided by competitors, or(2) to perform a value creating activity that competitors cannot perform. Only under these conditions does a firm create value for customers and have opportunities to capture that that value.

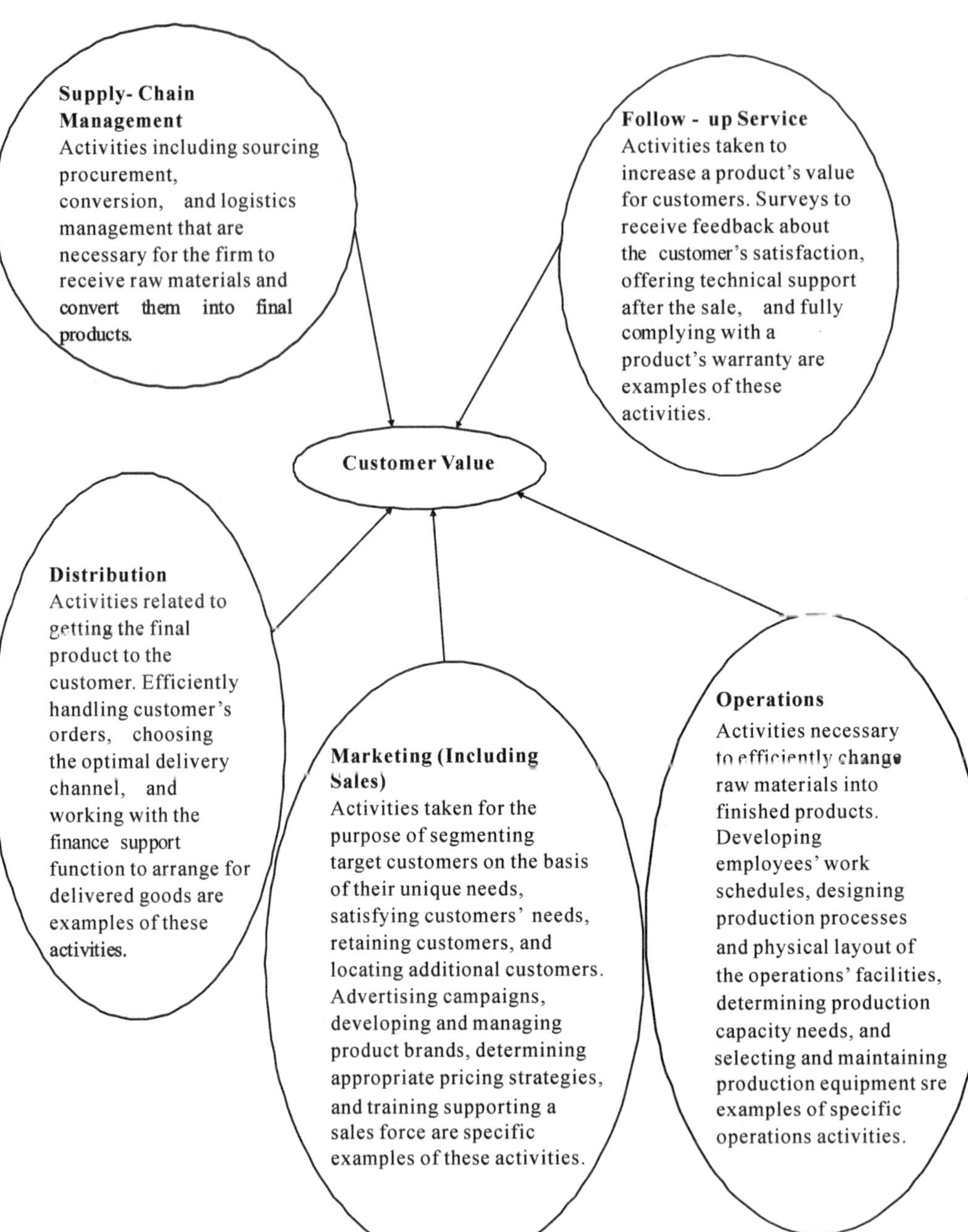

Figure 3. 4　Creating Value through Value Chain Activities

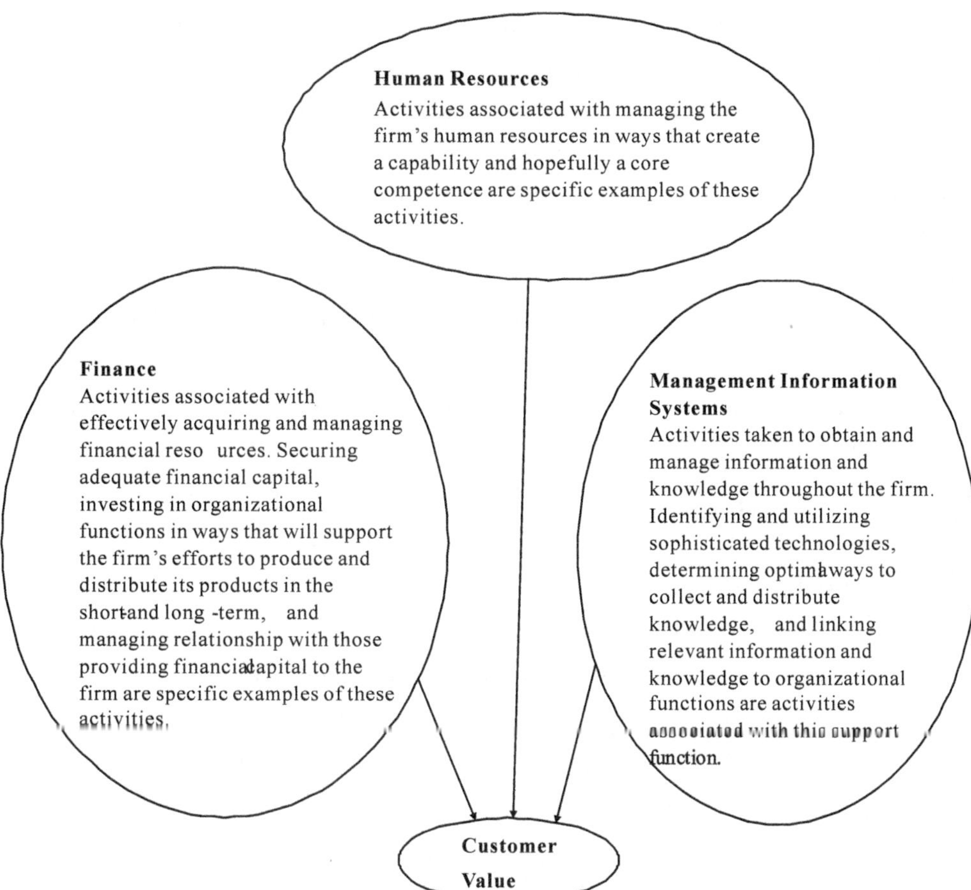

Figure 3.5　Creating Value through Support Functions

Creating value for customers by completing activities that are part of the value chain often require building effective alliances with suppliers (and sometimes others to which the firm outsources activities, as discussed in the next section) and developing strong positive relationships with customers. When firms have such strong positive relationships with suppliers and customers, they ate said to have "Social capital". The relationships themselves have value because they produce knowledge transfer and access to resources that a firm may not hold internally. To build social capital whereby resources such as knowledge are transferred across organizations requires trust between the parties. The partners must trust each other in order to allow their resources to be used in such a way that both parties will benefit over time and neither party will take advantage of the other. Trust and social capital usually evolve over time repeated interactions but firms can also establish special means to jointly manage alliances that promote greater trust with the outcome of enhanced benefits for both partners.

Evaluating a firm's capability to execute its value chain activities and support functions is challenging. Earlier in the chapter, we noted that identifying and assessing the value of a firm's resources and capabilities requires judgment. Judgment is equally necessary when using value chain analysis, because no obviously correct model or rule is universally available to help in the process.

The analysis on enterprise value chain—(the teacher plans to use enlighten education way)

There are two kinds of activities which can make profits:

(1) Primary activates: Inbound Logistics, Operations, Outbound Logistics, Marketing and Sales, Service

(2) Support Activities: Firm Infrastructure, Human Resource Management, Technology Development, Procurement

2. Primary Activities

(1) Inbound Logistics

concept introduction—(the teacher plans to use enlighten education way)

Activities: such as material handling, warehousing and inventory control

case study—(the teacher plans to use case study way)

TOYOTA—JUST IN TIME relationship between manufacturer and supplier

(2) Operations

concept introduction—(the teacher plans to use enlighten education way)

Activities: such as machining, packaging, assembly

case study—(the teacher plans to use case study way)

Federal Express — effective material assembly

(3) Outbound Logistics

concept introduction—(the teacher plans to use enlighten education way)

Activities: such as collecting, storing, distributing the final product

case study—(the teacher plans to use case study and scenario education way)

7-11—the same trigger of many stores in one target city

(4) Marketing and Sales

concept introduction—(the teacher plans to use enlighten education way)

Activities: such as advertising, promotional campaigns, pricing

case study—(the teacher plans to use case study way)

CITROEN—The advertising campaign on new kind of car

(5) Service

concept introduction—(the teacher plans to use enlighten education way)

Activities: such as installation, repair, training

case study—(the teacher plans to use case study way)

Little Swan—the repair activity in the night

3. Support Activities

(1) Firm Infrastructure

concept introduction—(the teacher plans to use enlighten education way)

Activities: such as planning, finance, accounting

case study—(the teacher plans to use case study way)

P&G—patents strategy on shampoo product

(2) Human Resource Management

concept introduction—(the teacher plans to use enlighten education way)

Activities: such as recruiting, hiring and training

case study—(the teacher plans to use case study way)

HP—The new qualification need of a professional receptionist

(3) Technology Development

concept introduction—(the teacher plans to use enlighten education way)

Activities: such as process improvement, basic R&D, design

case study—(the teacher plans to use case study way)

TOYOTA—The development of Ford Company testifies the importance of R&D

(4) Procurement

concept introduction—(the teacher plans to use enlighten education way)

Activities: such as raw material and supplies, fixed assets equipment, buildings

case study—(the teacher plans to use case study way)

APP—cultivating the own tree resource

Enterprise competitive simulation—(the teacher plans to use commutative education way)

Enterprise competitive simulation design—the teacher classify the students as 10 groups, and choosing 5 kinds of industries (Computer, Microwave Oven, Cosmetics, Hotel Service, Medicine), let these 10 groups assemble fixed—quantity operating resources in the above 9 kinds of value chain activities, and then, making the combination of value chain operating resources several simulating unit of every groups, the teacher will give evaluation in operating situation of every groups.

Competitive Force of Buyers Buyers are a strong competitive force when: They are large and purchase a sizable percentage of industry's product. They buy in large quantities. They can integrate backward Industry's product is standardized. Their costs in switching to substitutes or other brands are low. They can purchase from several sellers Product purchased does not save buyer money.

Competitive Pressures: Collaboration Between Sellers and Buyers Partnerships are an increasingly important competitive element in business-to-business relationships. Collaboration may result in mutual benefits regarding. Just-in-time deliveries Order processing Electronic invoice payments. On-line sharing of sales at the cash register Competitive advantage potential may accrue to industry rivals who do the best job of managing seller-buyer partnerships.

Principle of Competitive Markets Buyers are a stronger competitive force the more they have leverage to bargain over: Price Quality Service Other terms and conditions of sale.

Strategic Implications of the Five Competitive Forces Competitive environment is unattractive from the standpoint of earning good profits when: Rivalry is strong Entry barriers are low and entry is likely Competition from substitutes is strong Suppliers and customers have considerable bargaining power.

Strategic Implications of the Five Competitive Forces Competitive environment is ideal from a profit-making standpoint when: Rivalry is moderate Entry barriers are high and no firm is likely to enter Good substitutes do not exist Suppliers and customers are in a weak bargaining position.

Coping With the Five Competitive Forces Objective is to craft a strategy. To insulate firm from competitive forces. To help make the "rules, " placing added pressure on rivals Which allows firm to define the business model for the industry.

3.11 Outsourcing

Concerned with how components, finished goods, or services will be obtained, outsourcing is the purchase of a value-creating activity or a support function activity from an external supplier. Not-for-profit agencies as well as for-profit organizations actively engage in Out sourcing. Firms engaging in effective outsourcing increase their flexibility, mitigate risks, and reduce their capital investments. In multiple global industries, the trend toward outsourcing continues at a rapid pace. Moreover, in some industries virtually all firms seek the value that can be captured through effective outsourcing. As with other strategic management process decisions, careful analysis is required before the firm decides to outsource. And if outsourcing is to be used, firms must recognize that only activities where they cannot create value or where they are at a substantial disadvantage compared to competitors should be outsourced.

Outsourcing can be effective because few, if any, organizations possess the resources and capabilities required to achieve competitive superiority in all value chain activities and support functions. For example, research suggests that few companies can afford to develop internally all the technologies that might lead to competitive advantage. By nurturing a smaller number of capabilities, a firm increases the probability of developing core competencies and achieving a competitive advantage because it does not become overextended. In addition, by outsourcing activities in which it lacks competence, the firm can fully concentrate on those areas in which it can fully concentrate on those areas in which it can create value.

The consequences of outsourcing cause additional concerns. For the most part, these concerns revolve around the potential loss in firms' innovative ability and the loss of jobs within companies that decide to outsource some of their work activities to others. Thus, innovation and technological uncertainty are two important issues to consider when making outsourcing decisions. However, firms can also learn from outsource suppliers how to increase their own innovation capabilities. Companies must be aware of these issues and be prepared to fully consider the concerns about opportunities from outsourcing suggested by different stakeholders (e. g. , employees). The opportunities and foreign supply source (often referred to as off shoring). Bangalore and Belfast are the newest hotspots for technology outsourcing, competing with major operations in other nations such as China. Yet, IBM recently made the decision to keep outsourced activities in the United States instead of moving them to a foreign location.

3.12 Analyzing Driving Forces

Identify those forces likely to exert greatest influence over next 1—3 years. Usually no more than 3—4 factors qualify as real drivers of change. Assess impact What difference will the forces make-favorable or unfavorable?

Common Types of Driving Forces Internet and e-commerce opportunities. Increasing globalization of industry Changes in long-term industry growth rate Changes in who buys the product and how they use it Product innovation Technological change/process innovation Marketing innovation.

Common Types of Driving Forces Entry or exit of major firms Diffusion of technical knowledge Changes in cost and efficiency Market shift from standardized to differentiated products (or vice versa) Regulatory policies/government legislation Changing societal concerns, attitudes, and lifestyles Changes in degree of uncertainty and risk.

Environmental Scanning Definition Monitoring and interpreting sweep of social, political, economic, ecological, and technological events to spot budding trends that could eventually impact industry Purpose. Raise consciousness of managers about potential developments that could Have important impact on industry conditions Pose new opportunities and threats.

Which Companies are in Strongest/Weakest Positions? One technique for revealing the different competitive positions of industry rivals is strategic group mapping. A strategic group consists of those rivals with similar competitive approaches in an industry.

Strategic Group Mapping Firms in same strategic group have two or more competitive characteristics in common Sell in same price/quality range. Cover same geographic are as be vertically integrated to same degree. Have comparable product line breadth Emphasize same types of distribution channels Offer buyers similar services Use identical technological approaches

Procedure for Constructing a Strategic Group Map STEP 1: Identify competitive characteristics that differentiate firms in an industry from one another. STEP 2: Plot firms on a two-variable map using pairs of these differentiating characteristics. STEP 3: Assign firms that fall in about the same strategy space to same strategic group. STEP 4: Draw circles around each group, making circles proportional to size of group's respective share of total industry sales.

Market position refers to the selection of specific areas for marketing concentration and can be expressed in terms of markets, product, and geographical locations. Through market research, corporations are able to practice markets segmentation—tailoring products for specific market niches. 市场定位是指选择营销活动集中的特定领域，可以表现在市场、产品和地理位置等方面。借助市场调查，企业可以进行市场细分——为特定利基市场提供适合的产品。

The product life cycle is a graph showing time plotted against the dollar sales of a product as it moves from introduction through growth and maturity to decline. 产品生命周期以图表形式展示了产品销售额（以美元计）随着时间推移而发生的变化，经历了引入、成长、成熟和衰退等阶段。

Strategic Group Maps Variables selected as axes should not be highly correlated Variables chosen as axes should expose big differences in how rivals compete. Variables do not have to be either quantitative or continuous. Drawing sizes of circles proportional to combined sales of firms in each strategic group allows map to reflect relative sizes of each strategic group. If more than two good competitive variables can be used, several maps can be drawn

Interpreting Strategic Group Maps Driving forces and competitive pressures often favor some strategic groups and hurt others Profit potential of different strategic groups varies due to strengths and weaknesses in each group's market position. The closer strategic groups are on map, the stronger the competitive rivalry among member firms tends to be

What Strategic Moves Are Rivals Likely to Make Next? A firm's own best strategic moves are affected by Current strategies of competitors Future actions of competitors Profiling key rivals involves gathering competitive intelligence about their Current strategies Most recent moves Resource strengths and weaknesses Announced plans.

A brand is a name given to a company's product which identifies that item in the mind of the consumer. 品牌是公司的产品名称在消费者心目中的标识。

A corporate brand is a type of brand in which the company's name serves as the brand. 企业品牌是指采用公司的名称作为品牌名称。

Competitor Analysis Successful strategists take great pains in scouting competitors to Understand their strategies Watch their actions Evaluate their vulnerability to driving forces and competitive pressures Size up their resource strengths and weaknesses and their capabilities Try to anticipate rivals' next moves

Predicting Moves of Rivals Predicting rivals' next moves involves. Analyzing their current competitive positions. Examining public pronouncements about what it will take to be successful in industry. Gathering information from grapevine about current activities and potential changes. Studying past actions and leadership. Determining who has flexibility to make major strategic changes and who is locked into pursuing same basic strategy.

The flexible manufacturing permits the low-volume output of custom-tailored products at relatively low unit costs through economies of scope. 柔性制造允许借助范围经济为客户定制产品，以较低的单位成本实现小批量产出。

Autonomous (self-managing) work teams in which a group of people work together without a supervisor to plan, coordinate, and evaluate their work. 自主工作团队又称为自我管理工作团队。在自主工作团队中，团队成员一起工作，没有负责计划、协调和评估工作的主管。

Over two-third of large U. S. firms are successfully using autonomous work teams. 超过 2/3 的美国大型公司成功使用了自主工作团队。

Companies have begun using cross-functional work teams instead of developing products in a series of steps-beginning with a request from sales, which leads to design, to engineering and to purchasing, and finally to manufacturing (often resulting in customer rejection of a costly product)—companies are tearing down the traditional walls separating departments so that people from each discipline can get involved in projects early on. 公司使用跨职能工作团队替代传统的产品开发方式，消除横亘在各部门之间、将各部门分离开来的传统界限，确保来自各个学科的人员在项目早期就参与其中。

Virtual teams are groups of geographically and / or organizationally dispersed coworkers that are assembled using a combination of telecommunications and information technologies to accomplish an organizational task. 虚拟团队是指利用电信和信息技术，将

地理上和/或组织上分散的合作者组织起来，形成共同完成组织任务的团队。

Human diversity is the mix in the workplace of people from different races, cultures, and backgrounds. 人员多样性是指工作场所不同种族、文化和背景的人员的组合情况。

Supply chain management is the forming of networks for sourcing raw materials, manufacturing products or creating services, storing and distributing the goods, and delivering them to customers. 供应链管理是原材料采购、产品生产或服务创造、货物储存和分销，以及客户配送的网络形式。

Identifying Industry Key Success Factors Answers to three questions pinpoint KSFs On what basis do customers choose between competing brands of sellers? What resources and competitive capabilities does a seller need to have to be competitively successful? What does it take for sellers to achieve a sustainable competitive advantage? KSFs consist of the 3-5 really major determinants of financial and competitive success in an industry.

The concept of financial leverage (the ratio of total debt to total assets) helps describe the use of debt(versus equity)to finance the company's programs from outside. 财务杠杆概念帮助公司使用外部债务(相对于股权)进行融资的方案。

Capital budgeting is the analyzing and ranking of possible investments in fixed assets such as land, buildings, and equipment in terms of the additional outlays and additional receipts that will result from each investment. 资本预算是对固定资产，如土地、建筑物和设备，按照每项投资可能产生的额外支出和额外收入情况进行分析和排序。

A company's R&D intensity (its spending on R&D as a percentage of sales revenue) is a principal means of gaining market share in global competition. 一个公司的研发强度(即研发投入占销售收入的百分比)是在全球竞争中赢得市场份额的一种主要手段。

A company's R&D unit should be evaluated for technological competence, the proper management of technology, in both the development and the use of innovative technology. 评估一个公司研发部门的标准还包括技术竞争力、适当的技术管理，以及创新技术的发展和使用。

A company should also be proficient in technology transfer, the process of taking a new technology from the laboratory to the marketplace. 公司还应该擅长技术转让——新技术从实验室推向市场的过程。

The R&D mix involves basic R&D, product R&D, engineering or process R&D.

研发组合包括基础性研发、产品研发和工程或工艺研发。

The R&D mix is the balance of the three types of research. The mix should be appropriate to the strategy being considered and to each product's life cycle. 研发组合是三种研发类型研究的平衡。研发组合要适合所考虑的战略，以及每个产品的生命周期。

According to Richard Foster of McKinsey company, technological discontinuity is the displacement of one technology by another. 根据麦肯锡公司理查德·福斯特的研究，技术终结是一种技术替代另一种技术。

Even though the new technology may be more expensive to develop, it offers performance improvements in areas that are attractive to this small niche, but of no consequence to customers of the established competitors. 尽管新技术的开发可能更昂贵，但是新技术在很小的利基市场中所提供的绩效提升非常具有吸引力，对现有竞争对手的客户也没有什么影响。

Example: KSFs for Apparel Manufacturing Industry Fashion design—to create buyer appeal Low-cost manufacturing efficiency—to keep selling prices competitive.

Example: KSFs for Tin and Aluminum Can Industry Locating plants close to end-use customers—to keep costs of shipping empty cans low. Ability to market plant output within economical shipping distances

Things to Consider in Assessing Industry Attractiveness Industry's market size and growth potential Whether competitive conditions are conducive to rising/falling industry profitability. Will competitive forces become stronger or weaker. Whether industry will be favorably or unfavorably impacted by driving forces. Potential for entry/exit of major firms Stability/dependability of demand Severity of problems facing industry. Degree of risk and uncertainty in industry's future

Conducting an Industry and Competitive Situation Analysis Two things to keep in mind1. Evaluating industry and competitive conditions cannot be reduced to a formula-like exercise—thoughtful analysis is essential2. Sweeping industry and competitive analyses need to done every 1 to 3 years.

IFAS (Internal Factor Analysis Summary) table is one way to organize the internal factors into the generally accepted categories of strengths and weaknesses and to analyze how well a particular company's management is responding to these specific factors in light of the perceived importance of these factors to the company. 内部因素分析汇总表是将内部因素归类为普遍接受的优势和劣势，并分析特定公司的管理层是如何根据每个因素对于公司来说可感知的重要程度有所回应的。

Chapter 4 Evaluating Resources and Competitive Capabilities

4.1 A Model of Competitive Rivalry

Competitive rivalry evolves from the pattern of actions and responses as one firm's competitive actions have noticeable effects on competitors, eliciting competitive responses from them. This pattern suggests that firms are mutually interdependent, that they are affected by each other's actions and responses, and that marketplace success is a function of both individual strategies and the consequences of their use. Increasingly, too, executives recognize that competitive rivalry can have a major effect on the firm's financial performance. Research shows that intensified rivalry within an industry results in decreased average profitability for the competing firms. For example, Research in Motion (RIM) dominated the smartphone market with its Blackberry operating system platform until Apple's iPhone platform emerged. Likewise, the introduction of the Android platform by Google has cut into RIM's marked share and has thereby lowered the company's performance expectations.

Figure 4.1 presents a straightforward model of competitive rivalry at the firm level; this type of rivalry is usually dynamic and complex. The competitive actions and responses the firm takes are the foundation for successfully building and using its capabilities and core competencies to gain an advantageous market position. The model in Figure 4.1 presents the sequence of activities commonly involved in competition between a particular firm and each of its competitors' behavior and reduce the uncertainly associated with competitors' actions. Being able to predict competitors' actions and responses with competitors' actions. Being able to predict competitors' actions and responses has a positive effect on the firm's market position and its subsequent financial performance. The sum of all the individual rivalries modeled in Figure 4.1 that occur in a particular market reflect the competitive dynamics in that market.

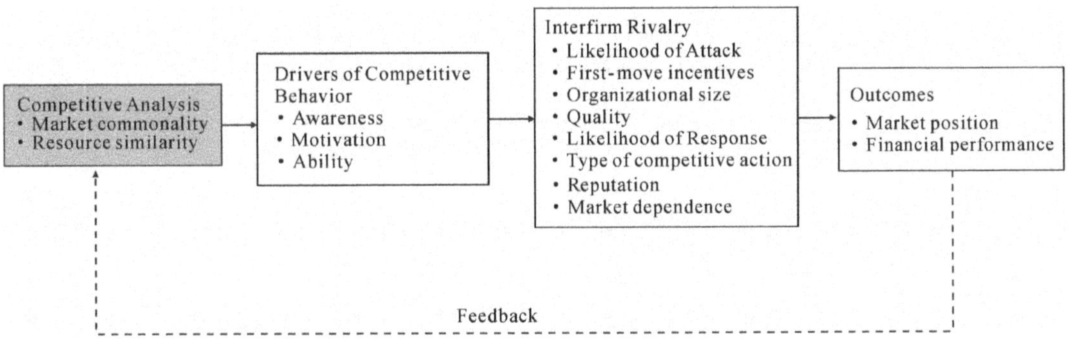

Figure 4.1 A Model of Competitive Rivalry

4.2 Competitor Analysis

As previously noted, a competitor analysis is the first step the firm takes to be able to predict the extent and nature of its rivalry with each competitor. The number of markets in which firms compete against each other and the similarity in their resources determine the extent to which the firms are competitors. Firms with high market commonality and highly similar resources are "clearly direct and mutually acknowledged competitors." The drivers of competitive behavior-as well as factors influencing the likelihood that a competitor will initiate competitive actions and will respond to its competitors' actions-influence the intensity of rivalry, even for direct competitors.

We discussed competitor analysis as a technique firms use to understand their competitive environment. Together, the general, industry, and competitive environments comprise the firm's external environment. We also described how competitor analysis is used to help the firm understand its competitors. This understanding results from studying competitors' future objectives, current strategies, assumptions, and capabilities.

Such competitive awareness is illustrated in the Strategic Focus on the competitors in the rivalry among the global automobile producers such as Toyota, Ford, General Motors, Honda, Chrysler, Nissan, and others. These analyses are highly important because they help managers to avoid "competitive blind spots," in which managers are unaware of specific competitors or their capabilities. If managers have competitive blind spots, they may be surprised by a competitor's actions, thereby allowing the competitor to increase its market share at the expense of the manager's firm. Competitor analyses are especially important when a firm enters a foreign market. Managers need to understand the local competition and foreign competitors currently operating in the market. Without such analyses, they are less likely to be successful.

4.3 Resource Similarity

Resource similarity is the extent to which the firm's tangible and intangible resources are comparable to a competitor's in terms of both type and amount. Firms with similar types and amounts of resources are likely to have similar strengths and weaknesses and use similar strategies. The competition between FedEx and United Parcel Service (UPS) in using information technology to improve the efficiency of their operations and to reduce costs demonstrates these expectations. Pursuing similar strategies that are supported by similar resource profiles, personnel in these firms work at a feverish pace to receive, sort, and ship packages. Rival DHL is trying to compete with the two global giants supported by the privatized German postal service, Deutsche Post World Net, which acquired it in 2002. DHL has made impressive gains in recent years; it competes strongly in Europe and Asia with resources and capabilities similar to those of FedEx and UPS and others to make its U. S. Deliveries. Such arrangements are often referred to as "coopertition" (cooperation between competitors).

When performing a competitor analysis, a firm analyzes each of its competitors in terms of market commonality and resource similarity. The results of these analyses can be mapped for visual comparisons. We show different hypothetical intersections between the firm and those with which it is compared are competitors. For example, the firm and its competitor displayed in quadrant I have similar types and amounts of resources. The firm and its competitor in quadrant. I would use their similar resource portfolios to compete against each other in many markets that are important to each. These conditions lead to the conclusion that the firms modeled in quadrant I are direct and mutually acknowledged competitors. In contrast, the firm and its competitor shown in quadrant III share few markets and have little similarity in their resources, indicating that they aren't direct and mutually acknowledged competitors. Thus, a small local, family-owned Italian restaurant does not compete directly against Olive. The firm's mapping of its competitive relationship with rivals is fluid as firms enter and exit markets and as companies' resources change in type and amount. Thus, the companies with which the firm is a direct competitor change across time.

4.4 Competitive Rivalry

The ongoing competitive action/response sequence between a firm and a competitor affects the performance of both firms, thus it is important for companies to carefully analyze and understand the competitive rivalry present in the markets they serve to select and implement successful strategies. Understanding a competitor's awareness, motivation, and ability helps the firm to predict the likelihood of an attack by that competitor and the probability that a competitor will respond to actions taken against it.

As we describe earlier, the predictions drawn from studying competitors in terms of awareness, motivation, and ability are grounded in market commonality and resource similarity. These predictions are fairly general. The value of the final set of predictions the firm develops about each of its competitors' competitive actions and responses is enhanced by studying the "likelihood of Attack" factors and the "Likelihood of Response" factors. Evaluating and understanding these factors allow the firm to refine the predictions it makes about its competitors' actions and responses.

4.5 Strategic and Tactical Actions

Firms use both strategic and tactical actions when forming their competitive actions and competitive response in the course of engaging in competitive rivalry. A competitive action is a strategic or tactical action the firm takes to build or defend its competitive advantages of improve its market position. A competitive response is a strategic or tactical action or a strategic response is a market-based move that involves a significant commitment of organizational resources and is difficult to implement and reverse. A tactical action or a tactical response is a market-based move that is taken to fine-tune a strategy; it involves fewer resources and is relatively easy to implement and reverse.

As noted in the Opening Case, Apple opened a service called "Game Center" once it found that users were using its iPhone, iPad, and iPod platforms for video games. With its update to its iOS (operating system) software, game producers began producing game applications to use the Apple system as its graphics became more advanced. This represents a strategic move by Apple. Game platform hardware and software producers such as Nintendo and Sony then created strategic responses to the Apple threat. For example, Sony, which produces the PlayStaion console, partnered with Sony Ericsson to make the Xperia PLAY phone, which uses "Play Station-certified games" and runs on Google's Android operating system.

Walmart prices aggressively as a mean of increasing revenues and gaining market share at the expense of competitors. However, pricing is a tactical strategy and Walmart's performance has lagged recently. In recent tactical moves, it has asserted that it will do a better job on competitive pricing. Although pricing aggressively is at the core of what Walmart is and how it competes, can the tactical action of aggressive pricing continue to lead to the competitive success the firm has historically enjoyed? Is Walmart achieving the type of balance between strategic and tactical competitive actions and competitive responses that is a foundation for all firm's success in marketplace competitions?

When engaging rivals in competition, firms must recognize the differences between strategic and tactical actions and responses and should develop an effective balance between the two types of competitive actions and responses. Airbus, Boeing's major competitor in commercial airliners, is aware that Boeing is strongly committed to taking actions it believers are necessary to successfully launch the 787 jetliner, because deciding to design, build and launch the 787 is a strategic action. In fact, many analysts believe that Boeing's development of the 787 airliner was a strategic response to Airbus's new A380 aircraft.

A corporation is a mechanism established to allow different parties to contribute capital, expertise, and labor for their mutual benefit. 公司是一种机制，其成立的目的是让各方人士为了共同利益投入资金、技术和劳动力。

The boards of most publicly owned corporations are composed of both inside and outside directors. Inside directors are typically officers or executives employed by the corporation. Outside directors may be executives of other firms but are not employees of the board's corporation. 大多数上市公司的董事会由内部董事和外部董事构成。内部董事通常由公司聘用的主管或执行官担任。外部董事可能是其他公司的执行官，但不是本公司董事会聘用的雇员。

4.6 Competitive Dynamics

Whereas competitive rivalry concerns the ongoing actions and responses between a firm and its direct competitors for an advantageous market position, competitive dynamics concern the ongoing action actions and responses among all firms competing within a market for advantageous positions. Building and sustaining competitive advantages are at the core of competitive rivalry, in that advantages are the key to creating value for shareholders.

To explain competitive dynamics, we explore the effects of varying rates of competitive speed in different markets on the behavior of all competitors within a given market. Competitive behaviors as well as the reasons for taking them are similar within each market type, but differ across the three markets. Thus, competitive dynamic differ in slow-cycle, fast-cycle and standard-cycle markets. The sustainability of the firm's competitive advantages differs across the three market types. Research has also shown how firms go through life-cycle stages as markets evolve overtime within which a firm is competing. However, understanding what happens within each type of market is more pertinent in knowing how to respond to the competition.

Firms want to sustain their competitive advantages for as long as possible, although no advantage is permanently sustainable. The degree of sustainability is affected by how quickly by how quickly competitive advantages can be imitated and how costly it is to do so.

The managers of business organizations have four responsibilities: economic, legal, ethical, and discretionary. 商业组织的管理者有四个责任:经济责任、法律责任、道德责任和任意责任。

A corporation's task environment includes a large number of groups with interest in the activities of a business organization. These groups are called stakeholders because they are groups that affect or are affected by the achievement of the firm's objectives. 公司的任务环境中包括大量与组织的活动具有利益关系的群体。这些群体称为利益相关者,因为这些群体影响公司目标的实现或受到公司目标实现的影响。

4.7 Slow-Cycle Markets

Slow-cycle markets are those in which the firm's competitive advantages are shielded from imitation, commonly for long periods of time, and where imitation is costly. Thus, competitive advantages are sustainable over longer periods of time in slow-cycle markets.

Building a unique and proprietary capability produces a competitive advantage and success in a slow-cycle market. This type of advantage is difficult for competitors to understand. A difficult-to-understand and costly-to-imitate resource or capability usually results from unique historical conditions, causal ambiguity, and/or social complexity. Copyrights, geography, patents, and ownership of an information resource are examples of resources. After a proprietary advantage is developed, the firm's competitive behavior in a slow-cycle market is oriented to protecting, maintaining, and extending that advantage. Thus, the competitive dynamics in slow-cycle markets usually concentrate on competitive actions and responses that enable firms to protect, maintain, and extend their competitive advantage. Major strategic actions in these markets, such as acquisitions, usually carry less risk than in faster cycle markets.

4.8 Fast-Cycle Markets

Fast-cycle markets are markets in which the firm's capabilities that contribute to competitive advantage aren't shielded from imitation and where imitation is often rapid and inexpensive. Thus, competitive advantages aren't sustainable in fast-cycle markets. Firms competing in fast-cycle markets recognize the importance of speed; these companies appreciate that "time is as precious a business resource as money or head count-and that the costs of hesitation and delay are just as steep as going over budget or missing a financial forecast." Such high-velocity environments place considerable pressures on top managers to quickly make strategic decisions that are also effective. The often substantial competition and technology-based strategic focus make the strategic decision complex, increasing the need for a comprehensive approach integrated with decision speed, two often-conflicting characteristics of the strategic decision process.

4.9 Company Situation Analysis

How well is firm's present strategy working? What are the firm's resource strengths and weaknesses and its external opportunities and threats? Are firm's prices and costs competitive? How strong is firm's competitive position relative to rivals? What strategic issues does firm face?

How Well is the Present Strategy Working? Two steps involved Determine current strategy of company Examine key indicators of strategic and financial performance.

What is the Strategy? Identify competitive approach Low-cost leadership Differentiation Focus on a particular market niche Determine competitive scope Stages of industry's production/distribution chain Geographic coverage Customer base Identify functional strategies Examine recent strategic moves.

Key Indicators of How Well the Strategy is Working Trend in sales and market share. Acquiring and/or retaining customers Trend in profit margins Trend in net profits, ROI, and EVA Overall financial strength and credit ranking Efforts at continuous improvement activities Trend in stock price and stockholder value Image and reputation with customers Leadership role(s)—technology, quality, innovation, e-commerce, etc.

Question :What Are the Firm's Strengths, Weaknesses, Opportunities and Threats? SWOT represents the first letter in Strengths, Weaknesses, Opportunities, Threats for a company's strategy to be well-conceived, it must be matched to both Resource strengths and weaknesses Best market opportunities and external threats to its well-being SWOT.

Identifying Resource Strengths and Competitive Capabilities. A strength is something a firm does well or a characteristic that enhances its competitiveness Valuable competencies or know-how Valuable physical assets Valuable human assets Valuable organizational assets Valuable intangible assets Important competitive capabilities. An attribute that places a company in a position of market advantage Alliances or cooperative ventures with capable partners Resource strengths and competitive capabilities are competitive assets!

Mobilizing Company Resources to Produce Competitive Advantage Competitive Advantage Strategic Assets and Market Achievements Core and Distinctive Competencies Competitive Capabilities Company Resources.

Identifying Resource Weaknesses and Competitive Deficiencies. A weakness is something a firm lacks, does poorly, or a condition placing it at a disadvantage Resource weaknesses relate to Deficiencies in know-how or expertise or competencies. Lack of important physical, organizational, or intangible assets Missing capabilities in key areas Resource weaknesses and deficiencies are competitive liabilities!

The enterprise strategy explicitly articulates the firm's ethical relationship with its stakeholders. 企业战略阐明了企业与利益相关者之间的道德责任关系。

SWOT Analysis-What to Look For Potential Resource Strengths Potential Resource Weaknesses Potential Company Opportunities Potential External Threats? Powerful strategy? Strong financial condition? Strong brand name image/reputation? Widely recognized market leader? Proprietary technology? Cost advantages? Strong advertising? Product innovation skills? Good customer service? Better product quality? Alliances or JVs? No clear strategic direction? Obsolete facilities? Weak balance sheet; excess debt? Higher overall costs than rivals? Missing some key skills/competencies? Subpar profits? Internal operating problems...? Falling behind in R&D? Too narrow product line? Weak marketing skills? Serving additional customer groups? Expanding to new geographic areas? Expanding product line? Transferring skills to new products? Vertical integration? Take market share from rivals? Acquisition of rivals? Alliances or JVs to expand coverage? Openings to exploit new technologies? Openings to extend brand name/image? Entry of potent new competitors? Loss of sales to substitutes? Slowing market growth? Adverse shifts in exchange rates &trade policies? Costly new regulations? Vulnerability to business cycle? Growing leverage of customers or suppliers? Reduced buyer needs for product? Demographic changes.

TOWS (SWOT backwards) Matrix illustrates how the external opportunities and threats facing a particular corporation can be matched with that company's internal strengths and weaknesses to result in four sets of possible strategic alternatives. TOWS 矩阵(SWOT 分析的反向形式)描述了特定公司所面临的外部的机会和威胁与公司内部的优势和劣势之间的匹配关系，可以产生四种可能的备选战略集。

Competencies vs. Core Competencies vs. Distinctive Competencies. A company competence is the product of organizational learning and experience and represents real proficiency in performing an internal activity. A core competence is a well-performed internal activity that is central(not peripheral or incidental)to a company's competitiveness and profitability. A distinctive competence is a competitively valuable activity that a company performs better than its rivals.

Company Competencies and Capabilities Stem from skills, expertise, and experience usually representing an Accumulation of learning over time and Gradual buildup of real proficiency in performing an activity. Involve deliberate efforts to develop the ability to do something, often entailing Selection of people with requisite knowledge and expertise Upgrading or expanding individual abilities. Molding work products of individuals into a cooperative effort to create organizational ability. A conscious effort to create intellectual capital.

Core Competencies：A Valuable Company Resource A competence becomes a core competence when the well-performed activity is central to the company's competitiveness and profitability. Often, a core competence results from collaboration among different parts of an organization. Typically, core competencies reside in a company's people, not in assets on the balance sheet. A core competence gives a company a potentially valuable competitive capability and represents a definite competitive asset.

The attractiveness of a particular strategic alternative is partially a function of the amount of risk it entails. Risk is composed not only of the probability that the strategy will be effective, but also of the amount of assets will be unavailable for other uses. 特定备选战略方案是否具有吸引力部分在于方案所涉及的大量风险。风险不仅包括战略结果最终是否有效，还包括公司必须分配给该战略的资产总额，以及这些资产不能为其他战略使用的时间长度。

The attractiveness of a strategic alternative is affected by its perceived compatibility with the key stakeholders in a corporation's task environment. 备选战略方案的吸引力受到公司与任务环境中关键利益相关者可感知的兼容性的影响。

Types of Core Competencies Expertise in building networks and systems to enable e-commerce Speeding new/next-generation products to market Better after-sale service capability Skills in manufacturing a high quality product Innovativeness in developing popular product features. Speed/agility in responding to new market trends System to fill customer orders accurately and swiftly Expertise in integrating multiple technologies.

Distinctive Competence—A Competitively Superior Resource ＃ 1A distinctive competence is a competitively significant activity that a company performs better than its competitors. A distinctive competence Represents a competitively valuable capability rivals do not have Presents attractive potential for being a cornerstone of strategy. Can provide a competitive edge in the marketplace—because it represents a competitively superior resource strength.

Strategic Management Principle A distinctive competence empowers a company to build competitive advantage!

Examples：Distinctive Competencies Sharp Corporation Expertise in flat-panel display technology Toyota, Honda, Nissan Low-cost, high-quality manufacturing capability and short design-to-market cycles Intel Ability to design and manufacture ever more powerful microprocessors for PCs Motorola Defect-free manufacture (six-sigma quality) of cell phones.

Determining the Competitive Value of a Company Resource To qualify as the basis for sustainable competitive advantage, a "resource" must pass 4 tests1. Is the resource hard to copy? Does the resource have staying power—is it durable? Is the resource really competitively superior? 4. Can the resource be trumped by the different capabilities of rivals?

Strategic Management Principle Successful strategists seek to capitalize on and leverage a company's resource strengths—its expertise, core competencies, and strongest competitive capabilities—by molding the strategy around the resource strengths!

Identifying a Company's Market Opportunities Opportunities most relevant to a company are those offering Best prospects for profitable long-term growth Potential for competitive advantage Good match with its financial and organizational resource capabilities.

Strategic Management Principle. A company is well-advised to pass on a particular market opportunity unless it has or can build the resource capabilities to capture it!

Identifying External Threats Emergence of cheaper/better technologies Introduction of better products by rivals Intensifying competitive pressures Onerous regulations Rise in interest rates Potential of a hostile take over Unfavorable demographic shifts Adverse shifts in foreign exchange rates Political upheaval in a country.

If a strategy is incompatible with the corporate culture, it probably will not succeed. 如果一家公司的战略与企业文化不相适应,那么这个战略可能不会成功。

In considering a strategic alternative, strategy makers must assess its compatibility with the corporate culture. 考虑到战略的备选性,战略制定者一定会评估战略与企业文化的适应程度。

Strategic Management Principle Successful strategists aim at capturing a company's best growth opportunities and creating defenses against external threats to its competitive position and future performance!

Role of SWOT Analysis in Crafting a Better Strategy Developing a clear understanding of a company's Resource strengths Resource weaknesses Best opportunities External threats Drawing conclusions about how Company's strategy can be matched to both its resource capabilities and market opportunities Urgent it is for company to correct resource weaknesses and guard against external threats.

Are the Company's Prices and Costs Competitive? Assessing whether a firm's costs are competitive with those of rivals is a crucial part of company analysis Key analytic tools Strategic cost analysis Value chain analysis Benchmarking.

Why Rival Companies Have Different Costs Companies do not have the same costs because of differences in Prices paid for raw materials, component parts, energy, and other supplier resources Basic technology and age of plant & equipment Economies of scale and experience curve effects Wage rates and productivity levels Marketing, promotion, and administration costs Inbound and outbound shipping costs Forward channel distribution costs.

Principle of Competitive Markets The higher a company's costs are above those of close rivals, the more competitively vulnerable it becomes!

What is Strategic Cost Analysis? Focuses on a firm's costs relative to its rivals Compares a firm's costs activity by activity against costs of key rivals From raw materials purchase to Price paid by ultimate customer Pinpoints which internal activities are a source of cost advantage or disadvantage.

The Concept of a Company Value Chain. A company consists of all the activities and function sit performs in trying to deliver value to its customers. A company's value chain shows the linked set of activities, functions, and business processes that it performs in the course of designing, producing, marketing, delivering, and supporting its product/service and thereby creating value for its customers. A company's value chain consists of two types of activities Primary activities (where most of the value for customers is created) Support activities that are undertaken to aid the individuals ands groups engaged in doing the primary activities.

4.10 Typical Company Value Chain

The Value Chain System for an Entire Industry. Assessing a company's cost competitiveness involves comparing costs all along the industry's value chain Suppliers' value chains are relevant because Costs, quality, and performance of inputs provided by suppliers influence a firm's own costs and product performance Forward channel allies' value chains are relevant because. Forward channel allies' costs and margins are part of price paid by ultimate end-user Activities performed affect end-user satisfaction.

Example: Key Value Chain Activities SOFT DRINK INDUSTRY Processing of basic ingredients Syrup manufacture Bottling and can filling Wholesale distribution Retailing Kroger.

Activity-Based Costing: A Key Tool in Strategic Cost Analysis Determining whether a company's costs are inline with those of rivals requires measuring how a company's costs compare with those of rivals activity-by-activity—from one end of the value chain to the other Requires having accounting data that measures the cost of each value chain activity. Activity-based accounting systems provide the data for determining the costs for each relevant value chain activity.

Benchmarking Costs of Key Value Chain Activities Focuses on cross-company comparisons of how certain activities are performed and the costs associated with these activities. Purchase of materials Payment of suppliers Management of inventories. Training of employees Processing of payrolls Getting new products to market Performance of quality control Filling and shipping of customer orders.

Even the most attractive might not be selected if it is contrary to the needs and desires of important managers. 即使这个战略是最有吸引力,但如果它与重要管理者的需求和愿望相违背,那么它也可能不会被选择。

Strategic choice is the evaluation of alternative strategies and the selection of the best alternative. 战略选择是评价备选战略方案并选择最佳战略方案的过程。

Objectives of Benchmarking Determine whether a company is performing particular value chain activities efficiently by studying the practices and procedures used by other companies. Understand the best practices in performing an activity—learn what is the "best" way to do a particular activity from those who have demonstrated they are "best-in-industry" or "best-in-world" Assess if company's costs of performing particular value chain activities are in line with competitors. Learn how other firms achieve lower costs. Take action to improve company's cost competitiveness.

Ethical Standards in Benchmarking: Do's and Don'ts Avoid talk about pricing or competitively sensitive costs. Don't ask rivals for sensitive data. Don't share proprietary data without clearance. Have impartial third party assemble and present competitively sensitive cost data with no names attached. Don't disparage a rival's business to outsiders based on data obtained.

What Determines Whether a Company is Cost Competitive? A company's cost competitiveness depends on how well it manages its value chain relative to how well competitors manage their value chains. When a company's costs are "out-of-line", the "high-cost" activities can exist in any of three areas in the industry value chain1. Suppliers'activities2. The company's own internal activities3. Forward channel activities Activities, Costs, &Margins of Forward Channel Allies &Strategic Partners Internally Performed Activities, Costs, & Margins. Activities, Costs, &Margins of Suppliers Buyer/ User Value Chains.

Correcting Supplier-Related Cost Disadvantages: Options Negotiate more favorable prices with suppliers Work with suppliers to help them achieve lower costs. Use lower-priced substitute inputs Collaborate closely with suppliers to identify mutual cost-saving opportunities Integrate backwards Make up difference by initiating cost savings in other areas of value chain.

Correcting Forward Channel Cost Disadvantages: Options Push for more favorable terms with distributors and other forward channel allies Work closely with forward channel allies and customers to identify win-win opportunities to reduce costs Change to a more economical distribution strategy Make up difference by initiating cost savings earlier in value chain.

Correcting Internal Cost Disadvantages: Options Reengineer how the high-cost activities or business processes are performed Eliminate some cost-producing activities altogether by revamping value chain system. Relocate high-cost activities to lower-cost geographic areas. See if high-cost activities can be performed cheaper by outside vendors/suppliers Invest in cost-saving technology Simplify product design. Make up difference by achieving savings in backward or forward portions of value chain.

From Value Chain Analysis to Competitive Advantage A company can create competitive advantage by managing its value chain to Integrate knowledge and skills of employees in competitively valuable ways. Leverage economies of learning/experience Coordinate related activities in ways that build valuable capabilities. Build dominating expertise in a value chain activity critical to customer satisfaction or market success.

From Value Chain Analysis to Competitive Advantage Strategy-Making Lesson of Value Chain Analysis Sustainable competitive advantage can be created by1. Managing value chain activities better than rivals and/or. Developing distinctive value chain capabilities to serve customers!

4.11 How Strong the Company's Competitive Position Is

The strength of a company's competitive position in the marketplace hinges on. Whether firm's position can be expected to improve or deteriorate if present strategy is continued. How firm ranks relative to key rivals on each industry KSF and relevant measure of competitive strength. Whether firm has a sustainable competitive advantage or finds itself at disadvantage relative to certain rivals. Ability of firm to defend its position in light of Industry driving forces Competitive pressures Anticipated moves of rivals.

Assessing a Company's Competitive Strength versus Key Rivals. List industry key success factors and other relevant measures of competitive strength. Rate firm and key rivals on each factor using rating scale of 1 to 10 (1 = very weak; 4 = average; 10 = very strong). Decide whether to use a weighted or unweighted rating system (a weighted system is usually superior because the chosen strength measures are unlikely to be equally important). Sum individual ratings to get an overall measure of competitive strength for each rival. Determine whether firm enjoys a competitive advantage or suffers from a competitive disadvantage based on the overall strength ratings.

Why Do a Competitive Strength Assessment? Reveals strength of firm's competitive position vis-à-vis key rivals Shows how firm stacks up against rivals, measure-by-measure—pinpoints firm's competitive strengths and competitive weaknesses. Indicates whether firm is at a competitive advantage/disadvantage against each rival. Identifies possible offensive attacks (pit company strengths against rivals' weaknesses) Identifies possible defensive actions(a need to correct competitive weaknesses).

Question: What Strategic Issues Does the Company Need to Address? Based on the answers to the preceding 4questions and the 7 questions posed in conducting industry and competitive analysis, what items should be on the company's "worry list"? Requires thinking strategically about Pluses and minuses in the industry and competitive situation Company's resource strengths and weaknesses and attractiveness its competitive position. A "good" strategy must address "what to do" about each and every strategic issue!

Identifying the Strategic Issues Is the present strategy adequate in light of competitive pressures and driving forces? Is the strategy well-matched to the industry's future key success factors? Does the company need new or different resource strengths and competitive capabilities? Does present strategy adequately protect against external threats and resource deficiencies? Is firm vulnerable to competitive attack by rivals? Where are strong/weak spots in present strategy?

Stating the Issues Clearly and Precisely. A well-stated issue involves such phrases as "What should be done about... ?""How to... ?""Whether to... ?""Should we... ?"Issues need to be precise, specific, an "cut straight to the chase "Issues on the "the worry list" raise questions about What actions need to be considered What to think about doing.

Chapter 5 Business-Level Strategies

5.1 Customers: Their Relationship with Business-Level Strategies

Strategic competitiveness results only when the firm satisfies a group of customers by using its competitive advantages as the basis for competing in individual product markets. A key reason firms must satisfy customers with their business-level strategy is that returns earned from relationships with customers are the lifeblood of all organizations.

The most successful companies try to find new ways to satisfy current customers and/or to meet the needs of new customers. Being able to do this can be even more difficult when firms and consumers face challenging economic conditions. During such times, firms may decide to reduce their workforce to control costs. This can lead to problems, however, when having fewer employees makes it more difficult for companies to meet individual customers' needs and expectations. In these instances, some suggest that firms should follow several courses of action, including paying extra attention to their best customers and developing a flexible workforce by cross-training employees so they can undertake a variety of responsibilities on their jobs. Amazon. com, insure USAA, and Lexus have been identified as "customer service champions" because they devote extra care and attention to customer service especially during challenging economic times.

Corporate strategy deals with three key issues facing the corporation as a whole that directional strategy, portfolio strategy and parenting strategy. 公司战略面对整个公司，把整个公司作为一个整体处理三个关键问题，即定向战略的问题、投资组合战略的问题及母合战略的问题。

Corporate strategy is therefore concerned with the direction of the firm and the management of its product lines and business units. This is true whether the firm is a small, one-product company or a large, multinational corporation. 公司战略主要关注企业的发展方向并管理公司的产品线和业务部门。无论这家公司是一家小型的、单一产品的企业还是大型的、多样化生产的企业，公司战略对它们而言都是真实存在的。

5.2 The Purpose of Business-Level Strategies

The purpose of a business-level strategy is to create differences between the firm's position and those of its competitors. To position itself differently from competitors, a firm must decide whether it intends to perform activities differently or to perform different activities. Strategy defines the path which provides the direction of actions to be taken by leaders of the organization. In fact, "choosing to perform activities differently or to perform different activities than rivals" is the essence of business-level strategy. Thus, the firm's business-level strategy is a deliberate choice about how it will perform the value chain's primary and support activities to create unique value. Indeed, in the current complex competitive landscape, successful use of a business-level strategy results from the firm learning how to integrate the activities it performs in ways that create superior value for customers.

Firms develop an activity map to show how they integrate the activities they perform. We show the Southwest Airlines activity map. The manner in which Southwest has integrated its activities is the foundation for the successful use of its primary cost leadership strategy (this strategy is discussed later in the chapter) but also includes differentiation through the unique services provided to customers. The tight integration among Southwest's activities is a key source of the firm's ability to at least historically operate more profitably than its competitors.

A corporation's directional strategy is composed of three general orientations toward growth: growth strategies, stability strategies, retrenchment strategies. 一个公司的定位战略是由增长战略、稳定战略或收缩战略这三个面对增长的总体方向组成的。

Southwest Airlines has conFigured the activities it performs into six strategic themes-limited passenger service; frequent, reliable departures; lean, highly productive ground and gate crews; high aircraft utilization; very low ticket prices; and short-haul. Point-to-point routes between mid-sized cities and secondary airports. Individual clusters of tightly linked activities make it possible for the outcome of a strategic theme to be achieved. For example, no meals, no seat assignments, and no baggage transfers form a cluster of individual activities that support the strategic theme of limited passenger.

Southwest's tightly integrated activities make it difficult for competitors to imitate the firm's cost leadership strategy. The firm's unique culture and customer service, both of which are sources of competitive advantages, are features that rivals have been unable to imitate, although some have tried and largely failed (e. g. , U. S. Airways' Metrojet subsidiary, United Shuttle, Delta's Song, and Continental Airlines' Continental Lite). Hindsight shows that these competitors offered low price to customers, but weren't able to operate at costs close to those of Southwest or to provide customers with any notable sources of differentiation, such as a unique experience while in the air. The key to Southwest's success has been its ability to continuously reduce its costs while providing customers with acceptable levels of differentiation such as an engaging culture. Firms using the cost leadership strategy must understand that in terms of sources of differentiation that accompany the cost leader's product, the customer defines acceptable. Fit among activities is a key to the sustainability of competitive advantage for all firms, including Southwest Airlines. Strategic fit among the many activities is critical for competitive advantage. It is more difficult for a competitor to match a configuration of integrated activities than to imitate a particular activity such as sales promotion, or a process technology.

Strategy formulation is often referred to as strategic planning or long-range planning and is concerned with developing a corporation's mission, objectives, strategies, and policies. 战略制定通常是指战略规划或长期规划，主要关注开发公司的使命、目标、战略和政策。

The SFAS (Strategic Factors Analysis Summary) Matrix summarize a corporation's strategic factors by combining the external factors from the EFAS Table with the internal factors form the IFAS Table. 战略因素分析汇总矩阵通过将外部因素分析汇总表中的外部因素与内部因素分析汇总表中的内部因素相结合，总结一家公司的战略因素。

Table 5.1 Strategic Factors Analysis Summary (SFAS) Matrix

<table>
<tr><th rowspan="2">Strategic Factors
(Select the most important opportunities/threats from the EFAS, Table 3-3, and the most important strengths and weaknesses from the IFAS, Table 4-2)</th><th rowspan="2">Weight</th><th rowspan="2">Rating</th><th rowspan="2">Weight Score</th><th colspan="3">Duration</th><th rowspan="2">comments</th></tr>
<tr><th>short</th><th>intermediate</th><th>long</th></tr>
<tr><td>• Quality Maytag Culture(S)</td><td>0.10</td><td>5</td><td>0.50</td><td></td><td></td><td>×</td><td>Quality key to success</td></tr>
<tr><td>• Hoover's international orientation(S)</td><td>0.10</td><td>3</td><td>0.30</td><td></td><td>×</td><td></td><td>Name recognition</td></tr>
<tr><td>• Financial position(W)</td><td>0.10</td><td>2</td><td>0.20</td><td></td><td>×</td><td></td><td>High debt</td></tr>
<tr><td>• Global positioning(W)</td><td>0.15</td><td>2</td><td>0.30</td><td></td><td></td><td>×</td><td>Only in New Zealand, U.K., and Australia</td></tr>
<tr><td>• Economic integration of European Union(O)</td><td>0.10</td><td>4</td><td>0.40</td><td></td><td></td><td>×</td><td>Acquisition of Hoover</td></tr>
<tr><td>• Demographics favor quality(O)</td><td>0.10</td><td>5</td><td>0.50</td><td></td><td>×</td><td></td><td>Maytag quality</td></tr>
<tr><td>• Trend to superstores(O+T)</td><td>0.10</td><td>2</td><td>0.20</td><td>×</td><td></td><td></td><td>Weak in this channel</td></tr>
<tr><td>• Whirlpool and Electrolux(T)</td><td>0.15</td><td>3</td><td>0.45</td><td>×</td><td></td><td></td><td>Dominate industry</td></tr>
<tr><td>• Japanese appliance companies (T)</td><td>0.10</td><td>2</td><td>0.20</td><td></td><td></td><td>×</td><td>Asian presence</td></tr>
<tr><td>Total</td><td>1.00</td><td></td><td>3.05</td><td></td><td></td><td></td><td></td></tr>
</table>

Corporate scenarios are pro forma balance sheets and income statements that forecast the effect that each alternative strategy and its various programs will likely have on division and corporate return on investment. 公司情境是使用预计资产负债表和利润表，预测每个备选战略及其方案可能对分部和公司的投资收益产生的影响。

Develop common-financial statements for the company's or business unit's previous years. 为公司或业务单位前些年的财务情况制定共同比财务报表。

Construct detailed pro forma financial statements for each strategic alternative. 为每一个备选战略构建详细的预测财务报表。

One approach is to appoint someone as devil's advocate, a person or group assigned to identify potential pitfalls and problems with a proposed alternative. Another approach, called dialectical inquiry, requires that two proposals using different assumptions be generated for each alternative strategy under consideration. 一种方法是任命某人为魔鬼代言人，指出其他人或群体提出的备选方案的潜在陷阱和问题。另一种方法称为辩证质询，要求两个提案采用不同的假设。

When crafted correctly, an effective policy accomplishes three things: 一项有效的政策被正确的执行和完成需要注意三件事：

It forces trade-offs between competing resource demands. 推动竞争性资源需求之间的权衡。

It tests the strategic soundness of a particular action. 测试特定战略行动的稳健性。

It sets clear boundaries within which employees must operate while granting them freedom to experiment within those constraints. 设置清晰的员工工作界限，同时赋予员工在允许范围内进行尝试的自由。

5.3 Types of Business-Level Strategies

Firms choose from among five business-level strategies to establish and defend their desired strategic position against competitor: cost leadership, differentiation, focused cost leadership. Focused differentiation, and integrated cost leadership/ differentiation. Each business-level strategy helps the firm to establish and exploit a particular competitive advantage within a particular competitive scope. How firms integrate the activities they perform within each different business-level strategy demonstrates how they differ from one another. For example, firms have different activity maps, and thus, a Southwest Airlines activity map differs from those of competitors JetBlue, Continental, American Airlines, and so forth. Superior integration of activities increases the likelihood of being able to gain an advantage over competitors and to earn above-average returns.

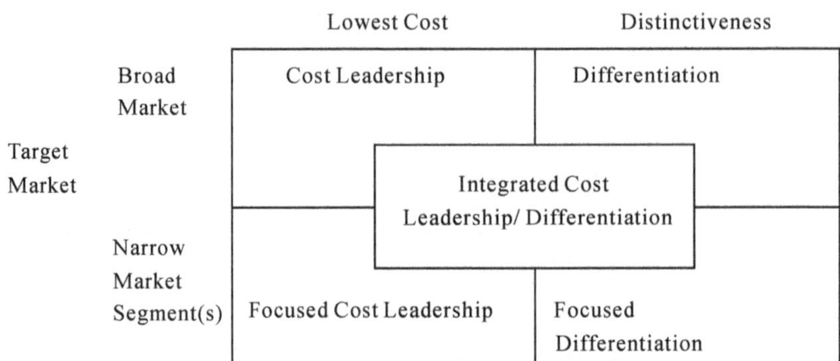

Figure 5.1 Five Business-Level Strategies

Business strategies focuses on improving the competitive position of a company's or business unit's products or services within the specific industry or market segment that the company of business unit serves. 业务战略关注改善公司或业务单位涉足的特定行业或细分市场中产品或服务的竞争地位。

Competitive strategy creates a defendable position in an industry so that a firm can outperform competitors. 竞争战略巩固了公司在行业中的防御地位，从而超越竞争对手。

Michael Porter proposes two "generic" competitive strategies for outperforming other corporations in a particular industry: lower cost and differentiation. These strategies are called generic because they can be pursued by any type or size of business firm, even by not-for-profit organizations. 迈克尔·波特认为有两种通用的竞争战略能在一个行业中有助于企业跑赢其他公司：低成本战略和差异化战略。它们之所以被称为通用战略是因为它们能被任何类型或规模的商业公司或非营利组织所利用。

By far the most widely pursued corporate strategies of business firms are those designed to achieve growth in sales, assets, profits, or some combination of these. there are two basic corporate growth strategies: concentration within one product line or industry and diversification into other products or industries. 到目前为止，最广泛追求的企业战略的是那些旨在实现销售，资产，利润，或一些组合增长的一些战略。有两种基本的企业成长战略，一种是集中于一个产品或一个产业的增长战略，另一种是在其他产品或行业多元化发展的增长战略。

5.4 Cost Leadership Strategies

The cost leadership strategy is an integrated set of actions taken to produce goods or services with features that are acceptable to customers at the lowest cost, relative to those of competitors. Firms using the cost leadership strategy commonly sell standardized goods or services (but with competitive levels of differentiation) to the industry's most typical customers. Process innovations, which are newly designed production and distribution methods and techniques that allow the firm to operate more efficiently, are critical to successful use of the cost leadership strategy.

Lower cost strategy is the ability of a company or a business unit to design, produce, and market a comparable product more efficiently than its competitors. 低成本战略是一个公司或业务单位在设计、生产和销售产品中表现出来的比其他竞争者更高效的能力。

As noted, cost leaders' goods and services must have competitive levels of differentiation that create value for customers. For example, in recent years Kia Motors has emphasized the design of its cars in the U. S. market as a source of differentiation while implementing a cost leadership strategy. Called "cheap chic", some analysts had a positive view of this decision, saying that "When they're done, Kia's cars will still be low-end (in price), but they won't necessarily look like it. It is important for firms using the cost leadership strategy to not only concentrate on reducing costs because it could result in the firm efficiently producing products that no customer wants to purchase. In fact, such extremes could limit the potential for important process innovations and lead to employment of lower-skilled workers, poor conditions on the production line, accidents, and a poor quality of work life for employees.

The firm using the cost leadership strategy targets a broad customer segment or group. Cost leaders concentrate on finding ways to lower their costs relative to competitors by constantly rethinking how to complete their primary and support activities to reduce costs still further while maintaining competitive levels of differentiation.

For example, cost leader Greyhound lines Inc. continuously seeks way to reduce the costs it incurs to provide bus service while offering customers have while they pay low prices for their service package. Interestingly, a number of customers have while they pay low prices trying to enhance the value of the experience customers have while they pay low prices for their service package. Interestingly, a number of customers now "insist on certain amenities that they receive on planes and trains-such as Internet access and comfortable seats, not to mention cleanliness". To maintain competitive levels of differentiation while using the cost leadership strategy, Greyhound recently starting using over 100" motor coaches" that have leather seats, additional legroom, Wi-Fi access, and power outlets in every row.

Greyhound enjoys economies of scale by serving more than 25million passengers annually with about 2300 destinations in the United States and almost 13000 daily departures. These scale economies allow the firm to keep its costs low while offering some of the differentiated services today's customers seek from the company. Demonstrating the firm's commitment to the physical environment segment of the general environment is the fact that "one Greyhound bus takes an average of 35 cars off the road".

Cost leadership is a low-cost competitive strategy that aims at the broad mass market and requires "aggressive construction of efficient-scale facilities, vigorous pursuit of cost reductions from experience, tight cost and overhead control, avoidance sales force, advertising, and so on". 成本领先是一种瞄准广阔的大众市场采取低成本方式竞争的战略，需要"积极建设高效的规模化设施，借助经验、成本和额外费用的严格控制，大力追求成本降低，避免客户账户边际化，在研发、服务、销售队伍、广告等领域实现成本最小化，等等"。

As primary activities, inbound logistics (e. g. , materials handling, warehousing, and inventory control) and outbound logistics (e. g. , collecting, storing, and distributing products to customers) often account for significant portions of the total cost to produce some goods and services. Research suggests that having a competitive advantage in logistics creates more with a cost leadership than with a differentiation strategy. Thus, cost leaders seeking competitively valuable ways to reduce costs may want to concentrate on the primary activities of inbound logistics and outbound logistics. In so doing many firms choose to outsource their manufacturing operations to low-cost firms with low-wage employees (e. g. , China). However, care must be taken because outsourcing also makes the firm more dependent on firms over which they have little control. At best, it creates interdependencies between the outsourcing firm and the suppliers. If dependencies become too great, it gives the supplier more power with which the supplier may increase price of the goods and services provided. Such actions could harm the firm's ability to maintain a low-cost competitive advantage.

Cost leader also carefully examine all support activities to find additional potential cost reductions. Developing new systems for finding the optimal combination of low cost and acceptable levels of differentiation in the raw materials required to produce the firm's goods or services is an example of how the procurement support activity can facilitate successful use of the cost leadership strategy.

Big Lost Inc. use the cost leadership strategy. With its vision of being "The World's Best Bargain Place," Big Lost is the large closeout retailer in the United States with annual sales of over5 billion from more than 1500 stores with approximately 13, 000 employees. For Big Lost, closeout goods are brand-name products sold by other retailers provided for sale at substantially lower prices.

Firms use value-chain analysis to identify the parts of the company's operations that create value and those that do not. The primary and support activities that allow a firm to create value through the cost leadership strategy. Companies unable to link the activities shown in this Figure through the activity map they form typically lack the core competencies needed to successfully use the cost leadership strategy.

Effective use of the cost leadership strategy allows a firm to earn above-average returns in spite of the presence of strong competitive force. The next sections explain how firms implement a cost leadership strategy.

5.5 Differentiation Strategies

The differentiation strategy is an integrated set of action taken to produce goods or services (at an acceptable cost) that customers perceive as being different in ways that are important to them. While cost leaders serve a typical customer in an industry, differentiators target customers for whom value is created by the manner in which the firm's products differ from those produced and marketed by competitors. Product innovation, which is "the result of bringing to life a new way to solve the customer's problem-through a new product or service development-that benefits both the customer and the sponsoring company is critical to successful use of the differentiation strategy.

Differentiation strategy is the ability to provide unique and superior(value) to the buyer in terms of product quality, special features, or after-sale service. 差异化战略是能长期为买方在产品质量、特殊功能或售后服务中提供独特的超价值的这样一种能力。

Porter further proposes that a firm's competitive advantage in an industry is determined by its competitive scope, that is, the breadth of the target market of the company or business unit. 波特预见一个公司在产业中的竞争优势取决于它的竞争范围，也就是这个公司或业务单位的目标市场的广度。

Firms must be able to produce differentiated products at competitive costs to reduce upward pressure on the price that customers pay. When a product's differentiated features are produced at noncompetitive costs, the price for the product may exceed what the firm's target customers are willing to pay. If the firm has a thorough understanding of what its target customers value, the relative importance they attach to the satisfaction of differentiation strategy can be effective in helping it earn above-average returns. Of course, to achieve these returns, the firm must apply its knowledge capital to provide customers with a different product that provides them with superior value.

Differentiation is aimed at the broad mass market and involves the creation of a product or service that is perceived throughout its industry as unique. 差异化是一种瞄准广阔的大众市场，创造全行业可感知独特性的产品或服务的竞争战略。

Through the differentiation strategy, the firm produces non-standardized (that is, distinctive) products for customers who value differentiated features more than they value low cost. For example, superior product reliability and durability and high-performance sound systems are among the differentiated features of Toyota Motor corporation's Lexus products. However, Lexus offers its vehicles to customers at a competitive purchase price relative to other luxury automobiles. As with Lexus products, a product's unique attributes, rather than its purchase price, provide the value for which customers are willing to pay.

To maintain success with the differentiation strategy results, the firm must consistently upgrade differentiated features that customers value and/or create new valuable features (innovate) without significant cost increases. This approach requires firms to constantly change their product lines. These firms may also offer a portfolio of products that complement each other, thereby enriching the differentiation for the customer and perhaps satisfying a portfolio of consumer needs. Because a differentiated product satisfies customers' unique needs, firms following the differentiation strategy are able to charge premium price. The ability to sell a good or service at a price that substantially exceeds the cost of creating its differentiated features allows the firm to outperform rivals and earn above-average returns. Rather than costs, a firm using the differentiation strategy primarily concentrates on investing in and developing features that differentiate a product in ways that create value for customers. Overall, a firm using the differentiation strategy seeks to be different from its competitors on as dimensions as possible. The less similarity between a firm's goods or service and those of competitors, the more buffered it is from rivals' actions. Commonly recognized differentiated goods include Toyota's Lexus, Ralph Lauren's wide array of product lines, Caterpillar's heavy-duty earth-moving equipment, and McKinsey & Co.'s differentiated consulting services.

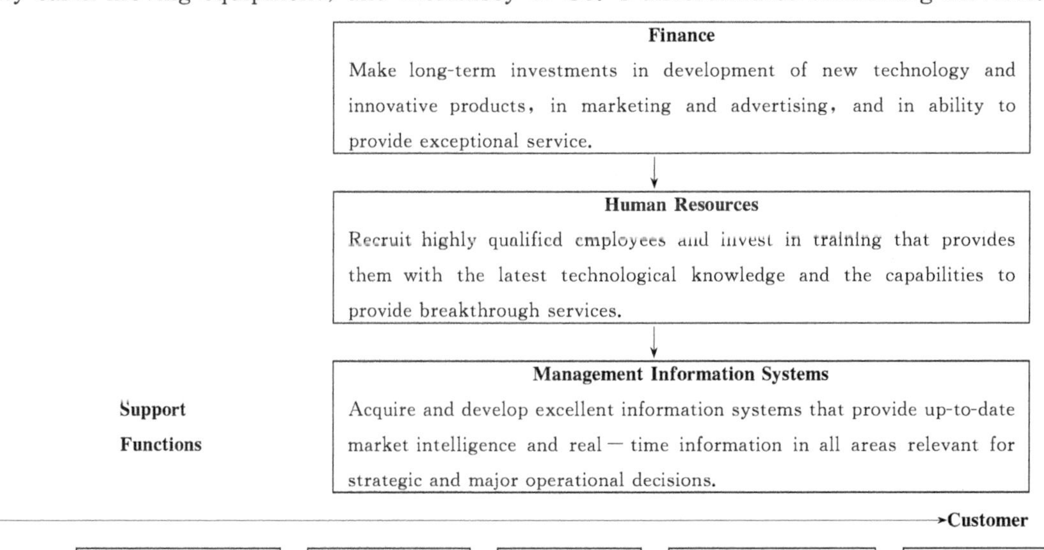

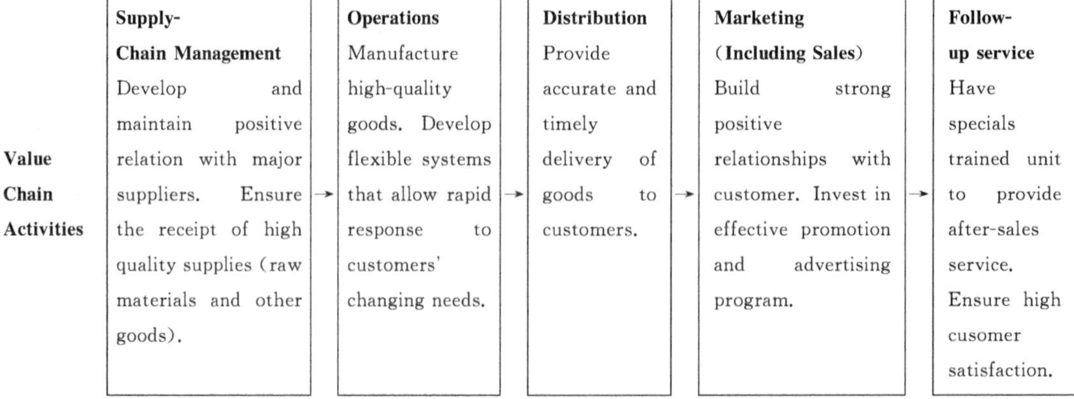

Figure 5.2 Examples of Value-Creating Activities Associated with the Differentiation Strategy

5.6 Focus Strategies

The focus strategy is an integrated set of actions taken to produce goods or services that serve the needs of a particular competitive segment. Thus, firms use a focus strategy when they utilize their core competencies to serve the needs of a particular industry segment or niche to the exclusion of others. Examples of specific market segments that can be targeted by a focus strategy include a particular buyer group (e. g. , youths or senior citizens), a different segment of a product line (e. g. , products for professional painters or the do-it-yourself group), or a different geographic market (e. g. , northern or southern Italy by using a foreign subsidiary).

There are many specific customer needs firms can serve by using a focus strategy. For example, Los Angeles-based investment banking firm Greif & Company positions itself as "The Entrepreneur's Investment Bank." Grief & Company is a leader in providing merger and acquisition advice to medium-sized businesses located in the western United States. Goya Foods is the largest U. S. -based Hispanic-owned food company in the United States. Segmenting the Hispanic market into unique groups, Goya offers more than 1600 products to consumers. The firm seeks "to be the be-all for the Latin community." By successful using a focus strategy, firms such as these gain a competitive advantage in specific market niches or segments, even though they do not possess an industry-wide competitive advantage.

Although the breadth of a target is clearly a matter of degree, the essence of the focus strategy "is the exploitation of a narrow target's differences from the balance of the industry." Firms using the focus strategy intend to serve a particular segment of an industry more effectively than can industry-wide competitors. They succeed when they effectively serve a segment whose unique needs are so specialized that broad-based competitors choose not to serve that segment or when they satisfy the needs of a segment being served poorly by industry-wide competitors.

When the lower cost and differentiation strategies have a broad (mass market) target, they are simply called cost leadership and differentiation. 当低成本战略和差异化战略具有广阔(大众市场)的目标时,则简单称之为成本领先和差异化。

When the lower cost and differentiation strategies are focused on a market niche (narrow target), however, they are called cost focus and differentiation focus. 当低成本战略和差异化战略专注于一个利基市场(狭窄目标)时,则称之为集中低成本和集中差异化。

Firms can create value for customers in specific and unique market segments by using the focused cost leadership strategy or the focused differentiation strategy.

A propitious niche is a company's specific competitive role that is so well suited to the firm's internal and external environment that other corporations are not likely to challenge or dislodge it. 适合利基是一家公司专有的竞争角色，与公司的内外部环境非常匹配，其他公司不太可能挑战或消除。

A firm's management must be always looking for strategic windows, that is, unique market opportunities available only for a limited time. 企业管理者必须一直努力寻找战略时机，即仅在有限时间内有效的独特市场机会。

Cost focus is a lower cost competitive strategy that focuses on a particular buyer group or geographic market and attempts to serve only this niche, to the exclusion of others. 集中低成本是一种低成本竞争战略，重点关注特定购买者群体或地域市场，并且试图只服务于这个利基市场，排斥其他市场细分。

Differentiation focus is a differentiation strategy that concentrates on a particular buyer group, product line segment, or geographic market. 集中差异化是一种差异化战略，重点关注特定购买者群体、产品线细分或地域市场。

5.7 Focused Cost Leadership Strategy

Based in Sweden, IKEA, a global furniture retailer with locations in 25 countries and territories and sales revenue of 21.1 billion euro's in 2008, uses the focused cost leadership strategy. Young buyers' desiring style at a low cost are IKEA's target customers. For these customers, the firm offers home furnishings that combine good design, function, and acceptable quality with low prices. According to the firm, "Low cost is always in focus. This applies to every phase of our activities."

IKEA emphasizes several activities to keep its costs low. For example, instead of relying primarily on third-party manufacturers, the firm's engineers design low-cost, modular furniture ready for assembly by customers. To eliminate the need for sales associates or decorators, IKEA positions the products in its stores so that customers can view different living combinations (complete with sofas, chairs, tables, etc.) in a single room like setting, which helps the customer imagine how furniture will look in the home. A third practice that helps keep IKEA's costs low is requiring customers to transport their own purchases rather than providing delivery service.

Although it is a cost leader, IKEA also offers some differentiated features that appeal to its target customers, including its unique furniture designs, in-store playrooms for children, wheelchairs for customer use, and extended hours. IKEA believes that these services and products "are uniquely aligned with the needs of customers, who are young, are not wealthy, are likely to have children, and, because they work, have a need to shop at odd hours." Thus, IKEA's focused cost leadership strategy also include some differentiated features with its low-cost products.

5.8 Competitive Risks of Focus Strategies

With either focus strategy, the firm faces the same general risks as does the company using the cost leadership or the differentiation strategy, respectively, on an industry-wide basis. However, focus strategies have three additional risks.

First, a competitor may be able to focus on a more narrowly defined competitive segment and thereby "out-focus" the focuser. This would happen to IKEA if another firm found a way to offer IKEA's customers additional sources of differentiation while charging the same price or to provide the same service with the same sources of differentiation at a lower price. Second, a company competing on an industry-wide basis may decide that the market segment served by the firm using a focus strategy is attractive and worthy of competitive pursuit. For example, women's clothiers such as Chico's, Ann Taylor, and Liz Claiborne might conclude that the profit potential in the narrow segment being served by Anne Fontaine is attractive and decide to design and sell competitively similar clothing items. Initially, Anne Fontaine designed and sold only white shirts for women. However, the shirts were distinctive. They were quite differentiated on the basis of their design, craftsmanship, and high quality of raw materials. The third risk involved with a focus strategy is that the needs of customers within a narrow competitive segment may become more similar to those of industry-wide customers as a whole over time. As a result, the advantage of a focus strategy are either reduced or eliminated. At some point, for example, the needs of Anne Fontaine's customers for high-quality, uniquely designed white shirts could dissipate. If this were to happen, Anne Fontaine's customers might choose to buy white shirts from chains such as Liz Claiborne that sell clothing items with some differentiation, but at a lower cost.

5.9 Integrated Cost Leadership/Differentiation Strategies

Most consumers have high expectations when purchasing a good or service. In general, it seems that most consumers want to pay a low price for products with somewhat highly differentiated features. Because of these customer expectations, a number of firms engage in primary value chain activities and support functions that allow them to simultaneously pursue low cost and differentiation. Firm seeking to do this use the integrated cost leadership/differentiation strategy. The objective of using this strategy is to efficiently produce products with some differentiated features. Efficient production is the source of maintaining low costs while differentiation is the source of creating unique value. Firms that successfully use the integrated cost leadership/differentiation strategy usually adapt quickly to new technologies and rapid changes in their external environments. Simultaneously concentrating on developing two sources of competitive advantage increase the number of primary and support activities in which the firm must become competent. Such firms often have strong networks with external parties that perform some of the primary and support activities. In turn, having skill in a larger number of activities makes a firm more flexible.

Porter argues that to be successful, a company or business unit must achieve one of the generic competitive strategies. Otherwise, the company or business unit is stuck in the middle of the competitive marketplace with no competitive advantage and is doomed to below-average performance. 波特认为,一个公司或业务单位要取得成功,必须采用一种通用竞争战略。否则,公司或业务单位会由于在竞争市场上没有竞争优势而卡在中间,注定只能具有平均水平的绩效表现。

Concentrating on the needs of its core customer group, Target Stores uses an integrated cost leadership/differentiation strategy as shown by its "Expect More. Pay Less' brand promise helped us to deliver greater convenience, increased savings and a more personalized shopping experience." In 2010, Target remodeled 351 stores and provided a grater assortment of merchandise to include more grocery items and innovative products. It added more privately branded products to offer lower prices, created new mobile applications, and introduced distinctive Web strategies to continue to differentiate the services provided to customers.

Although each of Porter's generic competitive strategies may be used in any industry, In some instances certain strategies are more likely to succeed than others. In a fragmented industry, for example, in which many small and medium-size local companies compete for relatively small shares of the total market, focus strategies will likely predominate. 尽管波特的通用竞争战略可以适用于任何产业,但在实际中某些战略更容易成功。比如,在一个细分的市场,一些小企业或中等规模的区域化企业利用聚焦化战略更容易在整个市场的相对小份额中获取市场地位。

As an industry matures, fragmentation is overcome and the industry tends to become a consolidated industry dominated by a few large companies. 当一个产业逐渐成熟和分化,那么这个产业就趋向于通过几家大的公司的控制来形成一个稳定的产业。

European-based Zara, which pioneered "cheap chic" in clothing apparel, is another firm using the integrated cost leadership/differentiation strategy. Zara offers current and desirable fashion goods at relatively low prices. To implement this strategy effectively requires sophisticated designers and means of managing costs, which fits Zara's capabilities. Zara can design and begin manufacturing a new fashion in three weeks, which suggests a highly flexible organization that can adapt easily to changes in the market or which competitors.

Vertical growth can be achieved by taking over a function previously provided by a supplier or distributor. 垂直增长通过接管以前由供应商或分销商所承担的职能来实现。

Vertical growth results in vertical integration, the degree to which a firm operates vertically in multiple locations on an industry's value chain from extracting raw materials to manufacturing to retailing. More specifically, assuming a function previously provided by a supplier is called backward integration. Assuming a function previously provide by a distributor is labeled forward integration. 垂直增长的结果是纵向一体化，是指一个公司在行业价值链上的多个节点垂直运作的程度，包括获取原材料、制造到零售。更具体地说，假设公司接管了以前由供应商承担的职能，称为后向一体化。假设公司接管了以前由分销商承担的职能，称为前向一体化。

Transaction cost economics proposes that vertical integration is more efficient than contracting for goods and services in the marketplace when the transaction costs of buying goods on the open market become too great. 交易成本经济学指出，当在公开市场上购买商品的交易成本过高的时候，纵向一体化比契约式商品和服务的提供方式更有效。

Horizontal Growth can be achieved by expanding the firm's products into other geographic locations and by increasing the range of products and services offered to current markets. Horizontal growth results in horizontal integration, the degree to which a firm operates in multiple locations at the same point in the industry's value chain. 水平增长通过将公司产品延伸到其他地域，以及扩大向目前市场所提供产品和服务的范围来实现。水平增长的结果是横向一体化，是指一个公司在多个地域的相同行业价值链节点上运作的程度。

When management realizes that the current industry is unattractive and that the firm lacks outstanding abilities or skills it could easily transfer to related products or services in other industries, the most likely strategy is conglomerate diversification-diversifying into an industry unrelated to its current one. 当管理层意识到目前行业缺乏吸引力，而公司又缺乏出色的能力或技巧轻易地将相关产品或服务转移到其他行业时，最可能选择的战略是通过集团多元化进入与当前行业无关的行业。

A corporation may choose stability over growth by continuing its current activities without any significant change in direction. 一个公司可以通过选择稳定战略，也就是通过继续现在这种在方向上没有明显改变的活动来形成增长。

A pause/proceed-with-caution strategy is, in effect, a time-out-an opportunity to rest before continuing a growth or retrenchment strategy. 暂停或谨慎开始战略实际上继续采取增长或紧缩战略之前的暂停休息机会。

A no-change strategy is a decision to do nothing new-a choice to continue current operations and policies for the foreseeable future. 维持战略是不做任何新尝试的决策——在可预见的未来一段时间内维持目前的经营和政策。

A profit strategy is a decision to do nothing new in a worsening situation, but instead to act thought the company's problems are only temporary. 利润战略是在日益恶化的情况下不采取任何新举措的决策,而只解决公司的暂时性问题。

The profit strategy is an attempt to artificially support profits when a company's sales are declining by reducing investment and short-term discretionary expenditures. 利润战略是在公司销售额下降的时候,通过减少投资和短期任意支出,人为支持利润的尝试。

Management may pursue retrenchment strategies when the company has a weak competitive position in some or all of its product lines resulting in poor performance when sales are down and profits are becoming losses. 当一家公司在销售和利润上的表现比较差,在某些或所有产品线中的业绩的微弱优势逐渐丧失的时候,管理层可能会倾向于紧缩战略。

The turnaround strategy emphasizes the improvement of operational efficiency and is probably most appropriate when a corporation's problems are pervasive but not yet critical. 转型战略强调提高经营效率,当一家公司存在的问题很普遍但尚未构成威胁时,转型可能是最合适的选择。

The two basic phases of a turnaround strategy include contraction and consolidation. 转型战略包括消化和吸收两个基本阶段。

Contraction is the initial effort to quickly "stop the bleeding" with a general, across-the-board cutback in size and costs. 收缩是全线缩减规模和成本,有如快速止血般的努力。

The second phase, consolidation, is the implementation of a program to stabilize the now leaner corporation. 吸收是第二阶段,是为了稳定精简后的公司所实施的过程。

A captive company strategy is becoming another company's sole supplier or distributor in exchange for a long-term commitment from that company. The firm, in effect, gives up independence in exchange for security. 专属公司战略是指成为另一家公司的唯一供应商或分销商,交换条件是获得该公司的长期支持承诺。公司实际上是放弃了独立性来交换安全。

In a sell-out strategy, the entire company is sold. 出售战略是指出售整个公司。

If the corporation has multiple business lines, it may choose divestment, that is, the selling of a business unit. 如果一家公司拥有多个业务,可能选择剥离战略,即出售一个业务单位。

Bankruptcy involves giving up management of the firm to the courts in return for some settlement of the corporation's obligations. 破产是指放弃对公司的管理,交给法院处理公司债务。

In contrast to bankruptcy, which seeks to perpetuate the corporation, liquidation is piecemeal sale of all of the firm's assets. 与破产旨在延续公司相反,清算是将公司的全部资产进行拆分出售。

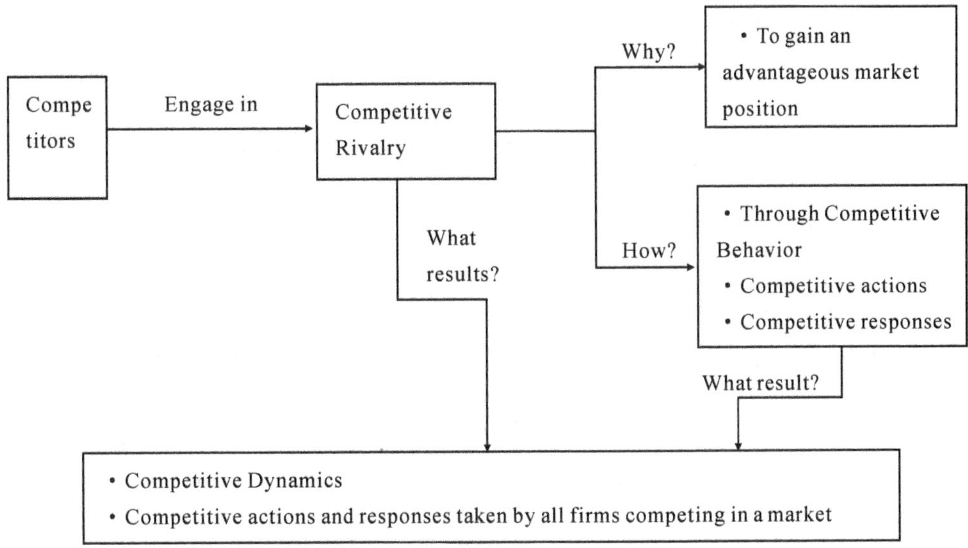

Figure 5.3 From Competitors to Competitive Dynamics

		Competitive Advantage	
		Lower Cost	Differentiation
Competitive Scope	Broad Target	Cost Leadership	Differentiation
	Narrow Target	Cost Focus	Differentiation Focus

Figure 5.4 Porter's Generic Competitive Strategies

5.10 Levels of Diversification

Diversified firms vary according to their level of diversification and the connections between and among their businesses. The single- and dominant-business categories denote relatively low levels of diversification; more fully diversified firms are classified into related and unrelated categories. A firm is related through its diversification when its businesses share several links; for example, businesses may share products, technologies, or distribution channels. The more links among businesses, the more "constrained" is the relatedness of diversification. "Unrelated" refers to the absence of direct links between businesses.

5.11 Low Levels of Diversification

A firm pursuing a low level of diversification uses either a single-or a dominant-business, corporate-level diversification strategy. A single-business diversification strategy is a corporate-level strategy wherein the firm generates 95 percent or more of its sales revenue from its core business area. For example, Wm. Wrigley Jr. Company, the world's largest producer of chewing and bubble gums, historically used a single-business strategy while operating in relatively few product markets. Wrigley's trademark chewing gum brands include Spearmint, Double mint, and Juicy Fruit, although the firm produces other products as well. Sugar-free Extra, which currently holds the largest share of the U.S. chewing gum market, was introduced in 1984.

5.12 Reasons for Diversification

A firm uses a corporate-level diversification strategy for a variety of reasons. Typically, a diversification strategy is used to increase the firm's value by improving its overall performance. Value is created either through related diversification or through unrelated diversification when the strategy allows a company's businesses to increase revenues or reduce costs while implementing their business-level strategies.

Other reasons for using a diversification strategy may have nothing to do with increasing the firm's value; in fact, diversification can have neutral effects or even reduce a firm's value. Value-neutral reasons for diversification include a desire to match and thereby neutralize a competitor's market power. Decisions to expand a firm's portfolio of businesses to reduce managerial risk can have a negative effect on the firm's value. Greater amounts of diversification reduce managerial risk in that if one of the businesses in a diversified firm fails, the top executive of that business does not risk total failure by the corporation. As such, this reduces the top executives' employment risk. In addition, because diversification can increase a firm's size and thus managerial compensation, managers have motives to diversify a firm to a level that reduce its value. Diversification rationales that may have a neutral or negative effect on the firm's value are discussed later in the chapter.

Operational relatedness and corporate relatedness ate two ways diversification strategies can create value. Studies of these independent relatedness dimensions show the importance of resources and key competencies. The Figure's vertical dimension depicts opportunities to share operational activities between businesses while the horizontal dimension suggests opportunities for transferring corporate-level core competencies. The firm with a strong capability in managing operational synergy, especially in sharing assets between its businesses, falls in the upper left quadrant, which also represents vertical sharing of assets through vertical integration. The lower right quadrant represents a highly developed corporate capability for transferring one or more core competencies across businesses.

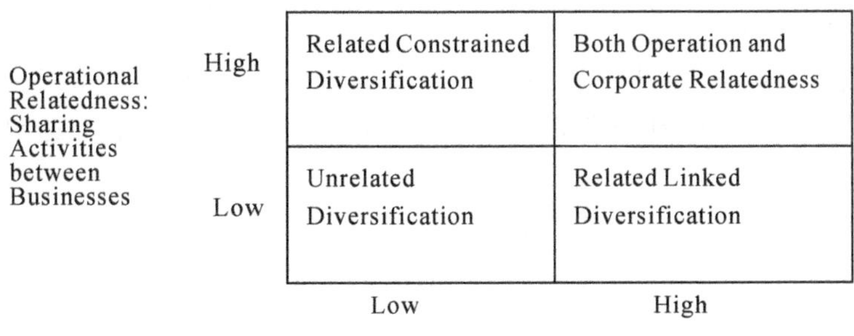

Figure 5. 5 Value-Creating Diversification Strategies: Operational and Corporate Relatedness

This capability is located primarily in the corporate headquarters office. Unrelated diversification is also illustrated in Figure 5. 5 in the lower left quadrant. Financial economies, rather than either operational or corporate relatedness, are the source of value creation for firms using the unrelated diversification strategy.

5. 13 Value-Creating Diversification: Related Constrained and Related Linked Diversification

With the related diversification corporate-level strategy, the firm builds upon or extends its resources and capabilities to build a competitive advantage by creating value for customers. The company using the related diversification strategy wants to develop and exploit economies of scope between its businesses. Available to companies operating in multiple product markets or industries, economies of scope are cost savings that the firm creates by successfully sharing some of its resources and capabilities or transferring one or more corporate-level core competencies that were developed in one of its businesses to another of its businesses.

As illustrated in Figure 5. 4, firms seek to create value from economies of scope through two basic kinds of operational economies: sharing activities and transferring corporate-level core competencies. The difference between sharing activities and transferring competencies is based on how separate resources are jointly used to create economies of scope. To create economies of scope tangible resources, such as plant and equipment or other business unit physical assets, often must be shared. Less tangible resources, such as manufacturing know-how transferred between separated activities with no physical or tangible resource involved is a transfer of a corporate-level core competence, not an operational sharing of activities.

Market stability is threatened by short product life cycles, short product design cycles, mew technologies, frequent entry by unexpected outsiders, repositioning by incumbents, and tactical redefinitions of market boundaries as diverse industries merge. 市场的稳定性正备受威胁:产品生命周期变短,产品设计周期变短,新技术层出不穷,未预期的外部企业频繁进入行业,现有企业重新定位,不同行业合并导致市场边界进行战术性重新定义。

One of the most popular aids to developing corporate strategy in a multi-business corporation is portfolio analysis. 在一家多元化公司的发展战略中,投资组合分析是最流行的目标之一。

In portfolio analysis, top management views its product lines and business units as a series of investments from which it expects a profitable return. 在投资组合分析过程中,高层管理者将各产品线和业务部门视为预期有收益的一系列投资。

The Boston Consulting Group (BCG) Growth-Share Matrix as depicted is the simplest way to portray a corporation's portfolio of investments. Each of the corporation's product lines or business units is plotted on the matrix according to the growth rate of the industry in which it competes, and its relative market share. 波士顿咨询集团(BCG)增长份额矩阵用最简单的方式描绘了一个公司的投资组合。公司的每条产品线或每个业务单位,根据所处行业的增长速度和相对市场份额绘入矩阵。

The GE Business Screen includes nine cells based on industry attractiveness, and business strength and competitive position. GE 业务荧屏基于行业吸引力、业务优势和竞争地位,分为 9 个单元。

How can portfolio analysis be used with strategic alliances? 投资组合分析如何用于战略联盟?

A study of 25 leading European corporations found four tasks of multi-alliance management that are necessary for successful alliance portfolio management: 25 家欧洲公司的一项研究发现,四项组合管理的任务对于成功的投资联盟管理是必要的:

1. Developing and implementing a portfolio strategy for each business unit and corporate policy for managing all the alliances of the entire company. 1. 为每个业务单位制定和实施投资组合战略和公司政策,用于管理整个企业的所有联盟

2. Monitoring the alliance portfolio in terms of implementing business unit strategies and corporate strategy and policies. 2. 从执行业务战略以及公司战略和政策等方面监控联盟的投资组合

3. Coordinating the portfolio to obtain synergies and avoid conflicts among alliances. 3. 协调投资组合，获得协同效应，避免联盟之间的冲突

4. Establishing an alliance management system to support other task of multi-alliance management. 4. 建立联盟管理系统，支持多联盟管理的其他任务

Corporate parenting, in contrast, views the corporation in terms of resources and capabilities that can be used to build business unit value as well as generate synergies across business units. 企业母合从资源和能力角度看待公司，这些资源和能力可用于建立业务单位价值，以及产生跨业务单位的协同效应。

Many people recommend that the search for appropriate corporate strategy involves three analytical steps: 许多人认为寻找合适的公司战略有三个分析步骤：

1. Examine each business unit(or target firm in the case of acquisition) in terms of its strategic factors. 按照自身的战略因素检查各业务单位(或收购案中的目标公司)

2. Examine each business unit(or target firm) in terms of area in which performance can be improved. 按照能够改善绩效的领域检查各业务单位(或目标公司)

3. Analyze how well the parent corporation fits with the business unit (or target firm). 分析母公司与业务单位(或目标公司)的匹配情况

When a horizontal strategy used to build synergy, it acts like a parenting strategy; when used to improve the competitive position of one or more business units, it can be thought of as a corporate competitive strategy. 当横向战略用于建立协同效应时，就是母合战略；当横向战略用来提高一个或多个业务单位的竞争地位时，则被认为是公司的竞争战略。

These multipoint competitors are firms that compete with each other not only in one business unit, but also in a number of business units. 这些多点竞争者不仅在一个业务单位与公司相互竞争，还在数个业务单位与公司相互竞争。

Chapter 6 Functional Strategies and Strategic Choices

6.1 Operational Relatedness: Sharing Activities

Firms can create operational relatedness by sharing either a primary activity or a support activity. Firms using the related constrained diversification strategy share activities in order to create value. Procter & Gamble (P&G) uses this corporate-level strategy. P&G's paper towel business and baby diaper business both use paper products as a primary input to the manufacturing process. The firm's paper production plant produces inputs for both businesses and is an example of a shared activity. In addition, because they both produce consumer products, these two businesses are likely to share distribution channels and sales networks.

Functional strategy is the approach a functional area takes to achieve corporate and business unit objectives and strategies by maximizing resource productivity. 职能战略是职能部门充分利用资源实现公司和业务单位的目标和战略的一种方法。

Activity sharing is also risky because ties among a firm's businesses create links between outcomes. For instance, if demand for one business's product is reduced, it may not generate sufficient revenues to cover the fixed costs required to operate the shared facilities. These types of organizational difficulties can reduce activity-sharing success. Additionally, activity sharing requires careful coordination between the businesses involved. The coordination challengers must be managed effectively for the appropriate sharing of activities.

A tactic is a specific operating plan detailing how a strategy is to be implemented in terms of when and where it is to be put into action. 战术是具体的运营计划,它详细说明了战略如何实施,以及付诸行动的时间和地点。

A timing tactic deals with when a company implements a strategy. The first company to manufacture and sell a new product or service is called the first mover(or pioneer). 时间战术解决公司何时执行战略的问题。第一家制造和销售新产品或服务的公司称为先行者(或开拓者)。

Although activity sharing across businesses is not risk-free, research shows that it can create value. For example, studies of acquisitions of firms in the same industry, such as the banking industry and software, found that sharing resources and activities and thereby creating economies of scope contributed to post-acquisition increases in performance and higher returns to shareholders. Additionally, firms that sold off related units in which resource sharing was a possible source of economies of scope have been found to produce lower returns than those that sold off businesses unrelated to the firm's core business. Still other research discovered that firms with closely related businesses have lower risk. These results suggest that gaining economies of scope by sharing activities across a firm's businesses may be important in reducing risk and in creating value. Further, more attractive results are obtained through activity sharing when a strong corporate headquarters office facilitates it.

A market location tactic deals with where a company implements a strategy. 市场位置战术解决公司在哪里执行战略的问题。

A company or business unit can implement a competitive strategy either offensively or defensively. 一个公司或业务单位能够通过采取进攻战术或防御战术来实施竞争战略。

An offensive tactic attempts to take market share from an established competitor. 进攻战术就是试图从一个确定的竞争对手那里瓜分市场。

In offensive tactics, some of the methods used to attack a competitor's position are: frontal assault, flanking maneuver, encirclement, bypass attack, guerrilla warfare. 进攻战术中根据进攻的位置被用来描述为一些竞争方法，它们是正面进攻、侧面进攻、合围之势、迂回之术、游击战争。

According to Porter, defensive tactics aim to lower the probability of attack, divert attacks to less-threatening avenues, or lessen the intensity of an attack. 根据波特理论，防御战术的目标就是降低攻击的可能性，向威胁较少的道路上转移攻击或减少密集的攻击。

These defensive tactics that deliberately reduce short-term profitability to ensure long-term profitability, such as raise structural barriers, increase expected retaliation, Lower the inducement for attack. 提高结构性壁垒、提高预期的报复、降低攻击的诱导这些防御战术能通过减少短期盈利来确保长期的盈利能力。

6.2 Market Power

Firms using a related diversification strategy may gain market power when successfully using a related constrained or related linked strategy. Mark power exists when a firm is able to sell its products above the existing competitive level or to reduce the costs of its primary and support activities below the competitive level, or both. Mars' acquisition of the Wrigley assets was part of its related constrained diversification strategy and added market share to the Mars/Wrigley above Cadbury and Nestle, which had 10.1 and 7.7 percent of the market share, respectively, at the time and left Hershey with only 5.5 percent of the market.

In addition to efforts to gain scale as a means of increasing market power, as Mars did when it acquired Wrigley, firms can create market power through multipoint competition and vertical integration. Multipoint competition exists when two or more diversified firms simultaneously compete in the same product areas or geographic markets. The actions taken by UPS and FedEx in two markets, overnight delivery and ground shipping, illustrate multipoint competition. UPS has moved into overnight delivery, FedEx's stronghold; FedEx has been buying trucking and ground shipping assets to move into ground shipping, UPS's stronghold. Moreover, geographic competition for markets increases. The strongest shipping company in Europe is DHL. All three competitors are moving into large foreign markets to either gain a stake or to expand their existing share. If one of these firms successfully gains strong positions in several markets while competing against its rivals, its market power may increase. Interestingly, DHL had to exit the U. S. market because it was too difficult to compete against UPS and FedEx, which are dominant in the United States.

Marketing strategy deals with pricing, selling, and distributing a product. 营销战略处理产品的定价、销售和分销等方面的事宜。

Using a market development strategy, a company or business unit can (1) capture a larger share of an existing market for current products through market saturation and market penetration or (2) develop new use and/or markets for current products. 使用市场开发战略，公司或业务单位可以：(1)通过市场饱和/市场渗透为目前产品在已有市场获取更大的市场份额；(2)为现有产品开发新用途或市场。

6.3 Simultaneous Operational Relatedness and Corporate Relatedness

Some firms simultaneously seek operational and corporate relatedness to create economies of scope. The ability to simultaneously create economies of scope by sharing activities and transferring core competencies is difficult for competitors to understand and learn how to imitate. However, if the cost of realizing both types of relatedness is not offset by the benefits created, the result is diseconomies because the cost of organization and incentive structure is very expensive.

Walt Disney Co. user a related diversification strategy to simultaneously create economies of scope through operational and corporate relatedness. Within the firm's Studio Entertainment business, for example, Disney can gain economies of scope by sharing activities among its different movie distribution companies such as Touchstone Pictures, Hollywood Pictures, and Dimension Films. Broad and deep knowledge about its customers is a capability on which Disney relies to develop corporate-level core competencies in terms of advertising and marketing. With these competencies, Disney is able to create economies of scope through corporate relatedness as it cross-sells products that are highlighted in its movies through the distribution channels that are part of its Parks and Resorts and Consumer Products businesses. Thus, characters created in movies become Figures that are marketed through Disney's retail stores. In addition, themes established in movies become the source of new rides in the firm's theme parks, which are part of the Parks and Resorts business and provide themes for clothing and other retail business products.

Thus, Walt Disney Co. has been able to successfully use related diversification as a corporate-level strategy through which it creates economies of scope by sharing some activities and by transferring core competencies. However, it can be difficult for investors to actually observe the value created by a firm as it shares activities and transfers core competencies. For this reason, the value of the assets of a firm using a diversification strategy to create economies of scope often is discounted by investors.

6.4 Value-Neutral Diversification: Incentives and Resources

The objectives firms seek when using related diversification and unrelated diversification strategies all have the potential to help the firm create value by using a corporate-level strategy. However, these strategies, as well as single-and dominant-business diversification strategies, are sometimes used with value-neutral rather than value-creating objectives in mind. As we discuss next, different incentives to diversify sometimes exist, and the quality of the firm's resources may permit only diversification that is value neutral rather than value creating.

Cooperative strategies are those strategies that are used to gain competitive advantage within an industry by working with rather than against other firms. 合作战略是采取与其他公司合作而不是针锋相对的方式获得行业内竞争优势的战略。

A strategic alliance is a partnership of two or more corporations or business units formed to achieve strategically significant objectives that are mutually beneficial. 战略联盟是指两个或两个以上的企业或业务单位构成战略伙伴关系,旨在实现显著的双赢战略目标。

6.5 Resources and Diversification

As already discussed, firms may have several value-neutral incentives as well as value-creating incentives to diversify. However, even when incentives to diversify exist, a firm must have the types and levels of resources and capabilities needed to successfully use a corporate-level diversification strategy. Although both tangible and intangible resources facilitate diversification, they vary in their ability to create value. Indeed, the degree to which resources are valuable, rare, difficult to imitate, and non-substitutable influences a firm's ability to create value through diversification. For instance, free cash flows are a tangible financial resource that may be used to diversify the firm. However, compared with diversification that is grounded in intangible resources, diversification based on financial resources only is more visible to competitors and thus more imitable and less likely to create value on a long-term basis. Tangible resources usually include the plant and equipment necessary to produce a product and tend to be less-flexible assets. Any excess capacity often can be used only for closely related products, especially those requiring highly similar manufacturing technologies. For example, large computer makes such as Dell and Hewlett-Packard have underestimated the demand for tablet computers, especially-Apple's iPad. Apple developed the iPad and may expect it to eventually replace the personal computer. In fact, HP's and Dell's sales of their PCs have been declining since the introduction of the iPad. Apple expects to sell 70 million IPads in 2011 and analysts projects sales of the iPad to reach 246 million in 2014. HP and Dell likely need to diversify their product lines.

A mutual service consortium is a partnership of similar companies in similar industries who pool their resources to gain a benefit that is too expensive to develop alone, such as access to advanced technology. 双边服务联盟伙伴关系中,类似行业的类似公司联合双方资源获得独自开发费用太高的收益,比如获得先进技术。

Joint venture is a cooperative business activity, formed by two or more separate organizations for strategic purposes, that creates an independent business entity and allocates ownership, operational responsibilities, and financial risks and rewards to each member, while preserving their separate identity and autonomy. 合资企业是一种合作性业务活动。出于战略目的,两个或多个独立组织构建一个独立的商业实体,并在每个成员间分配所有权、经营责任、金融风险和回报,同时保留独立的身份和自主权。

Extremely popular in international undertaking because of financial and political-legal constraints, joint ventures are a convenient way for corporations to work together without losing their independence. 由于金融和政治法律方面的约束,合资企业在国际市场上极其流行,是一种公司之间共同合作又不丧失独立性的便捷方式。合资企业的缺点包括丧失控制、利润降低、与合作伙伴产生冲突的可能性,以及技术优势向合作伙伴转移的可能性。

6.6 Value-Reducing Diversification: Managerial Motives to Diversify

Managerial motives to diversify can exist independent of value-neutral reasons and value-creating reasons. The desire for increased compensation and reduced managerial risk are two motives for top-level executives to diversify their firm beyond value-creating and value-neutral levels. In slightly different words, top-level executives may diversify a firm in order to diversify their own employment risk, as long as profitability does not suffer excessively.

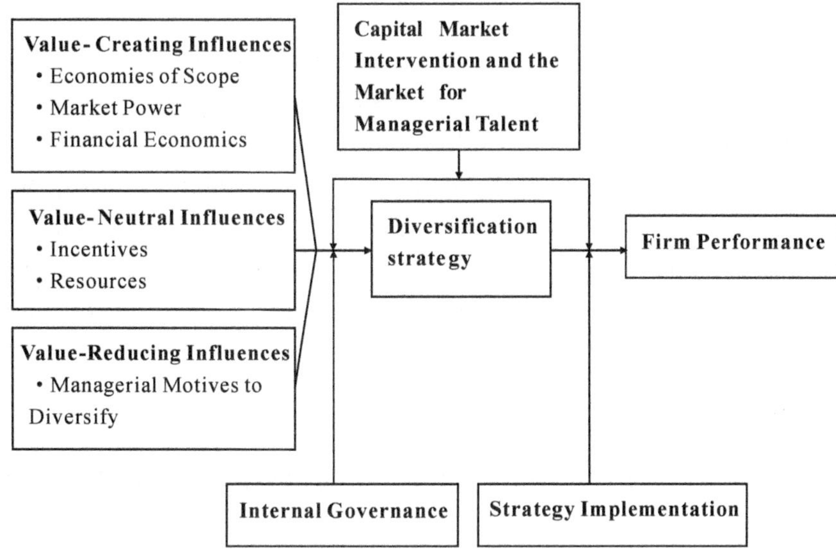

Figure 6.1 Summary Model of the Relationship Between Diversification and Performance

6.7 The Popularity of Merger and Acquisition Strategies

Merger and acquisition (M&A) strategies have been popular among U. S. firms for many years. Some believe that these strategies played a central role in the restructuring of U. S. businesses during the 1980s and 1990s and that they continue generating these types of benefits in the twenty-first century.

Although popular, and appropriately so, as a means of growth with the potential to lead to strategic competitiveness, it is important to emphasize that changing conditions in the external environment influence the type of M&A activity firms pursue. During the recent financial crisis, tightening credit markets made it more difficult for firms to complete "megadeals". However, the flow of deals picked up in 2011 in the United States, where "first-quarter deal volume rose a healthy 45 percent to $290.8 billion, compared with $200.6 billion" in 2010; "Europe saw a volume increase in the quarter, though not by as much as in the U. S., as worries over the health of government finances in the region lingered." Additionally, a relatively weak currency, such as the U. S. dollar, increases the interest of firms from other nations with a strong currency to pursue cross-border acquisitions in the country where the currency is weaker.

6.8 Increased Market Power

Achieving greater market power is a primary reason for acquisitions. Market power exists when a firm is able to sell its goods or services above competitive levels or when the costs of its primary or support activities are lower than those of its competitors. Market power usually is derived from the size of the firm and its resources and capabilities to compete in the marketplace; it is also affected by the firm's share of the market. Therefore, most acquisitions that are designed to achieve greater market power entail buying a competitor, a supplier, a distributor, or a business in a highly related industry to allow the exercise of a core competence and to gain competitive advantage in the acquiring firm's primary market.

6.9 Cost of New Product Development and Increased Speed to Market

Developing new products internally and successfully introducing them into the marketplace often requires significant investment of a firm's resources, including time, making it difficult to quick earn a profitable return. Because an estimated 88 percent of innovations fail to achieve adequate returns, firm managers are also concerned with achieving adequate returns from the capital invested to develop and commercialize new products. Potentially contributing to these less-than-desirable rates of return is the successful imitation of approximately 60 percent of innovations within four years after the patents are obtained. These types of outcomes may lead managers to perceive internal product development as a high-risk activity.

Acquisitions are another means a firm can use to gain access to new products and to current products that are new to the firm. Compared with internal product development processes, acquisitions provide more predictable returns as well as faster market entry. Returns are more predictable because the performance of the acquired firm's products can be assessed prior to completing the acquisition.

Medtronic is the world's largest medical device maker with $15.8 billion in sales. While most pharmaceutical firms invent many of their products internally, most of Medtronic's products are acquired form surgeons or other outside inventors. Research confirms that it can be a good strategy to buy early stage products, especially if you have strong R&D capability, even though there is risk and uncertainty in doing so.

A number of pharmaceutical firms use an acquisition strategy besides internal development because of the cost of new product development. Acquisitions can enable firms to enter markets quickly and to increase the predictability of returns on their

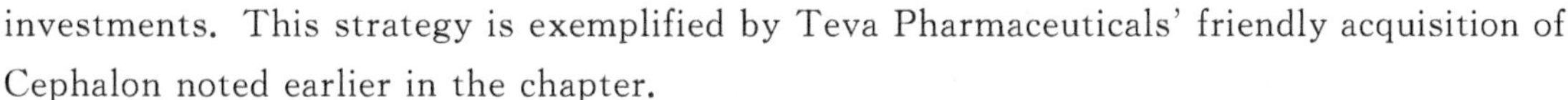

investments. This strategy is exemplified by Teva Pharmaceuticals' friendly acquisition of Cephalon noted earlier in the chapter.

6.10 Learning and Developing New Capabilities

Firms sometimes complete acquisitions to gain access to capabilities they lack. For example, acquisitions may be used to acquire a special technological capability. Research shows that firms can broaden their knowledge base and reduce inertia of their capabilities when they acquire diverse talent through cross-border acquisitions. Of course, firms are better able to learn these capabilities if they share some similar properties with the firm's current capabilities. Thus, firms should seek to acquire companies with different but related and complementary capabilities in order to build their own knowledge base.

Using the product development strategy, a company or unit can (1) develop new products for existing markets or (2) develop mew products for new markets. 使用产品开发战略,公司或业务单位可以:(1)为现有市场开发新产品;(2)为新市场开发新产品。

Many large food and consumer product companies in North America have followed a push strategy by spending a large amount of money on trade promotion in order to gain or hold shelf space in retail outlet. 北美许多大型食品和消费品公司遵循推动战略,在交易促进方面投入巨资,目的是增加或保持在零售店的铺货空间。

For new-product pioneers, skim pricing offers the opportunity to "skim the cream" from the top of the demand curve with a high price while the product is novel and competitors are few. 对于一些产品领先者来说,当产品新颖且竞争者较少时,撇脂定价以高价提供了"撇去奶油"的机会。

Penetration pricing, in contrast, use the experience curve to gain market share with a low price and then dominate the industry. 相反渗透定价用低价来获得市场份额,然后主导这个产业。

A number of large pharmaceutical firms are acquiring the ability to create "large molecule" drugs, also known as biological drugs, by buying biotechnology firms. Thus, these firms are seeking access to both the pipeline of possible drugs and the capabilities that these firms have to produce them. Such capabilities are important for large pharmaceutical firms because these biological drugs are more difficult to duplicate by chemistry alone. Biotech firms are focused on DNA research and have a biology base rather than a chemistry base. As an example, Sanofi-Aventis acquired Genzyme for \$20 billion. Sanofi's hope is that the biotech company will help it keep rare-disease drugs in the pipeline without losing sales to more generic competition such as this that Sanofi keep expertise an genetics and biomarkers back to Sanofi. Such biomarkers "are biological substances in the body that help show the body is responding to disease and medication."

If the acquisition is successful, there is added competitive advantage. Biological drugs must clear more regulatory barriers or hurdles which, when accomplished, add more to the advantage the acquiring firm develops through such acquisitions.

6.11 Managers Overly Focused on Acquisitions

Typically, a considerable amount of managerial time and energy is required for acquisition strategies to be used successfully. Activities with which managers become involved include (1) searching for viable acquisition candidates, (2) completing effective due-diligence processes, (3) preparing for negotiations, and (4) managing the integration process after completing the acquisition.

Top-level managers do not personally gather all of the data and information required to make acquisitions. However, these executives do make critical decisions on the firms to targeted, the nature of the negotiations, and so forth. Company experiences show that participating in and overseeing the activities required for making acquisitions can divert managerial attention from other matters that are necessary for long-term competitive success, such as identifying and taking advantage of other opportunities and interacting with important external stakeholders.

Both theory and research suggest that managers can become overly involved in the process of making acquisitions. One observer suggested, "Some executives can become preoccupied with making deals-and the thrill of selecting, chasing and seizing a target." The over involvement can be surmounted by learning from mistakes and by not having too much agreement in the boardroom. Dissent is helpful to make sure that all sides of a question are considered. When failure does occur, leaders may be tempted to blame the failure on others and on unforeseen circumstances rather than on their excessive involvement in the acquisition process.

The acquisitions strategy of Citigroup is a case in point. In 1998, Citigroup's CEO John Reed in a merger between Citicorp and Travelers Group set out to cross-sell financial services to the same customer and thereby reduce sales costs. Weil ultimately became the CEO. To accomplish this goal, the merged firm focused on a set of acquisitions including insurance and private equity investing beyond traditional banking services. However, as noted by one commentator, "More than once, ambitious executives, such as Sanford Weill of Citigroup fame, have assembled 'financial supermarkets,' and thinking that customers' needs for credit cards, checking accounts, wealth management services, insurance, and stock brokerage could be furnished most efficiently and effectively by the same company. Those efforts have failed, over and over again. Each function fulfills a different job that arises at a different point a customer's life, so a single source for all of them holds no advantage." As outlined in the Strategic Focus, Vikram Pandit, the CEO who took over after Charles Prince at Citigroup, was forced to sell off a lot of those peripheral financial service businesses.

6.12 Three Basic Benefits of International Strategies

As noted, effectively using one or more international strategies can result in three basic benefits for the firm. These benefits facilitate the firm's effort to achieve strategic competitiveness when using an international strategy.

Firms can expand the size of their potential market-sometimes dramatically-by using an international strategy to establish stronger positions in markets outside their domestic market. As noted, access to additional consumers is a key reason Carrefour sees China as a major source of growth.

Takeda, a large Japanese pharmaceutical company, recently acquired Swiss drug maker Nycomed for $13.7 billon. Buying Nycomed makes Takeda a major player in European markets. More significantly, the acquisition broadens Takeda's distribution capability in emerging markets "at a time when pharmaceutical firms world-wide are wrestling with the impact on revenue from the expiration of patents." In fact, the Nycomed deal will increase Takeda's sales in china about fourfold. Along with starbucks, Carrefour and Takeda are two additional companies relying on international strategy as the path to increased market size in china.

Firms such as Starbucks, Carrefour, and Takeda understand that effectively managing different consumer tastes and practices linked to cultural values or traditions in different markets is challenging. Nonetheless, they accept this challenge because of the potential to enhance the firm's performance. Other firms accept the challenge of successfully implementing an international strategy largely because of limited growth opportunities in their domestic market. This appears to be at least partly the case for major competitors Coca-Cola and PepsiCo, firms that have not been able to generate significant growth in their U. S. domestic markets for some time. Indeed, most of these firm's growth is occurring in international markets. These two firms approach international growth somewhat differently. PepsiCo, the world's largest snack-food maker as a result of its Frito-Lay division, relies "on chip sales overseas to make up for slower beverage sales volumes in North America." Less diversified than PepsiCo in terms of products but not in terms of geography, Coca-Cola is the world's largest producer of soft drink concentrates and syrups and the world's largest producer of Juice and Juice-related products. Selling its products in more than 200 countries, Coca-Cola derives only approximately 32 percent of its revenue from sales in North America as the cornerstone of its efforts to outperform PepsiCo, its chief rival.

6.13 International Strategies

Firms choose to use one or both basic types of international strategy: business-level international strategy and corporate-level international strategy. At the business level, firms select from among the generic strategies of cost leadership, differentiation, focused cost leadership, focused differentiation, and integrated cost leadership/differentiation. At the corporate level, multi-domestic, global, and transnational international strategies are considered. To contribute to the firm's efforts to achieve strategic competitiveness in the form of improved performance and enhanced innovation, each international strategy the firm uses must be based on one or more core competencies.

6.14 International Business-Level Strategies

Firms considering the use of any international strategy first develop domestic-market strategies. One reason this is important is that the firm may be able to use some of the capabilities and core competencies it has developed in its domestic market as the foundation for competitive success in international markets. However, research results indicate that the value created by relying on capabilities and core competencies developed in domestic markets as a source of success in international markets diminishes as a firm's geographic diversity increases.

Firms do not select and then use strategies in isolation of market realities. In the case of international strategies, conditions in a firm's domestic market affect the degree to which the firm can build on capabilities and core competencies it established in that market to create capabilities and core competencies in international markets. The reason for this is grounded in Michael Porter's analysis of why some nations are more competitive relative to those industries in other nations. Porter's core argument is that conditions of factors in a firm's home base that is, in its domestic market-either hinder the firm's efforts to use an international business-level strategy for the purpose of establishing a competitive advantage in international markets or support those efforts. Porter identifies four factors as determinants of a national advantage that some countries possess. Interactions among these four factors influence a firm's choice of international business-level strategy.

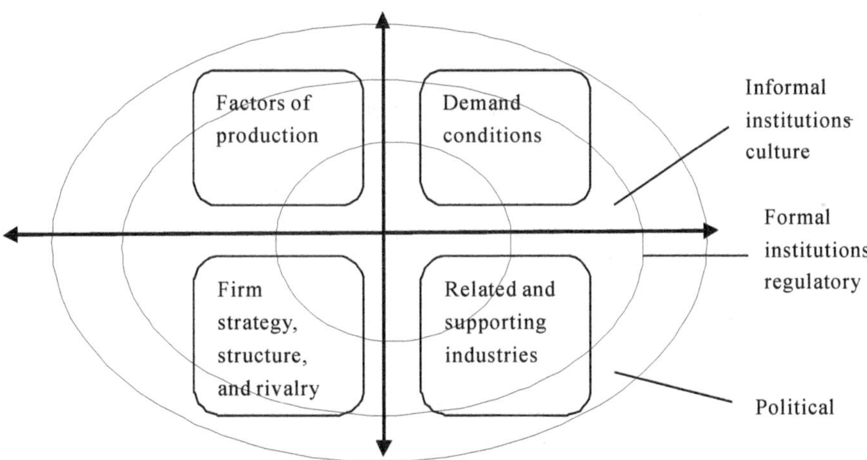

Figure 6. 2 Determinants of National Advantage

6. 15 Global Strategy

A global strategy is an international strategy in which a firm's home office determines the strategies business units are to use in each country or region. This strategy indicates that the firm has a high need for global integration and a low need for local responsiveness. These needs indicate that compared to a multi-domestic strategy, a global strategy seeks grater levels of standardization of products across country markets. The firm using a global strategy seeks to develop economies of scale as it produces the same or virtually the same products for distribution to customers throughout the world who are assumed to have similar needs. The global strategy offers greater opportunities to take innovations developed at the corporate level or in one market and apply them in other markets. Improvements in global accounting and financial reporting standards facilitate use of this strategy. A global is most effective for us when the differences between markets and the customers the firm is serving are insignificant.

6. 16 Acquisitions

When a firm acquires another company to enter an international market, it has completed a cross-border acquisition. Specifically, a cross-border acquisition is an entry mode through which a firm from one country acquires a stake in or purchases all of a firm located in another country acquires a stake in or purchases all of a firm located in another country.

As free trade expands in global markets, firms throughout the world are completing a large number of cross-border acquisitions. The ability of cross-border acquisitions to provide rapid access to new markets is a key reason for their growth. In fact, of the five entry modes, acquisitions often are the quickest means for firms to enter international markets.

Keys to Success in Achieving Low-Cost Leadership Scrutinize each cost-creating activity, identifying cost drivers Use knowledge about cost drivers to manage costs of each activity down year after year. Find ways to reengineer how activities are performed and coordinated—eliminate the costs of unnecessary work steps. Be creative in cutting low value-added activities out of value chain system—re-invent their industry value chain.

Financial strategy examines the financial implications of corporate and business level strategic options and identifies the best financial course of action. 财务战略检验公司和业务单位的战略选择对财务的影响,并确定行动的最佳财务过程。

The trade-off between achieving the desired debt-to-equity ratio and relying on internal long-term financing by way of cash flow is a key issue in financial strategy. 财务战略的关键问题是权衡实现既定债权比率,还是依赖现金流的内部长期融资方式。

In a leveraged buyout, a company is acquired in a transaction financed largely by debt, which is usually obtained from a third party such as an insurance company. Ultimately the debt is paid with money generated from the acquired company's operations or by sales of its assets. 在杠杆收购(LBO)中,在很大程度上,一个公司的收购交易通常依靠来自第三方的债务融资,如保险公司。最终的债务支付来自被收购公司的经营收入或资产出售。

Characteristics of a Low-Cost Provider Cost conscious corporate culture Employee participation in cost-control efforts. Ongoing efforts to benchmark costs. Intensive scrutiny of budget requests. Programs promoting continuous cost improvement Low-cost producers champion FRUGALITY while aggressively INVESTING in cost-saving improvements! Successful low-cost producers champion frugality but wisely and aggressively invest in cost-saving improvements!

When Does a Low-Cost Strategy Work Best? Price competition is vigorous Product is standardized or readily available from many suppliers. There are few ways to achieve differentiation that have value to buyers. Most buyers use product in same ways. Buyers incur low switching costs Buyers are large and have significant bargaining power Industry newcomers use introductory low prices to attract buyers and build customer base.

Pitfalls of Low-Cost Strategies Being overly aggressive in cutting price Low cost methods are easily imitated by rivals. Becoming too fixated on reducing costs and ignoring Buyer interest in additional features Declining buyer sensitivity to price. Changes in how the product is used Technological breakthroughs open up cost reductions for rivals.

Research and development (R&D) strategy deals with product and process innovation and improvement. One of the R&D choice is to be either a technological leader that pioneers an innovation or a technological follower that imitates the products of competitors. 研究与发展战略(简称研发战略)处理产品及流程创新和改进等事宜。研发选择包括作为开拓创新的技术领导者,或者作为模仿竞争对手产品的技术跟随者。

Differentiation Strategies Incorporate differentiating features that cause buyers to prefer firm's product or service over brands of rivals. Find ways to differentiate that create value for buyers and that are not easily matched or cheaply copied by rivals. Not spending more to achieve differentiation than the price premium that can be charged Objective Keys to Success.

Appeal of Differentiation Strategies A powerful competitive approach when uniqueness can be achieved in ways that Buyers perceive as valuable and are willing to pay for Rivals find hard to match or copy Can be incorporated at a cost well below the price premium that buyers will pay Which hat is unique?

Benefits of Successful Differentiation A product/service with unique and appealing attributes allows a firm to Command a premium price and/or Increase unit sales and/or Build brand loyalty=Competitive Advantage.

Operations strategy determines how and where a product or service is to be manufactured, the level of vertical integration, the deployment of physical resources, and relationship with suppliers. 运营战略决定产品或服务的生产方式和位置、垂直一体化水平、物理资源调配以及与供应商的关系。

Increasing competitive intensity in many industries has forced companies to switch from traditional mass production using dedicated transfer lines to a continuous improvement production strategy, in which cross-functional work teams strive constantly to improve production processes. 在很多行业,日益提高的竞争强度迫使企业从传统的规模化生产转向使用专用传输线,采取持续改进的生产战略。在持续改进生产战略中,跨职能工作团队共同努力,持续改进生产流程。

In contrast to continuous improvement, mass customization requires flexibility and quick responsiveness. 与持续改进相比,大规模定制需要灵活性和快速反应能力。

Purchasing strategy deals with obtaining the raw materials, parts, and supplies needed to perform the operations function. 采购战略处理执行运营职能所需的获得原材料、零部件和供应等事宜。

Logistics strategy deals with the flow of products into and out of the manufacturing process. 物流战略处理制造过程中的产品输入和输出事宜。

Types of Differentiation Themes Unique taste—Dr. Pepper Multiple features—Microsoft Windows and Office Wide selection and one-stop shopping—Home Depot and Amazon. com. Superior service—FedEx, Ritz-Carlton Spare parts availability—Caterpillar More for your money—McDonald's, Wal-Mart Prestige—Rolex Quality manufacture—

Honda, Toyota Technological leadership—3M Corporation, Intel Top-of-the-line image—Ralph Lauren, Chanel.

Sustaining Differentiation: The Key to Competitive Advantage. Most appealing approaches to differentiation Those hardest for rivals to match or imitate Those buyers will find most appealing Best choices for gaining a longer-lasting, more profitable competitive edge New product innovation. Technical superiority Product quality and reliability Comprehensive customer service Unique competitive capabilities.

Where to Find Differentiation Opportunities in the Value Chain Purchasing and procurement activities Product R&D and product design activities Production process/technology-related activities Manufacturing/production activities. Distribution-related activities Marketing, sales, and customer service activities Internally Performed Activities, Costs, &Margins Activities, Costs, &Margins of Suppliers Buyer/User Value Chains Activities, Costs, &Margins of Forward Channel Allies& Strategic Partners.

Human resource management(HRM) strategy attempts to find the best fit between people and the organization. 人力资源管理战略试图寻找员工与组织之间的最佳匹配方式。

Corporations are increasingly adopting information technology strategies to provide business units with competitive advantage. 越来越多的企业正在采用信息技术战略为业务单位提供竞争优势。

How to Achieve a Differentiation-Based Advantage Incorporate product features/attributes that lower buyer's overall costs of using product Approach 1Incorporate features/attributes that raise the performance a buyer gets out of the product. Approach Incorporate features/attributes that enhance buyer satisfaction in non-economic or intangible ways Compete on the basis of superior capabilities Approach.

Signaling Value as Well as Delivering Value Buyers seldom pay for value that is not perceived Signals of value may be as important as actual value when Nature of differentiation is hard to quantify Buyers are making first-time purchases Repurchase is infrequent Buyers are unsophisticated.

When Does a Differentiation Strategy Work Best? There are many ways to differentiate a product that have value and please customers Buyer needs and uses are diverse Few rivals are following a similar differentiation approach Technological change and product innovation are fast-paced.

Pitfalls of Differentiation Strategies Trying to differentiate on a feature buyers do not perceive as lowering their cost or enhancing their well-being Over-differentiating such that product features exceed buyers' needs Charging a price premium that buyers perceive is too high Failing to signal value Not understanding what buyers want or prefer and differentiating on the "wrong" things.

Outsourcing is purchasing from someone else a product or service that had been previously provided internally. 外包是从其他公司采购先前由公司内部提供的产品或服务。

Offshoring is the outsourcing of an activity or a function to a wholly owned company or an independent provider in another country. 离岸外包是将一项活动或一项职能外包给位于另一个国家的全资子公司或独立供应商。

Competitive Strategy Principle A low-cost producer strategy can defeat a differentiation strategy when buyers are satisfied with a standard product and do not see extra attributes as worth paying additional money to obtain! A low-cost provider strategy can defeat a differentiation strategy when buyers are satisfied with a standard product and do not see extra differentiating attributes as worth paying for!

Best Cost Provider Strategies Combine a strategic emphasis on low-cost with a strategic emphasis on differentiation Make an upscale product at a lower cost Give customers more value for the money Deliver superior value by meeting or exceeding buyer expectations on product attributes and beating their price expectations. Be the low-cost provider of a product with good-to-excellent product attributes, then use cost advantage to under price comparable brands Objectives.

Several strategies, which could be considered corporate, business, or functional, are very dangerous. Managers who have made a poor analysis or lack creativity may be trapped into considering them. 一些战略可能会被企业认为是十分危险的。那些不善于分析和缺乏创造力的管理者们可能会因为一些问题比如跟随领导者、再创本垒打、军备竞赛、全面出击、失控等而误入歧途。

How a Best-Cost Strategy Differs from a Low-Cost Strategy Aim of a low-cost strategy—Achieve lower costs than any other competitor in the industry. Intent of a best-cost strategy—Make a more upscale product at lower costs than the makers of other brands with comparable features and attributes. A best-cost provider cannot be the industry's absolute low-cost leader because of the added costs of incorporating the additional upscale features and attributes that the low-cost leader's product doesn't have.

Competitive Strength of a Best-Cost Provider Strategy. A best-cost provider's competitive advantage comes from matching close rivals on key product attributes and beating them on price Success depends on having the skills and capabilities to provide attractive performance and features at a lower cost than rivals. A best-cost producer can often out-compete both a low-cost provider and a differentiator when Standardized features/attributes won't meet the diverse needs of buyers Many buyers are price and value sensitive.

6.17 Risk of Best-Cost Provider Strategies

A best-cost provider may get squeezed between strategies of firms using low-cost and differentiation strategies Low-cost leaders may be able to siphon customers away with a lower price High-end differentiators may be able to steal customers away with better product attributes.

Focus/Niche Strategies Involve concentrated attention on a narrow piece of the total market Serve niche buyers better than rivals Choose a market niche where buyers have distinctive preferences, special requirements, or unique needs Develop unique capabilities to serve needs of target buyer segment Objective Keys to Success.

Focus/Niche Strategies and Competitive Advantage Approach Achieve lower costs than rivals in serving the segment—A low-cost strategy Which hat is unique? Approach Offer niche buyers something different from rivals—A differentiation strategy.

Examples of Focus Strategies eBay Online auctions Porsche Sports cars Horizon and Comair (commuter airlines) Link major airports with small cities Jiffy Lube International Maintenance for motor vehicles Bandag Specialist in truck tire recapping.

What Makes a Niche Attractive for Focusing? Big enough to be profitable and offers good growth potential Not crucial to success of industry leaders Costly or difficult for multi-segment competitors to meet specialized needs of niche members Focuser has resources and capabilities to effectively serve an attractive niche Few other rivals are specializing in same niche Focuser can defend against challengers via superior ability to serve niche members.

Risks of a Focus Strategy Competitors find effective ways to match a focuser's capabilities in serving niche Niche buyers' preferences shift towards product attributes desired by majority of buyers-niche becomes part of overall market Segment becomes so attractive it becomes crowded with rivals, causing segment profits to be splintered.

Cooperative Strategies Companies sometimes use strategic alliances or collaborative partnerships to complement their own strategic initiative sand strengthen their competitiveness. Such cooperative strategies go beyond normal company-to-company dealings but fall short of merger or formal joint venture.

Why Cooperative Strategies Are Integral to a Firm's Competitiveness Collaborative arrangements can help a company lower its costs or gain access to needed expertise and capabilities. Firms often lack the resources and competitive skills to be successful in very demanding competitive races. Allies can be useful in helping a company establish a stronger presence in global markets and helping it win the race for global market leadership. Allies with competitively useful technological know-how or expertise can greatly aid a company racing against rivals for leadership in the" industries of the future" now being created by today's technological and information age revolution Collaborative arrangements with foreign partners can be very helpful in pursuing opportunities in unfamiliar national markets.

Competitive Value of Strategic Alliances to the Partners Capacity of partners to defuse organizational frictions Ability to collaborate effectively over time and work through challenges Technological and competitive surprises. New market developments Changes in their own priorities and competitive circumstances. Competitive advantage emerges when a company acquires valuable capabilities via alliances it could not obtain on its own, providing an edge over rivals.

Why are Strategic Alliances Formed? To collaborate on technology development or new product development To fill gaps in technical or manufacturing expertise. To acquire new competencies. To improve supply chain efficiency To gain economies of scale in production and/or marketing. To acquire or improve market access via joint marketing agreements.

Potential Benefits of Alliances to Achieve Global and Industry Leadership Get into critical country markets quickly to accelerate process of building a global presence. Gain inside knowledge about unfamiliar markets and cultures. Access valuable skills and competencies concentrate din particular geographic locations Establish a beached for participating in target industry Master new technologies and build new expertise faster than would be possible internally. Open up expanded opportunities in target industry by combining firm's capabilities with resources of partners.

Why Alliances Fail Ability of an alliance to endure depends on. How well partners work together. Success of partners in responding and adapting to changing conditions. Willingness of partners to renegotiate the bargain Reasons for alliance failure include. Diverging objectives and priorities of partners. Inability of partners to work well together Emergence of more attractive technological paths Marketplace rivalry between one or more allies.

6.18 Merger and Acquisition Strategies

Combination and pooling of equals, with newly created firm often taking on a new name. Acquisition-One firm, the acquirer, purchases and absorbs operations of another, the acquired. Merger-acquisition Much-used strategic option Especially suited for situations where alliances do not provide a firm with needed capabilities or cost-reducing opportunities. Ownership allows for tightly integrated operations, creating more control and autonomy than alliances.

Benefits of Mergers and Acquisitions, Combining operations may result in. More or better competitive capabilities More attractive line-up of products/services. Wider geographic coverage Greater financial resources to invest in R&D, add capacity, or expand. Cost-saving opportunities Filling in of resource or technological gaps Stronger technological skills. Greater ability to launch next-wave products/services.

Pitfalls of Mergers and Acquisitions Combining operations may result in Resistance from rank-and-file employees. Hard-to-resolve conflicts in management styles and corporate cultures. Tough problems in combining and integrating the operations of the once-different companies. Greater-than-anticipated difficulties in Achieving expected cost-savings. Sharing of expertise Achieving enhanced competitive capabilities.

Vertical Integration Strategies Vertical integration extends a firm's competitive scope within same industry Backward into sources of supply Forward toward end-users of final product. Can aim at either full or partial integration Internally Performed Activities, Costs, &Margins Activities, Costs, &Margins of Suppliers Buyer/ User Value Chains Activities, Costs, & Margins of Forward Channel Allies& Strategic Partners. Competitive Strategy Principle A vertical integration strategy has appeal only if it significantly strengthens a firm's competitive position!

Strategic Advantages of Backward Integration Generates cost savings only if volume needed is big enough to capture efficiencies of suppliers. Potential to reduce costs exists when Suppliers have sizable profit margins Item supplied is a major cost component Resource requirements are easily met Can produce a differentiation-based competitive advantage when it results in a better quality part. Reduces risk of depending on suppliers of crucial raw materials/parts/components.

Strategic Advantages of Forward Integration. Advantageous for a firm to establish its own distribution network if Undependable distribution channels undermine steady production operations. Lacking a broad enough product line to justify integrating forward into stand-alone distributorships or retail outlets, a firm may sell directly to end users. Direct sales and Internet retailing may. Lower distribution costs Produce a relative cost advantage over rivals Enable lower selling prices to end users.

Strategic Disadvantages of Vertical Integration Boosts resource requirements Locks firm deeper into same industry. Results in fixed sources of supply and less flexibility in accommodating buyer demands for product variety Poses problems of balancing capacity at each stage of value chain May require radically different skills/capabilities Reduces manufacturing flexibility, lengthening design time and ability to introduce new products.

Pros and Cons of Integration vs. De-Integration Whether vertical integration is a viable or attractive strategy depends on. How much it can lower cost, build expertise, increase differentiation, or otherwise enhance performance of strategy-critical activities. Its impact on investment cost, flexibility, and administrative overhead. The contribution it makes to strengthening a company market position or helping it create competitive advantage. Many companies are finding that de-integrating, unbundling, and out-sourcing value chain activities are a better strategic option when it comes to lowering cost, improving their competitiveness, or gaining added operating flexibility.

6.19 Unbundling and Outsourcing Strategies

De-Integration or unbundling involves narrowing the scope of the firm's operations, focusing on performing certain "core" value chain activities and relying on outsiders to perform the remaining value chain activities Concept Internally Performed Activities Suppliers Support Services Functional Activities Distributors or Retailers.

When Does Outsourcing Make Strategic Sense? Activity can be performed better or more cheaply by outside specialists. Activity is not crucial to achieve a sustainable competitive advantage. Risk exposure to changing technology and/or changing buyer preferences is reduced Operations are streamlined to Cut cycle time Speed decision-making Reduce coordination costs Firm can concentrate on doing those "core" value chain activities that best suit its resource strengths and capabilities.

Strategic Advantages of Outsourcing Improves firm's ability to obtain high quality and/or cheaper components or services. Improves firm's ability to innovate by interacting with "best-in-world" suppliers. Enhances firm's flexibility should customer needs and market conditions suddenly shift. Increases firm's ability to assemble diverse kinds of expertise speedily and efficiently. Allows firm to concentrate its resources on performing those activities internally which it can perform better than outsiders.

Pitfalls of Outsourcing Farming out too many or the wrong activities, thus Hollowing out its capabilities. Losing touch with activities and expertise that determine its overall long-term success. Offensive and Defensive Strategies Offensive Strategies Used to build new or stronger market position and/or create competitive advantage Defensive Strategies Used to protect competitive advantage(rarely are they the basis for creating advantage).

The Building and Eroding of Competitive Advantage competitive Buildup Period Benefit Period Erosion Period Strategic moves produce competitive advantage Moves by rivals erode competitive advantage Size of competitive advantage achieved Time. Competitive Strategy Principle Any competitive advantage currently held will eventually be eroded by the actions of competent, resourceful competitors!

Options for Mounting Strategic Offensives. Initiatives to match or exceed competitor strengths. Initiatives to capitalize on competitor weaknesses. Simultaneous initiatives on many fronts. End-run offensives. Guerrilla warfare tactics. Preemptive strikes.

Attacking Competitor Strengths Objectives Whittle away at a rival's competitive advantage. Gain market share by out-matching strengths of weaker rivals Challenging strong competitors with a lower price is foolhardy unless the aggressor has a cost advantage or advantage of greater financial strength!

Options for Attacking a Competitor's Strengths Offer equally good product at a lower price Develop low-cost edge, then use it to under-price rivals. Leapfrog into next-generation technologies Add appealing new features Run comparison ads Construct new plant capacity ahead of the rival or in the rival's market strong holds Offer a wider product line. Develop better customer service capabilities.

Attacking Competitor Weaknesses Objective Concentrate company strengths and resources directly against a rival's weaknesses. Go after Those customers a rival has that it is least equipped to serve Rivals providing sub-par customer service. Rivals with weaker marketing skills Geographic regions where rival is weak Segments rival is neglecting Weaknesses to Attack.

Launching Simultaneous Offensive son Many Fronts Launch several major initiatives to. Throw rivals off-balance Splinter their attention Force them to use substantial resources to defend their position. Objective. Appeal. A challenger with superior resources can overpower weaker rivals by out-competing them across-the-board long enough to become a market leader.

End-Run Offensives Objectives Dodge head-to-head confrontations that escalate competitive intensity or risk cut throat competition Attempt to maneuver around strong competitors—concentrate on areas of market where competition is weakest.

Optional Approaches for End-Run Offensives Introduce new products that redefine market and terms of competition Build presence in geographic areas where rival shave little presence. Create new segments by introducing products with different features to better meet buyer needs. Introduce next-generation technologies to leapfrog rivals.

Guerrilla Offenses Approach Use principles of surprise and hit-and-run to attack in locations and at times where conditions are most favorable to initiator Well-suited to small challengers with limited resources and market visibility Appeal.

Options for Guerrilla Offenses Make random, scattered raids on leaders' customers Occasional low-balling on price Intense bursts of promotional activity. Special campaigns to attract buyers from rivals plagued with a strike or having problems meeting delivery schedules. Challenge rivals encountering problems with quality, meeting delivery times, or providing adequate technical support. File legal actions charging antitrust violations, patent infringements, or unfair advertising. Preemptive Strikes Approach Involves moving first to secure an advantageous position that rivals are foreclosed or discouraged from duplicating!

Preemptive Strike Options Acquire firm which has exclusive control of a valuable technology Secure exclusive/dominant access to best distributors Tie up best or most sources of essential raw materials Secure best geographic locations Obtain business of prestigious customers. Expand capacity ahead of demand in hopes of discouraging rivals from following suit Build an image in buyers' minds that is unique or hard to copy. Choosing Who to Attack Four types of firms can be the target of an fresh offensive Market leaders Runner-up firms Struggling rivals on verge of going under. Small local or regional firms not doing a good job for their customers.

6.20 Offensive Strategies and Competitive Advantage

Strategic offensive offering strongest basis for competitive advantage usually entail. Developing lower-cost product design Making changes in production operations that lower costs or enhance differentiation Developing product features that deliver superior performance or lower users' costs. Giving more responsive customer service Escalating marketing effort Pioneering a new distribution channel Selling direct to end-users.

Offensive Strategy Principle The chances for a successful offensive initiative are improved when it is based on a company's resource strengths and strongest competencies and capabilities! Defensive Strategy Fortify firm's present position Help sustain any competitive advantage held Lessen risk of being attacked Blunt impact of any attack that occurs Influence challengers to aim attacks at other rivals Objectives. Defensive Strategies: Approaches Approach 1 Block avenues open to challengers Signal challengers that vigorous retaliations likely Approach.

Block Avenues Open to Challengers Participate in alternative technologies Introduce new features, add new models, or broaden product line to close gaps rivals may pursuer Maintain economy-priced models Increase warranty coverage. Offer free training and support services Reduce delivery times for spare parts Make early announcements about new products or price changes. Challenge quality or safety of rivals' products using legal tactics Sign exclusive agreements with distributors.

Signal Challengers Retaliation Is Likely Publicly announce management's strong commitment to maintain present market share Publicly announce plans to put adequate capacity in place to meet forecasted demand. Give out advance information about new products, technological breakthroughs, and other moves. Publicly commit firm to policy of matching prices and terms offered by rivals Maintain war chest of cash reserves. Make occasional counter-response to moves of weaker rival.

6.21 First-Mover Advantages

When to make a strategic move is often as crucial as what move to make. First-mover advantages arise when Pioneering helps build firm's image and reputation. Early commitments to new technologies, new-style components, and distribution channels can produce cost advantage. Loyalty of first time buyers is high Moving first can be a preemptive strike.

First-Mover Disadvantages Moving early can be a disadvantage(or fail to produce an advantage) when Costs of pioneering are sizable and loyalty of first time buyers is weak Innovator's products are primitive, not living up to buyer expectations Rapid technological change allows followers to leapfrog pioneers.

Timing and Competitive Advantage Principle 1Being a first-mover holds potential for competitive advantage in some cases but not in others Principle Being a fast follower can sometimes yield as good a result as being a first mover Principle Being a late-mover may or may not be fatal—it varies with the situation.

Chapter 7 Strategy Implementation

7.1 Implementing Internal Innovations

An entrepreneurial mind-set is required to be innovative and to develop successful internal corporate ventures. Because of environmental and market uncertainty, individuals and firms must be willing to take risks to commercialize innovations. Although they must continuously attempt to identify opportunities, they must also select and pursue the best opportunities and do so with discipline. Employing an entrepreneurial mind-set entails not only developing new products and markets but also execution in order to do these things effectively. Often, firms provide incentives to managers to be entrepreneurial and to commercialize innovations.

Strategy implementation is the sum total of the activities and choices required for the execution of a strategic plan. It is the process by which strategies and policies are put into action through the development of programs, budgets, and procedures. 战略实施是执行一项战略计划所需要的活动和选择的总和。战略实施是通过开发各种方案、预算和流程，将战略和政策付诸行动的过程。

Having processes and structures in place through which a firm can successfully implement the outcomes of internal corporate ventures and commercialize the innovations is critical. Indeed, as the Strategic Focus on 3M illustrates, the successful introduction of innovations into the marketplace reflects implementation effectiveness. In the context of internal corporate ventures, managers must allocate resources, coordinate activities, communicate with many different parties in the organization, and make a series of decisions to convert the innovations resulting from either autonomous or induced strategic behaviors into successful market entries. Organizational structures are the sets of formal relationships that support processes managers use to commercialize innovations.

Effective integration of the various functions involved in innovation processes from engineering to manufacturing and, ultimately, market distribution is required to implement the incremental and radical innovations resulting from internal corporate ventures. Increasingly, product development teams are being used to integrate the activities associated with different organizational functions. Such integration involves coordinating and applying the knowledge and skills of different functional areas in order to maximize innovation. Teams must help to make decisions as to which projects should be commercialized and which ones should end. Although ending a project is difficult, sometimes because of emotional commitments to innovation-based projects, effective teams recognize when conditions change such that the innovation cannot create value as originally anticipated.

A program is a statement of the activities or steps needed to accomplish a single-use plan. The purpose of a program is to make the strategy action-oriented. 方案是对完成一个单独用途的计划所需活动或步骤的详细说明。方案的目的是确保战略立足于行动。

Procedures, sometimes termed standard operating procedures(SOPs), are a system of sequential steps or techniques that describe in detail how a particular task or job is to be done. 流程有时称为标准作业流程(SOPs),是一个系统,详细描述完成一项特定任务或工作的连续步骤或方法。

7.2 Facilitating Integration and Innovation

Shared values and effective leadership are important for achieving cross-functional integration and implementing innovation. Highly effective shared values are framed around the firm's vision and mission and become the glue that promotes integration between functional units. Thus, the firm's culture promotes unity and internal innovation.

Strategic leadership is also highly important for achieving cross-functional integration and promoting innovation. Leaders set the goals and allocate resources. The goals include integrated development and commercialization of new goods and services. Effective strategic leaders also ensure a high-quality communication system to facilitate cross-functional integration. A critical benefit of effective communication is the sharing of knowledge among team members. Effective communication thus helps create synergy and gains team members' commitment to an innovation throughout the organization. Shared values and leadership practices shape the communication systems that are formed to support the development and commercialization of new products.

7.3 Innovation Through Cooperative Strategies

Virtually all firms lack the breadth and depth of resources in their R&D activities needed to internally develop a sufficient number of innovations to meet the needs of the market and remain competitive. As indicated in the Opening Case, firms must be open to using external resources to help produce innovations. Alliances with other firms can contribute to innovations in several ways. First, they provide information on new business opportunities and how to exploit them. In other instances, firms use cooperative strategies to align what they believe are complementary assets with the potential to lead to future innovations. In fact, research suggests that such innovation will lead to "breakthroughs" and new product classes more often than other modes.

The rapidly changing technologies of the twenty-first-century competitive landscape, globalization, and the need to innovate at world-class levels are primary influences on firms' decisions to innovate by cooperating with other companies. Indeed, some believe that because of these conditions, firms are becoming increasingly dependent on cooperative strategies as a path to successful competition in the global economy. Even venerable old firms such as P&G and 3M have learned that they need help to create innovations necessary to be competitive in a twenty-first-century environment. As noted in the Opening Case, P&G produces Glad brand plastic bags in joint venture with Clorox.

Both entrepreneurial firms and established firms use cooperative strategies to innovate. An entrepreneurial firm, for example, may seek investment capital as well as established firms' distribution capabilities to successfully introduce one of its innovative products to the market. Alternatively, more established companies may need new technological knowledge and can gain access to it by forming a cooperative strategy with entrepreneurial ventures. Alliances between large pharmaceutical firms and biotechnology companies increasingly have been formed to integrate the knowledge and resources of both to develop new products and bring them to market.

Because of the importance of strategic alliances, particularly in the development of new technology and in commercializing innovations, firms are beginning to build networks of alliances that represent a form of social capital to them. Building social capital in the form of relationships with other firms provides access to the knowledge and other resources necessary to develop innovations. Knowledge from these alliances helps firms develop new capabilities. Some firms seek other companies to participate in their internal new capabilities. Some firms seek other companies to participate in their internal new product development processes. It is not uncommon, for example, for firms to have supplier or customer representative on their cross-functional innovation teams because of the importance of their input to ensure quality materials for any new product developed.

However, alliances formed for the purpose of innovation are not without risks. In addition to conflict that is natural when firms try to work together to reach a mutual goal, cooperative strategy participants also take a risk that a partner will appropriate a firm's technology or knowledge and use it to enhance its own competitive abilities. To prevent or at least minimize this risk, firms, particularly new ventures, need to select their partners carefully. The ideal partnership is one in which the firms have complementary skills as well as compatible strategic goals. However, because companies are operating in a network of firms and thus may be participating in multiple alliances simultaneously, they encounter challenges in managing the alliances. Research has shown that firms can become involved in too many alliances, which can harm rather than facilitate their innovation capabilities. Thus, effectively managing a cooperative strategy to produce innovation is critical.

As explained in the Strategic Focus, social networking Internet sites have become highly popular with the general public and with professionals as well. Furthermore, entrepreneurs have begun to use them in ways to facilitate their businesses. These sites provide many opportunities for businesses and especially for gaining access to ideas and information. Therefore, they can facilitate innovation. Firms can use them to identify unique product ideas, do market research, and access new markets and new customers. As the Strategic Focus illustrates, they are also being used to facilitate innovation communities such as application development for iPhone and Android smart phones. As a result, the social networking sites are highly valuable business mechanisms.

7.4 Organizational Structure and Controls

Research shows that organizational structure and the controls that are a part of the structure affect firm performance. In particular, evidence suggests that performance declines when the firm's strategy is not matched with the most appropriate structure and controls. Even though mismatches between strategy and structure do occur, research indicates that managers try to act rationally when forming of changing their firm's structure. His record of success at General Electric suggests that CEO Jeffrey Immelt pays close attention to the need to make certain that strategy and structure remain matched, as evidenced by restructuring alignments in GE Capital, GE's financial service group, during the economic downturn.

Organization structure specifies the firm's reporting relationships, procedures, controls, and authority and decision-making processes. Developing an organizational structure that effectively supports the firm's strategy is difficult, especially because of the uncertainty about cause-effect relationships in the global economy's rapidly changing and dynamic competitive environments. When a structure's elements are properly aligned with one another, the structure facilitates effective use of the firm's strategies. Thus, organizational structure is a critical component of effective strategy implementation processes.

A firm's structure specifies the work to be done and how to do it, given the firm's strategy or strategies. Thus, organizational structure influences how managers work and the decision resulting from that work. Supporting the implementation of strategies, structure is concerned with processes used to complete organizational tasks. Having the right structure and process is important. For example, many product-oriented firms have been moving to develop service businesses associated with those products. This strategy has been used by GE. However, research suggests that developing a separate division for such services in product-oriented companies, rather than managing the service business within the product divisions, leads to additional growth and profitability in the service business. GE developed a separate division for its financial services businesses and this helped facilitate GE's growth over the last two decades.

Organizational controls are an important aspect of structure. Organizational controls guide the use of strategy, indicate how to compare actual results with expected results, and suggest corrective actions to take when the difference is unacceptable. When fewer differences separate actual from expected outcomes, the organization's controls are more effective. It is difficult for the company to successfully exploit its competitive advantages without effective organizational controls. Properly designed organizational controls provide clear insights regarding behaviors that enhance firm performance. Firms use both strategic controls and financial controls to support the implementation and use of their strategies.

Strategic controls are largely subjective criteria intended to verify that the firm is using appropriate strategies for the conditions in the external environment and the company's competitive advantages. Thus, strategic controls are concerned with examining the fit between what the firm might do and what it can do. Effective strategic controls help the firm understand what it takes to be successful. Strategic controls demand rich communications between managers responsible for using them to judge the firm's performance and those with primary responsibility for implementing the firm's strategies. These frequent exchanges are both formal and informal in nature.

Strategic controls are also used to evaluate the degree to which the firm focuses on the requirements to implement its strategies. For a business-level strategy, for example, the strategic controls are used to study primary and support activities to verify that the critical activities are being emphasized and properly executed. In fact, Nokia failed to employ effective strategic controls and is now fighting for survival as a result. With related corporate-level strategies, strategic controls are used by corporate strategic leaders to verify the sharing of appropriate strategic factors such as knowledge, markets, and technologies across businesses. To effectively use strategic controls when evaluating related diversification strategies, headquarter executives must have a deep understanding of each unit's business-level strategy. As we described in the Opening Case, Borders' significant strategic problems likely stemmed at least partly from the ineffective use of strategic controls.

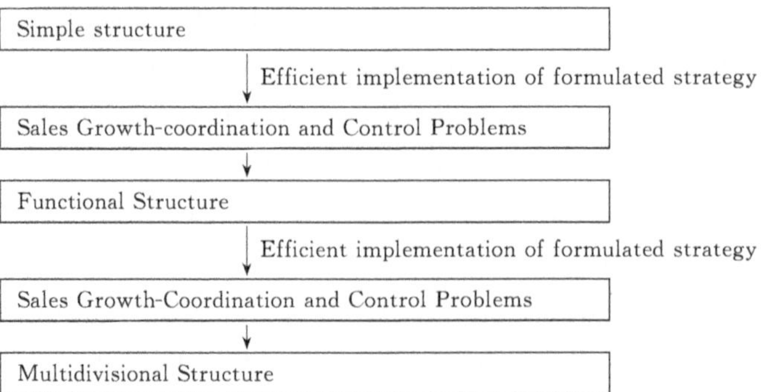

Figure 7.1 Strategy and Structure Growth Pattern

7.5 Functional Structure

The functional structure consists of a chief executive officer and a limited corporate staff, with functional line managers in dominant organizational areas such as production, accounting, marketing, R&D, engineering, and human resources. This structure allows for functional specialization, thereby facilitating active sharing of knowledge within each functional area. Knowledge sharing facilitates career paths as well as professional development of functional specialists. However, a functional orientation can negatively affect communication and coordination among those representing different organizational functions. For the reason, the CEO must verify that the decisions and actions of individual business functions promote the entire firm rather than a single function. The functional structure supports implementing business-level strategies with low levels of diversification. When changing from a simple to a functional structure, firms want to avoid introducing value-destroying bureaucratic procedures such as failing to promote innovation and creativity.

Matches between Corporate-Level Strategies and the Multidivisional Structure

As explained earlier, Chandler's research shows that the firm's continuing success leads to product or market diversification or both. The firm's level of diversification is a function of decisions about the number and type of businesses in which it will compete as well as how it will manage the businesses. Geared to managing individual organizational functions, increasing diversification eventually creates information processing, coordination, and control problems that the functional structure cannot handle. Thus, using a diversification strategy requires the firm to change from the functional structure to the multidivisional structure to develop an appropriate strategy/structure match.

Corporate-level strategies have different degrees of product and market diversification. The demands created by different levels of diversification highlight the need for a unique organizational structure to effectively implement each strategy (see Figure 7.2).

Cisco must use a differentiation strategy in order to compete in its several high technology product market segments. However, given the presence of major competitors in those markets, such as Hewlett-Packard and Huawei, and its loss of market share in its core market of routers, Cisco must also be sensitive to costs. Thus, the horizontal structure can be useful to integrate the two disparate dimensions of structure needed to implement Cisco's integrated cost leadership-differentiation strategy. In addition, Cisco needs to coordinate several related product units, and the horizontal structure should facilitate this cooperation. Therefore, Cisco's approach is similar to the cooperative M-form structure, discussed next.

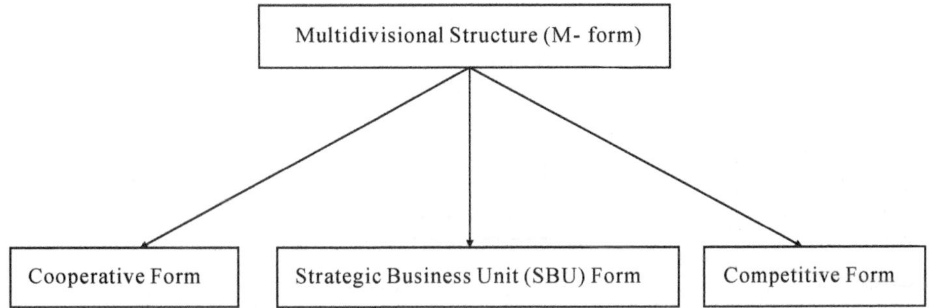

Figure 7.2 Three Variations of the Multidivisional Structure

Using the Strategic Business Unit Form of the Multidivisional Structure to implement the Related Linked Strategy

Firms with fewer links or less constrained links among their divisions use the related linked diversification strategy. The strategic business unit form of the multidivisional structure supports implementation of this strategy. The strategic business unit (SBU) form is an M-form structure consisting of three levels: corporate headquarters, strategic business units, and SBU divisions. The SBU structure is used by large firms and can be complex, given associated organization size and product and market diversity.

The divisions within each SBU are related in terms of shared products or markets or both, but the divisions of one SBU have little in common with the divisions of the other SBUs. Divisions within each SBU share product or market competencies to develop economies of scope and possibly economies of scale. The integrating mechanisms use by the divisions in this structure can be equally well used by the divisions within the individual strategic business units that are part of the SBU form of the multidivisional structure. In this structure, each SBU is a profit center that is controlled and evaluated by the headquarters office. Although both financial and strategic controls are important, on a relative basis financial controls are vital to headquarters' evaluation of each SBU; strategic controls are critical when the heads of SBUs evaluate their divisions' performances. Strategic controls are also critical to the headquarters' efforts to determine whether the company has formed an effective portfolio of businesses and whether those businesses are being successfully managed. Therefore, there is need for strategic structures that promote exploration to identify new products and markets, but also for actions that exploit the current product lines and markets.

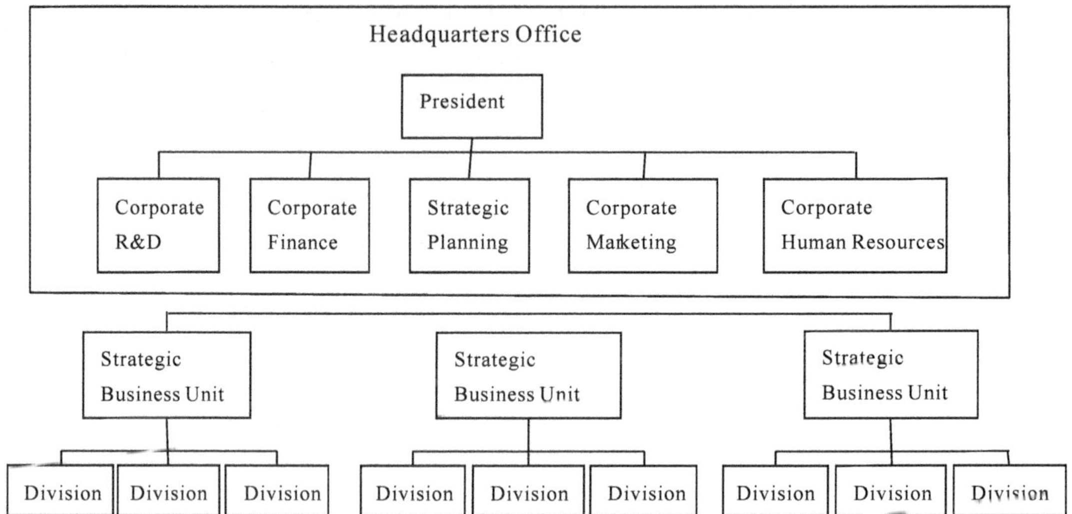

Figure 7.3 SUB Form of the Multidivisional Structure for Implementing a Related Linked Strategy

7.6 The Role of Top-Level Managers

Top-level managers play a critical role in that they are charged to make certain their firm is able to effectively formulate and implement strategies. Top-level managers' strategic decisions influence how the firm is designed and goals will be achieved. Thus, a critical element of organizational success is having a top management team with superior managerial skills.

Managers often use their discretion when making strategic decisions, including those concerned with effectively implementing strategies. Managerial discretion differs significantly across industries. The primary factors that determine the amount of decision-making discretion held by a manager are (1) external environmental sources such as the industry structure, the rate of market growth in the firm's primary industry, and the degree to which products can be differentiated; (2) characteristics of the organization, including its size, age, resources, and culture; and (3) characteristics of the manager, including commitment to the firm and its strategic outcomes, tolerance for ambiguity, skills in working with different people, and aspiration levels. Because strategic leaders' decisions are intended to help the firm gain a competitive advantage, how managers exercise discretion when determining appropriate strategic actions is critical to the firm's success.

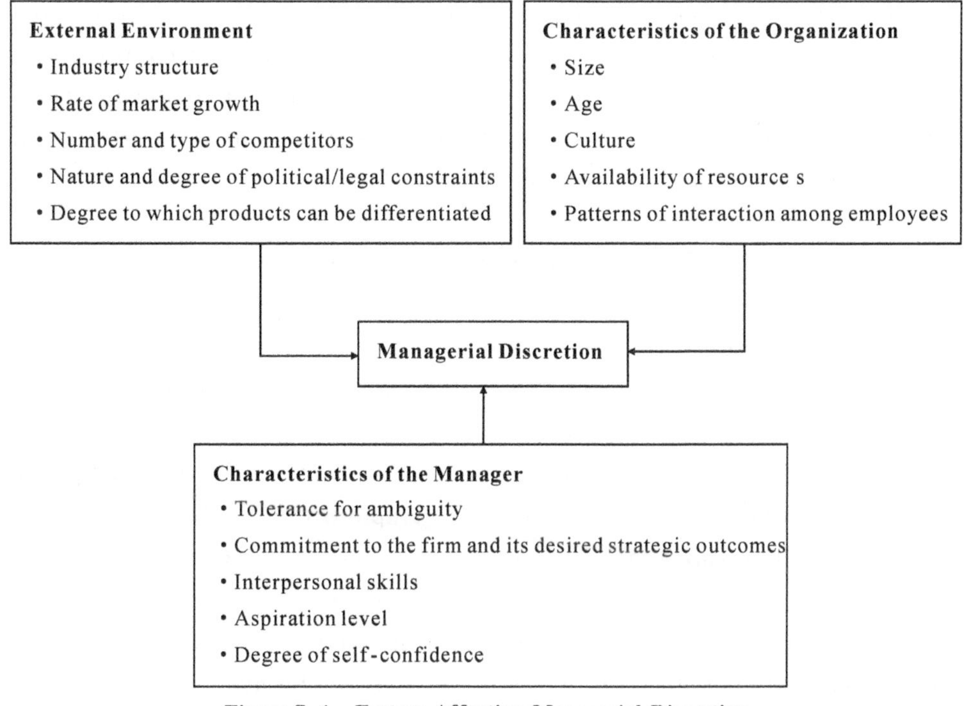

Figure 7.4 Factors Affecting Managerial Discretion

In addition to determining new strategic initiatives, top-level managers develop a firm's organizational structure and reward systems. Top executives also have a major effect on a firm's culture. Evidence suggests that managers' values are critical in shaping a firm's cultural values. Accordingly, top-level managers have an important effect on organizational activities and performance. Because of the challenges top executives face, they often are more effective when they operate as top management teams.

7.7 Top Management Teams

In most firms, the complexity of challenges and the need for substantial amounts of information and knowledge require strategic leadership by a team of executives. Using a team to make strategic decisions also helps to avoid another potential problem when these decisions are made by the CEO alone: managerial hubris. Research evidence shows that when CEOs begin to believe glowing press accounts and to feel that they are unlikely to make errors, they are more likely to make poor strategic decisions. Top executives need to have self-confidence but must guard against allowing it to become arrogance and a false belief in their own invincibility. To guard against CEO overconfidence and poor strategic decisions, firms often use the top management team to consider strategic opportunities and problems and to make strategic decisions. The top management team is composed of the key individuals who are responsible for selecting and implementing the firm's strategies. Typically, the top management team includes the officers of the corporation, defined by the title of vice president and above or by service as a member of the board of directors. The quality of the strategic decisions made by a top management team affects the firm's ability to innovate and engage in effective strategic change.

7.8 Managerial Succession

The choice of top executives-especially CEOs is a critical decision with important implications for the firm's performance. Many companies use leadership screening systems to identify individuals with managerial and strategic leadership potential as well as to determine the criteria individuals should satisfy to be candidates for the CEO position.

The most effective of these systems assesses people within the firm and gains valuable information about the capabilities of other companies' managers, particularly their strategic leaders. Based on the results of these assessments, training and development programs are provided for current individuals in an attempt to preselect and shape the skills of people who may become tomorrow's leaders. Because of the quality of its programs, General Electric "is famous for developing leaders who are dedicated to turning imaginative ideas into leading products and services." However, there are many companies that do not have succession plans for their top executives. For example, a recent survey found that 43 percent of the largest public companies in the United States had no formal succession plan for their CEOs. Of those companies with plans, only about 20 percent were satisfied with their succession processes.

Synergy can take place in one of six ways: shared know-how, coordinated strategies, shared tangible resources, economies of scale or scope, pooled negotiating power, and new business creation. 产生协同效应的方式有六种:共享知识、协调战略、共享有形资源、规模经济或范围经济、集中谈判力量以及创造新业务。

7.9 Sustaining an Effective Organizational Culture

We defined organizational culture as a complex set of ideologies, symbols, and core values that are shared throughout the firm and influence the way business is conducted. Evidence suggests that a firm can develop core competencies in terms of both the capabilities it possesses and the way the capabilities are leveraged when implementing strategies to produce desired outcomes. In other words, because the organizational culture influences how the firm conducts its business and helps regulate and control employees' behavior, it can be a source of competitive advantage. Given its importance, it may be that a vibrant organizational culture is the most valuable competitive differentiator for business organizations. Thus, shaping the context within which the firm formulates and implements its strategies-that is, shaping the organizational culture-is an essential strategic leadership action.

In a classic study of large U. S. corporations such as DuPont, General Motors, Chandler concluded that structure follows strategy—that is, changes in corporate strategy lead to changes in organizational structure. 钱德勒在一项经典研究中总结说,美国大型公司如杜邦、通用汽车都采取组织结构遵循战略的方式,即公司在战略上的变化导致组织结构的变化。

7.10 Establishing Balanced Organizational Controls

Organizational controls are basic to a capitalistic system and have long been viewed as an import part of strategy implementation processes. Controls are necessary to help ensure that firms achieve their desired outcomes. Defined as the "formal, information-based... procedures used by managers to maintain or alter patterns in organizational activities," controls help strategic leaders build credibility, demonstrate the value of strategies to the firm's stakeholders, and promote and support strategic change. Most critically, controls provide the parameters for implementing strategic change. Most critically, controls provide the parameters for implementing strategies as well as the corrective actions to be taken when implementation-related adjustments are required. For example, Alibaba exercised control to identify and eliminate the fraud. Furthermore, it developed additional controls to prevent such actions from occurring again.

Successful firms tend to follow a pattern of structural development, called stages of corporate development, as they grow and expand. 随着公司不断成长壮大,成功企业往往遵循某种形式的结构性发展,称为企业的发展阶段。

Stage 1: simple structure 第 1 阶段:简单结构

Stage 1 is completely centralized in the entrepreneur, who founds the company to promote an idea(product or service). 第一阶段完全集中于创立公司来推广某个想法(产品或服务)的企业家。

Stage 2: functional structure 第 2 阶段:职能结构

Stage 2 is the point when the entrepreneur is replaced by a team of managers who have functional specializations. 在第二阶段,企业家往往被具有专业职能的管理者团队取代。

Stage 3: divisional structure 第 3 阶段:分部结构

Stage 3 is typified by the corporation's managing diverse product lines in numerous industries; it decentralizes the decision-making authority. 第三阶段的典型特征是公司在许多不同的行业管理着多元化的产品线,需要分散决策权。

Stage 4: beyond SBUS 第四阶段:超越战略业务单位结构

The matrix and the network are two possible candidates for a fourth stage in corporate development-a stage that not only emphasizes horizontal over vertical connections between people and groups, but also organizes work around temporary projects in which sophisticated information systems support collaborative activities. 矩阵结构和网络结构是第四阶段公司进一步发展的两种可能候选阶段——不仅强调人与群体之间的水平和垂直连接,还围绕借助先进的信息系统支持协作活动的临时项目来组织工作。

The organizational life cycle describes how organizational grow, develop, and eventually decline. It is the organizational equivalent of the product life cycle in marketing. The stages of the organizational life cycle are Birth(stage1),Growth(stage2), Maturity(stage 3), Decline(stage 4), and Death(stage 5). 组织生命周期描述了组织如何成长、发展并最终衰退的过程,等同于营销中的产品生命周期。组织生命周期的各个阶段包括出生期(第一阶段)、成长期(第二阶段)、成熟期(第三阶段)、衰退期(第四阶段)和死亡(第五阶段)。

7.11 Entrepreneurship and Entrepreneurial Opportunities

Entrepreneurship is the process by which individuals, teams, or organizations identify and pursue entrepreneurial opportunities without being immediately constrained by the resources the currently control. Entrepreneurial opportunities are conditions in which new goods or services can satisfy a need in the market. These opportunities exist because of competitive imperfections in markets and among the factors of production used to produce them or because they were independently developed by entrepreneurs. Entrepreneurial opportunities come in many forms such as the chance to develop and sell a new product and the chance to sell an existing product in a new market. Firms should be receptive to pursuing entrepreneurial opportunities whenever and wherever they may surface.

As these two definitions suggest, the essence of entrepreneurship is to identify and exploit entrepreneurship is to identify and exploit entrepreneurial opportunities-that is, opportunities others do not see or for which they do not recognize the commercial potential-and manage risks appropriately as they arise. As a process, entrepreneurship results in the "creative destruction" of existing products or methods of producing them and replaces them with new products and production methods. Thus, firms engaging in entrepreneurship place high value on individual innovations as well as the ability to continuously innovate across time.

7.12 Innovation

Peter Drucker argued that "innovation is the specific function of entrepreneurship, whether in an existing business, a public service institution, or a new venture started by a lone individual." Moreover, Drucker suggested that innovation is "the means by which the entrepreneur either creates new wealth-producing resources or endows existing resources with enhanced potential for creating wealth." Thus, entrepreneurship and the innovation resulting from it are critically important for all firms. The realities of competition in the competitive landscape of the twenty-first century suggest that to be market leaders, companies must regularly develop innovative products desired by customers. This means that innovation should be an intrinsic part of virtually all of a firm's activities.

Innovation is a key outcome firms seek through entrepreneurship and is often the source of competitive success, especially in turbulent, highly competitive environments. For example, research results show that firms competing in global industries that invest more in innovation also achieve the highest returns. In fact, investors often react positively to the introduction of a new product, thereby increasing the price of a firm's stock. Furthermore, "innovation may be required to maintain or achieve competitive parity, much less a competitive advantage in many global markets". Investing in the development of new technologies can increase the performance of firms that operate in different but related product markets. In this way, the innovations can be used in multiple markets, and return on the investments is eared more quickly.

In his classic work, Schumpeter argued that firms engage in three types of innovative activities. Invention is the act of creating a commercial product from an invention. Invention begins after an invention is chosen for development. Thus, an invention brings something new into being, while an innovation brings something new into use. Accordingly, technical criteria are used to determine the success of an invention, whereas commercial criteria are used to determine the success of an innovation. Finally, imitation is the adoption of a similar innovation by different firms. Imitation usually leads to product or process standardization, and products based on imitation often are offered at lower prices, but without as many features. Entrepreneurship is critical to innovative activity in that it acts as the linchpin between invention and innovation.

Briefly, Six sigma is an analytical method for achieving near-perfect results on a production line. 简单来说，六西格玛是实现生产线近乎完美结果的分析方法。

Although the emphasis is on reducing product variance in order to boost quality and efficiency, it is increasingly being applied to accounts receivable, sales, and R&D. 尽管六西格玛的重点是减少产品差异，提高质量和效率，但是现在越来越的应用到应收账款、销售

和研发中。

The process of six sigma encompasses five steps：六西格玛的过程包括五个步骤：

Define a process where results are poor than average. 定义一个比平均值差的过程

Measure the process to determine exact current performance. 测量过程以确定精确的目前的性能

Analyze the information to pinpoint where things are going wrong. 分析信息，找出哪里出错

Improve the process and eliminate the error. 完善过程，消除误差

Control the process to prevent future defects from occurring. 从目前发生的事情中防止未来发生错误的过程控制

In the United States in particular, innovation is the most critical of the three types of innovative activities. Many companies are able to create ideas that lead to inventions, but commercializing those inventions has, at times, proved difficult. This difficulty is suggested by the fact that approximately 80 percent of R&D occurs in large firms, but these same firms produce fewer than 50 percent of the patents. Patents are a strategic asset and the ability to regularly produce them can be an important source of competitive advantage, especially when a firm intends to commercialize the invention and when the firm competes in a knowledge-intensive industry.

7.13 Internal Innovation

In established organizations, most innovation comes from efforts in research and development (R&D). Effective R&D often leads to firms filing for patents to protect their innovative work. Increasingly, successful R&D results from integrating the skills available in the global workforce. Thus, the ability to have a competitive advantage based on innovation is more likely to accrue to firms capable of integrating the talent of human capital from countries around the world.

Increasingly, it seems possible that in the twenty-first-century competitive Landscape, R&D may be the most critical factor in gaining and sustaining a competitive advantage in some industries, such as pharmaceuticals. Larger, established firms, certainly those competing globally, often try to use their R&D labs to create disruptive new technologies and products. Being able to innovate in this manner can create a competitive advantage for firms in many industries. Although critical to long-term corporate success, the outcomes of R&D investments are uncertain and often not achieved in the short term, meaning that patience is required as firms evaluate the outcomes of their R&D efforts.

7.14 Incremental and Radical Innovation

In contrast to incremental innovations, radical innovations usually provide significant technological breakthroughs and create new knowledge. Radical innovations, which are revolutionary and nonlinear in nature, typically use technologies to serve newly created markets. The development of the original personal computer was a radical innovation at the time. Reinventing the computer by developing a "radically new computer-brain chip" is an example of a radical innovation. Obviously, such a radical innovation would seem to have the capacity to revolutionize the tasks computers could perform. Perhaps some of the new products to be produced by the joint venture between Intel and Nokia integrating smartphones and computers will be considered to be radical innovations.

Because they establish new functionalities for users, radical innovations have strong potential to lead to significant growth in revenue and profits. For example, Toyota's innovation, embodied in the Prius, "the first mass-produced hybrid-electric car," changed the industry in this segment. Developing new processes is a critical part of producing radical innovations. Both types of innovations can create value, meaning that firms should determine when it is appropriate to emphasize either incremental or radical innovation. However, radical innovations have the potential to contribute more significantly to a firm's efforts to earn above-average returns, although they may be more risky.

Radical innovations are because of the difficulty and risk involved in developing them. The value of the technology and the market opportunities are highly uncertain. Because radical innovation creates new knowledge, creativity is required. However, creativity does not produce something from nothing. Rather, creativity discovers, combines, or synthesizes current knowledge, often from diverse areas. This knowledge is then used to develop new products that can be used in an entrepreneurial manner to move into new markets, capture new customers, and gain access to new resources. Such innovations are often developed in separate business units that start internal ventures.

Internally developed incremental and radical innovations result from deliberate efforts. These deliberate efforts are called internal corporate venturing, which is the set of activities firms use to develop internal inventions and especially innovations. Autonomous and induced strategic behaviors are the two types of internal corporate venturing. Each venturing type facilitates incremental and radical innovations. However, a large number of radical innovations spring from autonomous strategic behavior while the greatest percentage of incremental innovations come from induced strategic behavior.

7.15 Autonomous Strategic Behavior

Autonomous strategic behavior is a bottom-up process in which product champions pursue new ideas, often through a political process, by means of which they develop and coordinate the commercialization of a new good or service until it achieves success in the marketplace. A product champion is an organizational member with an entrepreneurial vision of a new good or service who seeks to create support for its commercialization. Product champions play critical roles in moving innovations forward. Indeed, in many corporations, "Champions are widely acknowledged as pivotal to innovation speed and success." Champions are vital to sell the ideas to others in the organization so that the innovations will be commercialized. Commonly, product champions use their social capital to develop informal networks within the firm. As progress is made, these networks become more formal as a means of pushing an innovation to the point of successful commercialization. Internal innovations springing from autonomous strategic behavior frequently differ from the firm's current strategy, taking it into new markets and perhaps new ways of creating value for customers and other stakeholders.

Autonomous strategic behavior is based on a firm's wellspring of knowledge and resources that are the sources of the firm's innovation. Thus, a firm's technological capabilities and competencies are the basis for new products and processes. As described in the Strategic Focus, 3M uses autonomous strategic behavior extensively to identify new technologies and products that can better serve its customers. Similarly, the iPod likely resulted from autonomous strategic behavior at Apple, thought the development of the iPhone was more the result of induced strategic behavior discussed in the next section.

Changing the concept of corporate-level strategy through autonomous strategic behavior results when a product is championed within strategic and structural contexts (see Figure 7.5). Such a transformation occurred with the development of the iPod and introduction of iTunes at Apple. The strategic context is the process used to arrive at strategic decisions. The best firms keep changing their strategic context and strategies because of the continuous changes in the current competitive landscape. Thus, some believe that the most competitively successful firms reinvent their industry or develop a completely new one across time as they compete with current and future rivals.

To be effective, an autonomous process for developing new products requires that new knowledge be continuously diffused throughout the firm. In particular, the diffusion of tacit knowledge is important for development of more effective new products. Interestingly, some of the processes important for the promotion of autonomous new product development behavior vary by the environment and country in which a firm operates. For example, the Japanese culture is high on uncertainty avoidance. As such, research has found that Japanese firms are more likely to engage in autonomous behaviors under conditions of low uncertainty because they prefer stability.

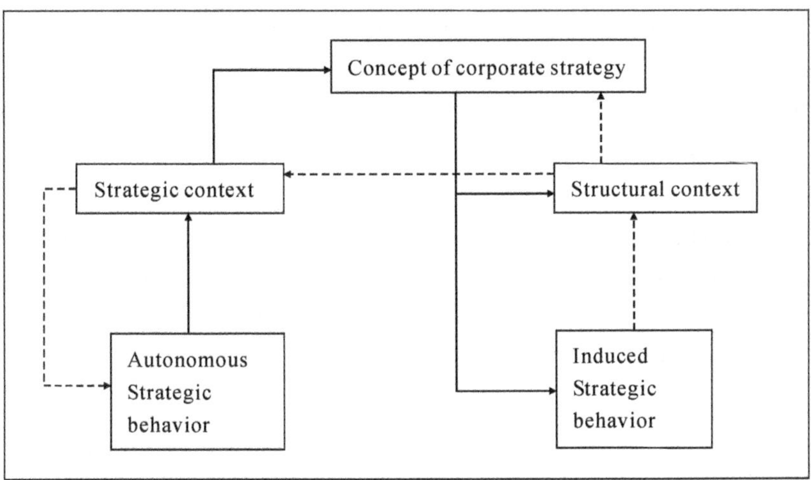

Figure 7.5 Model of Internal Corporate Venturing

7.16 Why the World Economy Is Globalizing

Previously closed national economies are opening up their markets to foreign companies. Importance of geographic distance is shrinking due to the Internet Growth-minded companies are racing to stake out positions in the markets of more and more countries.

What is the Motivation for Competing Internationally? Gain access to new customers. Capitalize on resource strengths and competencies Help achieve lower costs. Spread business risk across wider market base Obtain access to valuable natural resources.

International vs. Global Competition International or Multinational Competitor Company operates in a few foreign countries, with modest ambitions to expand further Global Competitor Company markets products in 50 to 100 countries and is expanding operations into additional country markets annually.

Cross-Country Differences in Cultural, Demographic, and Market Conditions. Cultures and life styles differ among countries. Differences in market demographics. Variations in manufacturing and distribution costs Fluctuating exchange rates Differences in host government trade policies.

How Markets Differ from Country to Country Consumer tastes and preferences. Consumer buying habits Market size and growth potential Distribution channels Driving forces Competitive pressures One of the biggest concerns of companies competing in foreign markets is whether to customize their product offerings in each different country market to match the tastes and preferences of local buyers or whether to offer a mostly standardized product worldwide.

Potential Locational Advantages Stemming from Cost Variations Among Countries Manufacturing costs vary based on Wage rates Worker productivity. Natural resource availability Inflation rates Energy costs Tax rates Quality of a country's business environment. Clustering of suppliers, trade associations, and makers of complementary products.

Differences in Host Government Trade Policies Local content requirements Import tariffs or quotas Restrictions on exports Regulations regarding prices of imports Other regulations. Technical standards Product certification Prior approval of capital spending projects. Withdrawal of funds from country Minority ownership by local citizens.

The Role of Strategy: Actions managers take to attain the goals of the firm. Need to identify and take action that lowers the cost of value creation and/or differentiates the firm's product through superior design, quality, service, or functionality.

7.17 Multi-domestic Strategy Maximizes Local Responsiveness

Customize the product and marketing strategy to national demands. Skill and product transfer. Transfer all value-creation activities, no experience curve rewards. Good for high local responsiveness and low cost reduction pressures.

Global Strategy Best use of the experience curve and location economies. This is the low cost strategy. Utilize product standardization. Not good where local responsiveness demand is high.

Transnational StrategyCore competencies can develop in any of the firm's worldwide operations. Flow of skills and product offerings occurs throughout the firm-not only from home firm to foreign subsidiary (global learning). Makes sense where there is pressure for both cost reduction and local responsiveness.

Four Basic Strategies Global Strategy Transnational Strategy Multi domestic Strategy Low High International Strategy Pressures for local responsiveness High Cost pressures Low.

Cost Pressures and Pressures for Local Responsiveness Facing Caterpillar Caterpillar Tractor High Cost pressures Low High Pressures for local responsiveness.

Characteristics of Multi-Country Competition Each country market is self-contained Competition in one country market is independent of competition in other country markets Rivals competing in one country market differ from set of rivals competing in another country market. Rivals vie for national market leadership No"international"market, just a collection of country markets.

Characteristics of Global Competition Competitive conditions across country markets are strongly linked together. Many of same rivals compete in many of the same country markets Rivals vie for worldwide leadership. A true international market exists A firm's competitive position in one country is affected by its position in other countries. Competitive advantage (or disadvantage) is based on a firm's world-wide operations and overall global standing.

Strategy Options for International Markets Exporting Licensing Franchising strategy Multi-country strategy. Global strategy based on Low cost Differentiation Best-cost Focusing Strategic alliances or joint ventures.

Characteristics of Export Strategies Involves using domestic plants as a production base for exporting to foreign markets Excellent initial strategy to pursue international sales. Advantages Minimizes both risk and capital requirements Conservative way to test international waters. Minimizes direct investments in foreign countries. An export strategy is vulnerable when Manufacturing costs in home country are higher than in foreign countries where rivals have plants High shipping costs are involved.

Characteristics of Licensing Strategies Licensing makes sense when a firm Has valuable technical know-how or a patented product but does not have international capabilities or resources to enter foreign markets. Desires to avoid risks of committing resources to markets which Are unfamiliar Present economic uncertainty. Are politically volatile Disadvantage Risk of providing valuable technical know-how to foreign firms and losing some control over its use.

Characteristics of Franchising Strategies Often is better suited to global expansion efforts of service and retailing enterprises Advantages Franchisee bears most of costs and risks of establishing foreign locations Franchisor has to expend only the resources to recruit, train, and support franchisee Disadvantage Maintaining cross-country quality control.

Strategy is matched to local market needs Different country strategies are called for when Significant country-to-country differences in customers' needs exist. Buyers in one country want a product different from buyers in another country. Host government regulations preclude uniform global approach. Two drawbacks Poses problems of transferring competencies across borders. Works against building a unified competitive advantage Multi-Country Strategy.

Global Strategy for competing is similar in all country markets Involves Coordinating strategic moves globally Selling in many, if not all, nations where a significant market exists Works best when products and buyer requirements are similar from country to country.

Competitive Strategy Principle A multi-country strategy is appropriate for industries where multi-country competition dominates! A global strategy works best in markets that are globally competitive or beginning to globalize!

Pursuing Competitive Advantage by Competing Multi-nationally Three ways to gain competitive advantage. Locating activities among nations to lower costs or achieve greater product differentiation. Efficient/effective transfer of competitively valuable competencies and capabilities from domestic to foreign markets. Coordinating dispersed activities in ways a domestic-only competitor.

7.18 Locating Activities to Build a Global Competitive Advantage

Whether to Concentrate each activity in a few countries or Disperse activities to many different nations Where to locate activities-Which country is best location for which activity?

Concentrating Activities to Build a Global Competitive Advantage Activities should be concentrated when Costs of manufacturing or other value chain activities are meaningful lower in certain locations than in others There are sizable scale economies in performing the activity There is a steep learning curve associated with performing an activity in a single location Certain locations have superior resources, allow better coordination of related activities, oroffer other valuable advantages

Dispersing Activities to Build a Global Competitive Advantage Activities should be dispersed when They need to be performed close to buyers Transportation costs, scale diseconomies, or trade barriers make centralization expensive. Buffers for fluctuating exchange rates, supply interruptions, and adverse politics are needed.

Transferring Valuable Competencies to Build a Global Competitive Advantage Transferring competencies, capabilities, and resource strengths across borders contributes to Development of broader competencies and capabilities. Achievement of dominating depth in some competitively valuable area Dominating depth in a competitively valuable capability is a strong basis for sustainable competitive advantage over Other multinational or global competitors and Small domestic competitors in host countries.

Coordinating Cross-Border Activities to Build a Global Competitive Advantage. Aligning activities located in different countries contributes to competitive advantage in several ways. Choose where and how to challenge rivals Shift production from one location to another to take advantage of most favorable cost or trade conditions or exchange rates Enhance brand reputation by incorporating same differentiating attributes in its products in all markets where it competes.

7.19 What Profit Sanctuaries Are

Profit sanctuaries are country markets where a firm has a strong or protected market position and Derives substantial profits. Generally, a firm's most strategically crucial profit sanctuary is its home market Profit sanctuaries are a valuable competitive asset in global industries!

What is Cross-Market Subsidization? Involves supporting competitive offensives in one market with resources/profits diverted from operations in other markets. Competitive power of cross-market subsidization results from a multinational firm's ability to Draw upon its organizational resources and profits in other country markets to help mount an attack on single-market or one-country rivals and try to lure away their customers with lower prices, discount promotions, heavy advertising, or other offensive tactics.

Achieving Global Competitiveness via Cooperation Cooperative agreements/ strategic alliances with foreign companies are a means to Enter a foreign market or Strengthen a firm's competitiveness in world markets. In purpose of alliances Joint research efforts Technology-sharing Joint use of production or distribution facilities Marketing/promoting one another's products.

Benefits of Strategic Alliances Gain scale economies in production and/or marketing Fill gaps in technical expertise or knowledge of local markets Share distribution facilities and dealer networks. Direct combined competitive energies toward defeating mutual rivals. Useful way to gain agreement on important technical standards.

Pitfalls of Strategic Alliances Becoming too dependent on another firm for essential expertise over the long-term Different motives and conflicting objectives Time consuming; slows decision-making Language and cultural barriers Mistrust when collaborating in competitively sensitive areas Clash of egos and company cultures.

Guidelines in Forming Strategic Alliances Pick a good partner, one that shares a common vision. Be sensitive to cultural differences. Recognize the alliance must benefit both sides Both parties have to deliver on their commitments in the agreement Structure decision-making process so actions can be taken swiftly when needed Parties must do a good job of managing the learning process, adjusting the alliance agreement over time to fit new circumstances.

Characteristics of Competing in Emerging Foreign Markets. Tailoring products for the big, emerging markets often involves Making more than minor product changes and Becoming more familiar with the local cultures Companies have to attract buyers with bargain prices as well as better products. Specially designed and/or specially packaged products may be needed to accommodate local market circumstances. Management team must usually consist of a mix of expatriate and local managers.

Strategies for Local Companies in Emerging Markets Optimal strategic approach hinges on. Whether a firm's competitive assets are suitable only for the home market or can be transferred abroad Whether industry pressures to move toward global competition are strong or weak.

Strategy Options for Local Companies in Competing Against Global Challengers industry Resources and Competitive Capabilities Dodge Rivals by Shifting to a New Business Model or Market Niche Initiate Actions to Contend on a Global Level Defend by Using "Home-field" Advantages Transfer Company Expertise to Cross-Border Markets Tailored for Home Market Transferable to Other Countries Low High.

7. 20 Advantages and Disadvantages of the Four Strategies

Strategy Advantages Disadvantages Global Exploit experience curve effects Exploit location economies Lack of local responsiveness International Transfer distinctive competencies to Foreign Markets Lack of local responsiveness. Inability to realize location economies Failure to exploit experience curve effects.

The Advantages and Disadvantages of the Four Strategies Strategy: Advantages Disadvantages Multi-domestic Inability to realize location economies Failure to exploit experience curve effects. Failure to transfer distinctive competencies to foreign markets Customize product offerings and marketing in accordance with local responsivenessTransnational Exploit experience curve effects. Exploit location economies Customize product offerings and marketing in accordance with local responsiveness. Reap benefits of global learning Difficult to implement due to organizational problems.

7. 21 New Business Model for the Internet Economy

Impact of the Internet and E-Commerce Impact on external industry environment Changes character of the market and competitive environment. Creates new driving forces and key success factors Breeds formation of new strategic groups Impact on internal company environment. Having, or not having, e-commerce capabilities tilts the scales toward valuable resource strengths or threatening weaknesses Creatively reconfiguring the value chain will affect a firm's competitiveness vis-à-vis rivals.

Characteristics of Internet Market Structure Internet is composed of Integrated network of users' connected computers. Banks of servers and high-speed computers Digital switches and routers Telecommunications equipment and lines

Supply Side of the Internet Economy Major groups of Internet and e-commerce firms comprising the supply side include Makers of specialized communications components and equipment. Providers of communications services Suppliers of computer components and hardware Developers of specialized software E-commerce enterprises Business-to-business merchants Business-to-consumer merchants Media companies Content providers.

Strategy-Shaping Characteristics of the E-Commerce Environment Internet makes it feasible for companies everywhere to compete in global markets Competition in an industry is greatly intensified by new e-commerce strategic initiatives of existing rivals and by entry of new, enterprising e-commerce rivals. Entry barriers into e-commerce world are relatively low On-line buyers gain bargaining power.

Strategy-Shaping Characteristics of the E-Commerce Environment (continued) Internet makes it feasible for firms to reach beyond their borders to find the best suppliers and, further, to collaborate closely with them to achieve efficiency gains and cost-savings Internet and PC technologies are advancing rapidly, often in uncertain and unexpected directions Internet results in much faster diffusion of new technology and new ideas across the world E-commerce environment demands that firms move swiftly-"at Internet speed".

E-commerce technology open up a host of opportunities for reconfiguring industry and company value chains Internet can be an economical means of delivering customer service Capital for funding potentially profitable e-commerce businesses is readily available Needed e-commerce resource in short supply is human talent, in the form of both technological expertise and managerial know-how.

Effects of the Internet and E-Commerce Can produce important shifts in an industry's competitive forces Alters industry value chains, spawning substantial opportunities for increasing efficiency and reducing costs. Affects a company's resource strengths and weaknesses Rapid pace of technological change with an often uncertain direction.

Overview of E-Commerce Business Models and Strategies Provide new opportunities to put a globally-connected Internet infrastructure in place Build out telecommunications system install millions of servers Provide high-speed Internet connections to billions of businesses and households Develop software and networks to create a wired global economy. Offer potential to exploit business opportunities in aglobally wired e-commerce environment Business-to-business sales E-procurement Business-to-consumer sales E-retailing Provide content Provide services to users.

Business Models: Suppliers of Communications Equipment Traditional business model of a manufacturer Is being used by most firms to make money sell products to customers at prices above costs. Produce a good return on investment Strategic issues facing equipment makers. Several competing technologies for various components of the Internet infrastructure exist Competing technologies may. Have different performance pluses and minuses Be incompatible.

Strategy Options for Suppliers of Communications Equipment Invest aggressively in R&D to win the technological race against rivals. Form strategic alliances to build consensus for favored technological approaches Acquire other companies with complementary technological expertise. Hedge firm's bets by investing sufficient resources in mastering one or more of the competing technologies.

Business Models: Suppliers of Communications Services Business models are based on profitably selling services for a fee based on a flat rate per month or volume of use Firms must invest heavily in extending line sand installing equipment to have capacity to Provide desired point-to-point service and Handle traffic load Investment requirements are particularly heavy for backbone providers, creating sizable up-front expenditures and heavy fixed costs Key to success-Establish networks ahead of rivals to get in position to sign up customers.

Business Models: Suppliers of Communications Services (continued) Fierce competition has emerged among "last mile" providers selling high-speed Internet access. Strategic options Provide high-speed (broadband) Internet connections using new digital signal line technology Provide wireless broadband services or cable Internet service Bundle local telephone service, long distance service, cable TV service and Internet access into a single package for a single monthly fee Key strategic weapons for last mile providers-Name recognition and advertising.

Business Models: Suppliers of Computer Components and Hardware Traditional business model is used-Make money by selling products at prices above costs Strategic approaches. Stay on cutting edge of technology Invest in R&D Move quickly to imitate technological advances and product innovations of rivals Key to success-Stay with or ahead of rivals in introducing next-generation products Competitive advantage will most likely be based on strategies keyed to low-cost.

Business Models: Developers of Specialized E-Commerce Software Business model involves Investments in designing and developing specialized software Marketing and selling software to other firms. Profitability hinges on volume Strategic approaches Sell software at a set price per copy Collect a fee for every transaction provided by the software Rent or lease the software.

Business Models: E-Commerce Retailers Sell products at or below cost and make money byselling advertising to other merchandisers Use traditional model of Purchasing goods from manufacturers and distributors. Marketing items at a Web store Filling orders from inventory at a warehouse Operate Web site to market and sell product/service and outsource manufacturing, distribution and delivery activities to specialists.

Strategic Approaches: E-Commerce Retailers Spend heavily on advertising to build widespread brand awareness, draw traffic, and start process of developing customer loyalty Add new product offerings to help attract traffic to firm's Web site Be a first-mover or at worst an early mover Pay consideration attention to Web site attractiveness to generate"buzz" about the siteamong surfers. Keep Web site innovative, fresh, and entertaining.

Business Models: Suppliers of E-Commerce Services Key strategic issue for e-commerce retailers-Handling warehousing and delivery activities. Firms are using services of"Internet middlemen"to efficiently sort all the supplier choices Firms are using focus strategies to zero in on specific niches, pursuing competitive advantage based on First-mover mastery of a particular technology Product superiority Unique product attributes Convenience and ease of use Speed More value for the money.

Business Models: Media Companies and Content Providers Using intellectual capital to develop music, games, video, and text, media firms Charge subscription fees or Rely on a pay-per-use model Business model of content providers involves creating content to attract users, then selling advertising to firms wanting to deliver a message Key success factors for content providers Create a sense of community Deliver convenience and entertainment value as well as information.

7.22 Internet Strategies for Traditional Businesses

Use Internet technology to communicate and collaborate closely with suppliers and distribution channel allies Reengineer company and industry value chains to revamp how certain activities are performed and to eliminate or by pass others Make greater use of build-to-order manufacturing and assembly. Build systems to pick and pack products that are shipped individually.

Internet Strategies for Traditional Businesses(continued)Use Internet to give both existing and potential customers another choice of how to interact with the company Adopt Internet as an integral distribution channel for accessing new buyers and geographic markets Gather real-time data on customer tastes and buying habits, doing real-time market research, and use results to respond more precisely to customer needs and wants.

Key Success Factors: Competing in the E-Commerce Environment Employ an innovative business model Develop capability to quickly adjust business model and strategy to respond to changing conditions. Focus on a limited number of competencies and perform a relatively specialized number of value chain activities Stay on the cutting edge of technology Use innovative marketing techniques that are efficient in reaching the targeted audience and effective in stimulating purchases Engineer an electronic value chain that enables differentiation or lower costs or better value for the money.

7.23 Tailoring Strategy to Fit Specific Industry Situations

Features of an Emerging Industry New and unproven market Proprietary technology Low entry barriers Experience curve effects may permit cost reductions as volume builds Buyers are first-time users. Marketing involves inducing initial purchase and overcoming customer concerns Possible difficulties in securing raw materials Firms struggle to fund R&D, operations and build resource capabilities for rapid growth.

Strategy Options for Competing in Emerging Industries Win early race for industry leadership by employing a bold, creative strategy Push hard to perfect technology, improve product quality, and develop attractive performance features Move quickly when technological uncertainty clears and a dominant technology emerges. Form strategic alliances with Key suppliers Companies having related technological expertise.

Strategy Options for Competing in Emerging Industries(continued) Capture potential first-mover advantages Pursue New customers and user applications Entry into new geographical areas Focus advertising emphasis on. Increasing frequency of use Creating brand loyalty Use price cuts to attract price-sensitive buyers.

Features of High Velocity Markets Rapid-fire technological change Short product life-cycles Rapidly evolving customer expectations Frequent launches of new competitive moves Entry of important new rivals.

Meeting the Challenge of High-Velocity Change Source: Adapted from Shona L. Brown and Kathleen M. Eisenhardt, Competing on the Edge: Strategy as Structured Chaos. Strategic Posture Actions Strategy Reacting to Change? Introduce better products in response to new offerings of rivals? Respond to unexpected changes in buyer needs and preferences? Adjust to new government policies? React and respond as needed? Analyze prospects for market globalization? Research buyer needs, preferences, and expectations? Monitor new technological developments to predict future? Plan ahead for future changes? Add/adapt competitive capabilities? Improve product line? Strengthen distribution Leading Change? Pioneer new and better technologies? Introduce innovative products that open new markets and spur creation of whole new industries? Seek to set industry standards? Seize the offensive? Be the agent of industry change? Influence rules of the game? Force rivals to follow.

Strategy Options for Competingin High Velocity Markets Invest aggressively in R&D Develop quick response capabilities Shift resources Adapt competencies Create new competitive capabilities Speed new products to market Use strategic partnerships to develop specialized expertise and capabilities. Initiate fresh actions every few months Keep products/services fresh and exciting.

Keys to Success in Competing in High Velocity Markets Cutting-edge expertise Speed in responding to new developments Collaboration with others Agility Innovativeness Opportunism Resource flexibility First-to-market capabilities.

Characteristics of Industry Maturity Slowing demand breeds stiffer competition More sophisticated buyers demand bargains Greater emphasis on cost and service "Topping out" problem in adding production capacity Product innovation and new end uses harder to come by International competition increases Industry profitability falls Mergers and acquisitions reduce the number of industry rivals.

Strategy Options for Competing in a Mature Industry Prune marginal products and models Emphasize innovation in the value chain Strong focus on cost reduction Increase sales to present customers Purchase rivals at bargain prices Expand internationally Build new, more flexible competitive capabilities.

Strategic Pitfalls in a Maturing Industry Employing a ho-hum strategy with no distinctive features thus leaving firm "stuck in the middle" Concentrating on short-term profits rather than strengthening long-term competitiveness. Being slow to adapt competencies to changing customer expectations. Being slow to respond to price-cutting. Having too much excess capacity Overspending on marketing Failing to pursue cost reductions aggressively.

Stagnant or Declining Industries: The Standout Features Demand grows more slowly than economy as whole (or even declines) Competitive pressures intensify—rivals battle for market share To grow and prosper, firm must take market share from rivals Industry consolidates to a smaller number of key players via mergers and acquisitions.

Strategy Options for Competing in a Stagnant or Declining Industry Pursue focus strategy aimed at fastest growing market segments Stress differentiation based on quality improvement or product innovation Work diligently to drive costs down Cut marginal activities from value chain Use outsourcing Redesign internal processes to exploit e-commerce Consolidate under-utilized production facilities. Add more distribution channels Close low-volume, high-cost distribution outlets Prune marginal products.

Competing in a Stagnant Industry: The Strategic Mistakes Getting embroiled in a profitless battle for market share with stubborn rivals Diverting resources out of the business too quickly Being overly optimistic about industry's future (believing things will get better).

Competitive Features of Fragmented Industries Absence of market leaders with large market shares Buyer demand is so diverse and geographically scattered that many firms are required to satisfy buyer needs Low entry barriers Absence of scale economies Buyers require small amounts of customized or made-to-order products Market for industry's product/service may be globalizing, thus putting many companies across the world in same market arena Exploding technologies force firms to specialize just to keep up in their area of expertise Industry is young and crowded with aspiring contenders, with no firm having yet developed recognition to command a large market share.

Examples of Fragmented Industries Book publishing Landscaping and plant nurseries Auto repair Restaurant industry Public accounting Women's dresses Meat packing Paperboard boxes Hotels and motels Furniture.

Competing in a Fragmented Industry: The Strategy Options Construct and operate "formula" facilities Become a low-cost operator Specialize by product type Specialize by customer type Focus on limited geographic area.

Strategies for Sustaining Rapid Growth Companies desirous of growing revenues and earnings rapidly year-after-year have to have a portfolio of strategies. Horizon 1: Strategic initiatives to fortify and extend their position in existing businesses. Horizon 2: Strategic initiatives to leverage existing resources and capabilities by entering new businesses with promising growth potential. Horizon 3: Strategic initiatives to plant new seeds for venturing into businesses that are just emerging or do not even exist yet.

Figure 8. 2: Three Strategy Horizons for Sustaining Rapid Growth Portfolio of Strategy Initiatives? "Short-jump" initiatives to fortify and extend current businesses? Immediate gains in revenues and profits? "Medium-jump" initiatives to leverage existing resources and capabilities to pursue growth in new businesses? Moderate revenue and profit gains now, but foundation laid for sizable gains over next 2-5 years? "Long-jump" initiatives to sow theseeds for growth inbusinesses of the future? Minimal revenue gains now and likely losses, but potential for significant contributions to revenues and profits in 5-10 years Source: Adapted from Eric D. Beinhocker, "Robust Adaptive Time Strategies, "Sloan Management Review 40, No. 3(Spring 1999), p. 101.

Risks of Pursuing Multiple Strategy Horizons Firm should not pursue all options to avoid stretching itself too thin Pursuit of medium-and long-jump initiatives may cause firm to stray too far from its core competencies. Competitive advantage may be difficult to achieve in medium-and long-jump businesses that do not mesh well with firm's present resource strengths. Payoffs of long-jump initiatives may prove elusive.

Characteristics of Industry Leaders Stronger-than-average to powerful position Well-known reputation Proven strategies Strategic concern—How to sustain dominant leadership position Strategy Options: Industry Leaders Stay-on-the-offensive strategy Fortify-and-defend strategy Muscle-flexing strategy.

Stay-on-the-Offensive Strategies Be a first-mover, leading industry change best defense is a good offense Relentlessly pursue continuous improvement and innovation Force rivals to scramble to keep up Launch initiatives to keep rivals off balance Grow faster than industry, taking market share from rivals.

Fortify-and-Defend Strategy: Objectives Make it harder for new firms to enter and for challengers to gain ground Hold onto present market share Strengthen current market position Protect competitive advantage.

Fortify-and-Defend: Strategic Options Increase advertising and R&D Provide higher levels of customer service Introduce more brands to match attributes of rivals Add personalized services to boost buyer loyalty Keep prices reasonable and quality attractive. Build new capacity ahead of market demand Invest enough to remain cost competitive Patent feasible alternative technologies Sign exclusive contracts with best suppliers and distributors.

Muscle-Flexing Strategy: Objectives Play competitive hardball with smaller rivals that threaten leader's position Signal smaller rivals that moves to cut into leader's business will be hard fought Convince rivals they are better off playing "follow-the-leader" or else attacking each other rather the industry leader.

Muscle-Flexing: Strategic Options Be quick to meet price cuts of rivals Counter with large-scale promotional campaigns if rivals boost advertising Offer better deals to rivals' major customers Dissuade distributors from carrying rivals' products Provide sales persons with documentation about weaknesses of competing products. Make attractive offers to key executives of rivals Use arm-twisting tactics to pressure present customers not to use rivals' products.

Types of Runner-up Firms Market challengers Use offensive strategies to gain market share Focusers Concentrate on serving a limited portion of market Perennial runners-up Lack competitive strength to do more than continue in trailing position I'm trying!

Obstacles Runner-Up Firms Must Overcome When big size is a competitive asset, firms with low market share face obstacles Less access to economies of scale Difficulty in gaining customer recognition Inability to afford mass media advertising Difficulty in funding capital requirements.

Strategic Options for Runner-Up Firms When big size provides larger rivals with a cost advantage, runner-up firms have two options Build market share Lower costs and prices to grow sales or Out-differentiate rivals in ways to grow sales Withdraw from market.

Competitive Strategies for Runner-Up Firms: Building Market Share Strategic options for building market share to overcome cost advantage of larger rivals. Use lower prices to win customers from weak, higher-cost rivals Merge or acquire rivals to achieve size needed to capture greater scale economies. Invest in new cost-saving facilities and equipment, perhaps relocating operations to countries where costs are lower Pursue technological innovations or radical value chain revamping to achieve cost.

Strategic Options for Runner-Up Firms Not Disadvantaged By Smaller Size Where big size does not yield a cost advantage, runner-up firms have seven options. Offensive strategies to build market share. Growth-via-acquisition strategy. Vacant niche strategy. Specialist strategy. Superior product strategy. Distinctive image strategy. Content follower strategy.

Strategies for Runner-Up Firms Not Disadvantaged By Smaller Size Best"mover-and-shaker"offensives Pioneer a leapfrog technological breakthrough Get new/better products into market ahead of rivals and build reputation for product leadership Be more agile and innovative in adapting to evolving market conditions and customer needs Forge attractive strategic alliances with key distributors and/or marketers of similar products Find innovative ways to dramatically drive down costs to win customers from higher-cost rivals Craft an attractive differentiation strategy.

Rule of Offensive Strategy Runner-up firms should avoid attacking a leader head-on with an imitative strategy, regardless of resources and staying power an underdog may have!

Frequently used strategy of ambitious runner-up firms To succeed, top managers must have skills to Assimilate operations of acquired firms, eliminating duplication and overlap, Generate efficiency and cost savings, and Structure combined resources to create stronger competitive capabilities Growth-via-Acquisition Strategies for Runner-Up Firms.

Vacant Niche Strategies for Runner-Up Firms Focus strategy concentrated on end-use applications market leaders have neglected Characteristics of an ideal vacant niche Sufficient size to be profitable Growth potential Well-suited to a firm's capabilities Hard for leaders to serve.

Specialist Strategy for Runner-Up Firms Strategy concentrated on being a leader based on Specific technology Product uniqueness. Expertise in Special-purpose products Specialized know-how Delivering distinctive customer services.

Superior Product Strategy for Runner-Up Firms Differentiation-based focused strategy based on Superior product quality or Unique product attributes Approaches Fine craftsmanship Prestige quality Frequent product innovation Close contact with customers to gain in put for better quality product.

Distinctive Image Strategy for Runner-Up Firms Strategy concentrated on ways to stand out from rivals Approaches Reputation for charging lowest price Prestige quality at a good price Superior customer service Unique product attributes New product introductionsUnusually creative advertising.

Content Follower Strategy for Runner-Up Firms Strategy involves avoiding Trend-setting moves and Aggressive moves to steal customers from leaders Approaches Do not provoke competitive retaliation React and respond Defense rather than offense Keep same price as leaders Attempt to maintain market position.

Weak Businesses: Strategic Options Launch a strategic offensive (if resources permit) Play aggressive defense (to the extent that resources permit) Pursue immediate abandonment Adopt an end-game strategy.

The implementation of new strategies and policies often calls for new human resource management priorities and a different utilization of personnel. This may mean hiring new people with new skills, firing people with inappropriate or substandard skills, and/or training existing employees to learn new skills. 新战略和政策的实施往往需要新的人力资源管理的优先顺序和人员的不同利用。这可能意味着雇用掌握新技术的新员工，解雇技能不合适或不合格的员工，以及/或者培训现有员工学习新技能。

If growth strategies are to be implemented, new people may need to be hired and trained. 如果增长战略要实施，新人可能需要雇用和培训。

Training and development is one way to implement a company's corporate or business strategy. 培训和发展是实施一个企业的公司战略或业务战略的一种方式。

Training is also important when implementing a retrenchment strategy. 培训对于实施紧缩战略来说也是重要的。

Achieving a Turnaround: The Strategic Options Sell off assets to generate cash and/or reduce debt Revise existing strategy Launch efforts to boost revenues Cut costs Combination of efforts.

Liquidation Strategy Wisest strategic option in certain situations Lack of resources. Dim profit prospects May serve stockholder interests better than bankruptcy Unpleasant strategic option Hardship of job eliminations Effects of closing on local community.

What is an End-Game Strategy? Steers middle course between status quo and exiting quickly Involves gradually sacrificing market position in return for bigger near-term cash flow /profit Objectives Short-term-Generate largest feasible cash flow Long-term-Exit market.

Types of End-Game Options Reduce operating budget to rock-bottom Hold reinvestment to minimum. Emphasize stringent internal cost controls Place little priority on new capital investments Raise price gradually Trim promotional expenses Reduce quality in non-visible ways Curtail non-essential customer services Shave equipment maintenance.

When Should an End-Game Strategy be Considered? Industry's long-term prospects are unattractive Building up business would be too costly Market share is increasingly costly to maintain. Reduced levels of competitive effort will not trigger immediate fall-off in sales Firm can re-deploy freed-up resources in higher opportunity areas. Business is not a major component of diversified firm's portfolio of businesses Business does not contribute other desired features to overall business portfolio.

Commandments for Crafting Successful Business Strategies. Always put top priority on crafting and executing strategic moves that enhance a firm's competitive position for the long-term and that serve to establish it as an industry leader. Be prompt in adapting and responding to changing market conditions, unmet customer needs and buyer wishes for something better, emerging technological alternatives, and new initiatives of rivals. Responding late or with too little often puts a firm in the precarious position of playing catch-up.

A company can identify and prepare its people for important positions in several ways. One approach is to establish a sound performance appraisal system, which not only evaluates a person's performance, but also identifies promotion potential. 公司可以采取以下多种方式识别并准备身居重要职位的人员。一种方法是建立健全考核体系，不仅评价一个人的表现，还识别其晋升的潜力。

Many large organizations are using assessment centers, a method of evaluating a person's suitability for an advanced position. 许多大型组织使用评价中心作为评估员工是否适合未来更高层级职位的方法。

Downsizing refers to the planned elimination of positions or jobs. Companies commonly use this program to implement retrenchment strategies. 机构精简是指按照计划精简职位或工作。公司通常使用此方案实施紧缩战略。

Commandments for Crafting Successful Business Strategies. Invest in creating a sustainable competitive advantage, for it is a most dependable contributor to above-average profitability. Avoid strategies capable of succeeding only in the best of circumstances. Don't underestimate the reactions and the commitment of rival firms.

Commandments for Crafting Successful Business Strategies. Consider that attacking competitive weakness is usually more profitable than attacking competitive strength. Be judicious in cutting prices without an established cost advantage. Employ bold strategic moves in pursuing differentiation strategies so as to open up very meaningful gaps in quality or service or advertising or other product attributes.

Commandments for Crafting Successful Business Strategies. Endeavor not to get "stuck back in the pack" with no coherent long-term strategy or distinctive competitive position, and little prospect of climbing into the ranks of the industry leaders. Be aware that aggressive strategic moves to wrest crucial market share away from rivals often provoke aggressive retaliation in the form of a marketing "arms race" and/or price wars.

Implementation also involves leading: motivating people to use their abilities and skills most effectively and efficiently to achieve organizational objectives. 战略实施还涉及领导：激励员工最有效地利用自身能力和技能，高效地实现组织目标。

Leading may take the form of management leadership, communicated norms of behavior from the corporate culture, or agreements among workers in autonomous work groups. It may also be accomplished more formally through action planning or through programs such as Management by Objectives (MBO) and Total Quality Management (TQM). 领导需要领导的管理形式,沟通行为规范或与工作组的工人协调一致的企业文化。它还可能被更多的正式通过的行动计划,比如目标管理(MBO)或全面质量管理(TQM)等方式实现。

Top management responsibilities, especially those of CEO, involve getting things accomplished through and with others in order to meet the corporate objectives. 高层管理者尤其是首席执行官的责任,涉及借助他人并与他人一起实现企业目标的所有事情。

Executive leadership is the directing of activities toward the accomplishment of corporate objectives. Executive leadership is important because it sets the tone for the entire corporation. 行政领导是指导实现企业目标的各种活动。行政领导的重要性在于规定了整个公司的基调。

The CEO are able to command respect and influence strategy formulation and implementation because they tend to have three key characteristics: 首席执行官可能影响公司战略的制定和实施,他们通常有三种特征:

The CEO articulates a strategic vision for the corporation. 首席执行官拟就了公司的战略愿景。

The CEO presents a role for others to identify with and to follow. 首席执行官扮演着他人认同和遵循的角色。

The CEO not only communicates high performance standards, but also shows confidence in the followers' abilities to meet these standards. 首席执行官不仅传达高绩效标准,还给予下属有能力实现这些标准的信心。

Because an organization's culture can exert a powerful influence on the behavior of all employees, it can strongly affect a company's ability to shift its strategic direction. 因为一个组织的文化能够明显作用于所有雇员的行为,它能强烈影响一个公司转移战略方向的能力。

7.24 Competitive Advantage in Diversified Companies

Strategies for Entering New Businesses Strategy Options for Diversified Companies Strategies to Broaden a Diversified Company's Base Divestiture Strategies Corporate Restructuring and Turn around Strategies.

Diversification and Corporate Strategy A company is diversified when it is in two or more lines of business Strategy-making in a diversified company is a bigger picture exercise than crafting a strategy for a single line-of-business. A diversified company needs a multi-industry, multi-business strategy A strategic action plan must be developed for several different businesses competing in diverse industry environments.

Four Main Tasks in Crafting Corporate Strategy Pick new industries to enter and decide on means of entry. Initiate actions to boost combined performance of businesses Pursue opportunities to leverage cross-business value chain relationships and strategic fits into competitive advantage. Establish investment priorities, steering resources into most attractive business units.

Competitive Strengths of a Single Business Strategy Less ambiguity about"who we are" Energies of firm can be directed down one business path and keeping strategy responsive to industry change Less chance resources will be stretched thinly over too many competing activities. Resources can be focused on building competencies and capabilities that make the firm better at what it does.

Competitive Strengths of a Single Business Strategy(continued) Higher probability innovative ideas will emerge Top executives can maintain hands-on contact with core business Important competencies more likely to emerge Ability to parlay experience and reputation in to Sustainable competitive advantage Prominent leadership position.

Risks of a Single Business Strategy Putting all the"eggs"in one industry basket. If market becomes unattractive, a firm's prospects can quickly dim Unforeseen changes can undermine a single business firm's prospects Changing customer needs Technological innovation New substitutes.

When Does Diversification Start to Make Sense? Strong competitive position, rapid market growth—Not a good time to diversify Weak competitive position, rapid market growth—Not a good time to diversify Strong competitive position, slow market growth—Diversification is to priority consideration Weak competitive position, slow marketgrowth—Diversification merits consideration.

When to Diversify? Diminishing growth prospects in present business Opportunities to add value for customers or gain competitive advantage by broadening present business to include complementary products. Attractive opportunities to transfer existing competencies to new businesses. Potential cost-saving opportunities to be realized by entering related businesses Availability of adequate financial and organizational resources.

Why Diversify? To build shareholder value1 + 1 = 3Diversification is capable of increasing shareholder value if it passes three tests1. Industry Attractiveness Test2. Cost of Entry Test3. Better-Off Test.

Strategic Management Principle To create shareholder value, a diversifying firm must get into businesses that can perform well under common management.

Related vs. Unrelated DiversificationRelated Diversification Involves diversifying into businesses whose value chains possess competitively valuable"strategic fits"with the value chain(s) of the firms present business(es). Unrelated Diversification Involves diversifying into businesses where there is no deliberate effort to seek out businesses having strategic fit with the firm's other business(es).

Strategy Alternatives fora Company Looking to Diversify Strategy Options for a Company Looking to Diversify? Build shareholder value by capturing cross-business strategic fits-Transfer skills and capabilities from one business to another-Share facilities or resources to reduce costs-Leverage use of a common brand name-Combine resources to create new competitive strengths and capabilities Diversify into Related Businesses? Spread risks across diverse businesses? Build shareholder value by doing a superior job of choosing businesses to diversify into and of managing the whole collection of businesses in the company's portfolio Diversify into Unrelated Businesses Diversify into Both Related and Unrelated Businesses.

What is Related Diversification? Involves diversifying into businesses whose value chains possess competitively valuable"strategic fits"with the value chain(s) of the present business(es) Capturing the "strategic fits" makes related diversification a 1 + 1 = 3phenomenon.

Concept:Strategic Fit Exists whenever one or more activities in the value chains of different businesses are sufficiently similar to present opportunities for Transferring competitively valuable expertise or technological know-how from one business to another Combining performance of common value chain activities to achieve lower costs Exploiting use of a well-known brand name Cross-business collaboration to create competitively valuable resource strengths and capabilities.

Value Chains for Related Businesses Supply Chain Activities Sales and Marketing Customer Service Technology Operations Distribution Support Activities Supply Competitively valuable opportunities for technology or skills transfer, cost reduction, common brand name usage, and cross-business collaboration exist at one or more points along the value chains of A and Business BA Representative Value Chain Activities Chain Activities Sales and Marketing Customer Service Technology Operations Distributionne Bsssui Support Activities.

Strategic Appeal of Related Diversification Reap competitive advantage benefits of Skills transfer Lower costs Common brand name usage Stronger competitive capabilities Spread investor risks over a broader base Preserves strategic unity in its business activities. Achieve consolidated performance greater than the sum of what individual businesses can earn operating independently.

Types of Strategic Fits Cross-business strategic fits can exist anywhere along the value chain R&D and technology activities Supply chain activities Manufacturing activities Distribution activities Sales and marketing activities Managerial and administrative support activities.

R&D and Technology Fits Offer potential for sharing common technology or transferring technological know-how Potential benefits. Cost-savings in technology development and new product R&D Shorter times in getting new products to market Interdependence between resulting products leads to increased sales.

Supply Chain Fits Offer potential opportunities for skills transfer Procuring materials Greater bargaining power in negotiating with common suppliers. Benefits of added collaboration with common supply chain partners. Added leverage with shippers in securing volume discounts on incoming parts.

Manufacturing Fits Potential source of competitive advantage when adiversifier's expertise can be beneficially transferred to another business Quality manufacture Cost-efficient production methods Just-in-time inventory practices Training and motivating workers Cost-saving opportunities arise from ability to perform manufacturing/assembly activities jointly in same facility, making it feasible to Consolidate production into fewer plants Significantly reduce overall manufacturing.

Distribution Fits Offer potential cost-saving opportunities Share same distribution facilities Use many of the same wholesale distributors and retail dealers to access customers.

7.25 Sales and Marketing Fits

Types of Potential Benefits Reduction in sales costs Single sales force for related products Advertising related products together Combined after-sale service and repair work Joint delivery and shipping. Joint order processing and billing Joint promotion tie-in Similar sales and marketing approaches provide opportunities to transfer selling, merchandising, and advertising/promotional skills Transfer of a strong company's brand name and reputation

Managerial and Administrative Support Fits Emerge when different business units require comparable types of Entrepreneurial know-how. Administrative know-how Operating know-how Different businesses often entail same types of administrative support facilities Customer data network Billing and customer accounting systems Customer service infrastructure.

Concept: Economies of Scope Stem from cross-business cost-saving opportunities Arise from ability to eliminate costs by operating two or more businesses under same corporate umbrella Exist when it is less costly for two or more businesses to operate under centralized management than to function independently Cost saving opportunities can stem from interrelationships anywhere along businesses' value chains.

Related Diversification and Competitive Advantage Competitive advantage can result from related diversification if opportunities exist to Transfer expertise/capabilities/technology Combine related activities into a single operation and reduce costs Leverage use of firm's brand name reputation. Conduct related value chain activities in a collaborative fashion to create valuable competitive capabilities.

Capturing Benefits of Strategic Fit Benefits don't occur just because a company has diversified into related businesses! Businesses with sharing potential must be reorganized to coordinate activities Means must be found to make skills transfer effective Benefits of some strategic coordination must exist to justify sacrificing business-unit autonomy Competitive advantage potential exists to Expand resources and strategic assets and Create new ones faster and cheaper than rivals.

7.26 What Unrelated Diversification Is

Involves diversifying into businesses with No strategic fit No meaningful value chain relationships. No unifying strategic theme Approach is to venture into "any business in which we think we can make a profit" Firms pursuing unrelated diversification are often referred to as conglomerates.

Basic Premise of Unrelated Diversification Any company that can be acquired on good financial terms and offers good prospects for profitability is a good business to diversify into!

Value Chains for Unrelated Businesses Supply Chain Activities Sales and Marketing Customer Service Technology Operations Distribution Support Activitiesusiness BA Representative Value Chain Activities Supply Chain Activities Sales and Marketing Customer Service Technology Operations Distributionne Bsssui Support Activities An absence of competitively valuable strategic fits between the value chain for Business A and the value chain for Business.

Acquisition Criteria For Unrelated Diversification Strategies Can business meet corporate targets for profitability and ROI? Will business require substantialin fusions of capital? Is business in an industry with growth potential? Is business big enough to contribute to the parent firm's bottom line? Is there potential for union difficulties or adverse government regulations? Is industry vulnerable to recession, inflation, highinterest rates, or shifts in government policy?

Attractive Acquisition Targets Companies with undervalued assets Capital gains may be realized Companies in financial distress May be purchased at bargain prices and turned around.

Appeal of Unrelated Diversification Business risk scattered over different industries Financial resources can be directed to those industries offering best profit prospects Stability of profits—Hard times in one industry may be offset by good times in another industry. If bargain-priced firms with big profit potential are bought, shareholder wealth can be enhanced.

Drawbacks of Unrelated Diversification Difficulties of competently managing many diverse businesses Lack of strategic fits which can be leveraged into competitive advantage Consolidated performance of unrelated businesses tends to be no better than sum of individual businesses on their own(and it maybe worse) Likely effect is 1+1=2, rather than 1 + 1 = 3. Promise of greater sales-profit stability over business cycles seldom realized.

7.27 How Broadly a Company Should Diversify

Two questions should guide unrelated diversification efforts. What is the least diversification it will take to achieve acceptable growth and profitability? What is the most diversification that can be managed, given its added complexity? Need to strike a balance between too few different businesses and too many different businesses!

How Many Unrelated Businesses Can a Company Diversify Into? With unrelated diversification, corporate managers have to be shrewd enough to Discern good acquisitions from bad ones Select capable managers to run many different businesses. Judge soundness of strategic proposals of business-unit managers Know what to do if a subsidiary stumbles.

Diversification and Shareholder Value Related Diversification. A strategy-driven approach to creating shareholder value Unrelated Diversification. A finance-driven approach to creating shareholder value.

Combination Related-Unrelated Diversification Strategies Dominant-business firms One major core business accounting for 50-80 percent of revenues, with several small related or unrelated businesses accounting for remainder. Narrowly diversified firms Diversification includes a few(2-5)related or unrelated businesses Broadly diversified firms Diversification includes a wide ranging collection of either related or unrelated businesses or a mixture Multi-business firms Diversification portfolio includes several unrelated groups of related businesses.

When implementing a new strategy, management should consider the following questions regarding the corporation's strategy-culture compatibility-the fit between the new strategy and the existing culture：当实施一个新战略的时候，管理层应该针对公司的战略与文化的兼容性—新战略与现有文化之间的匹配，考虑以下几个问题：

Is the planned strategy compatible with the company's current culture? 公司计划的战略与目前的文化兼容吗？

Can the culture be easily modified to make it more compatible with the new strategy? 文化可以轻松改变以适应新的战略吗？

Is management willing and able to make major organizational changes and accept probable delays and a likely increase in costs? 管理层愿意并且能够做出重大组织变革，并接受可能的拖延以及成本增加吗？

Is management still committed to implementing the strategy? 管理层仍然致力于实施这一战略吗？

Strategies for Entering New Businesses Acquire existing company Internal start-up Joint venture/strategic partnerships. Acquisition of an Existing Company Most popular approach to diversification Advantages Quicker entry into target market Easier to hurdle certain entry barriers Technological in experience Gaining access to reliable suppliers. Being of a size to match rivals in terms of efficiency and costs Getting adequate distribution access.

Internal Startup More attractive when Ample time exists to create anew business from ground up Incumbents slow in responding to new entry Less expensive than buying an existing firm Company already has most of needed skills Additional capacity will not adversely impact supply-demand balance in industry New start-up does not have to go head-to-head against powerful rivals.

Joint Ventures and Strategic Partnerships Good way to diversify when Uneconomical or risky to go it alone Pooling competencies of two partners provides more competitive strength. Foreign partners are needed to surmount Import quotas Tariffs Nationalistic political interests Cultural road blocks Lack of knowledge about marketsof particular countries.

Drawbacks of Joint Ventures Raises questions Which partner will do what Who has effective control Potential conflicts Control over strategy and long-term direction How operations will be conducted Control over cash flows and profits Personalities and cultures of partners.

Strategy Options for a Company Already Diversified Make new acquisitions and/or enter into additional strategic partnerships Divest some of the company's existing businesses Restructure the company's portfolio of businesses Become a multinational, multi-industry enterprise Strategy Options for a Diversified Company.

Strategies to Broaden a Diversified Company's Business Base Conditions making this approach attractive Slow grow in current business Eminently transferablc resources and capabilities to other related businesses. Unexpected opportunity arises to acquire an attractive company Rapidly-changing conditions in one core industry are blurring boundaries with adjoining industries Desirable conditions favor new acquisitions to complement and strengthen market position of one or more of present businesses.

Management by Objectives (MBO) is an organization-wide approach to help assure purposeful action toward desired objectives by linking organizational objectives with individual behavior. 目标管理(MBO)是在整个组织范围内，通过将个人行为与预期目标相联系，通过将个人行为与预期目标相联系，确保有目的的行动朝着既定目标前进的方法。

MBO provides an opportunity for the corporation to connect the objectives of people at each level to those at the next higher level. 目标管理可以给公司提供一个机会,即联系每一层次的人们的目标并促使这一目标能越来越高。

Divestiture Strategies Aimed at Retrenching to a Narrower Diversification Base Strategic options Retrenchment Divestiture Spin it off as independent company Sell it Leveraged buyout Retrench? Divest? Sell? LBO?

Retrenchment Strategies Objective Reduce scope of diversification to smaller number of"core"businesses Strategic options involve divesting businesses. Having little strategic fit with core businesses Too small to contribute to earnings.

Conditions That Make Retrenchment Attractive Diversification efforts have become too broad Difficulties encountered in profitably managing broad diversification Continuing losses in certain businesses Lack of funds or resources to support operating and investment needs of all businesses. Misfits cannot be completely avoided Unfavorable changes in industry attractiveness Diversification may lack compatibility of values essential to cultural fit.

Options for Accomplishing Divestiture Spin it off as independent company Involves deciding whether to retain partial ownership or forego any ownership interest. Sell it Involves finding a company which views the business as a good deal and good fit Leveraged buy out Involves selling business to the managers who have been running it for a minimal equity down payment and loaning balance of purchase price to new owners.

Corporate Restructuring and Turnaround Strategies Strategy options for a diversified firm wit-hailing subsidiaries Why consider these options? Large losses in one or more subsidiaries Large number of businesses in unattractive industries Bad economic conditions Excessive debt load Acquisitions performing worse than expected. New technologies threatening survival of one or more core businesses. Corporate Restructuring Strategy Objective Make radical changes in mix of businesses in portfolio via both Divestitures and New acquisitions.

Conditions That Make Portfolio Restructuring Attractive Long-term performance prospects are unattractive Core business units fall upon hard times. New CEO takes over and decides to redirect where company is headed "Wave of the future"technologies emerge prompting a shakeup to build position in a new industry"Unique opportunity"emerges and existing businesses must be sold to finance new acquisition. Major businesses in portfolio become unattractive Changes in markets of certain businesses proceed in such different directions, it's better to de-merge.

Corporate Turnaround Strategies Objectives Restore money-losing businesses to profitability rather than divest them Get whole firm back in the back by curing problems of ailing businesses in portfolio Most appropriate where Reasons for poor performance are short-term Ailing businesses are in attractive industries Divesting money-losers doesn't make long-term strategic sense,

7.28 Turnaround Strategies

The Options Sell or close down a portion of operations Shift to a different, and hopefully better, business-level strategy Launch new initiatives to boos trevenues Pursue cost reduction Combination of efforts.

Comment: Trend in Diversification The present trend toward narrower diversification has been driven by a growing preference to gear diversification around creating strong competitive positions in a few, well-selected industries as opposed to scattering corporate investments across many industries!

Multinational Diversification Strategies Distinguishing characteristic Diversity of businesses and diversity of national markets Presents a big strategy-making challenge Strategies must be conceived and executed for each business, with as many multinational variations as appropriate.

Appeal of Multinational Diversification Strategies Offer two avenues for long-term growth in revenues and profits Enter additional businesses. Extend operations of existing businesses into additional country markets.

Opportunities to Build Competitive Advantage via Multinational Diversification Full capture of economies of scale and experience curve effects Capitalize on cross-business economies of scope Transfer competitively valuable resources from one business toanother and/or from one country to another Leverage use of a competitively powerful brand name Coordinate strategic activities and initiatives across businesses and countries Use cross-business or cross-country subsidization toout-compete rivals.

Total Quality Management (TQM) is an operational philosophy that stresses commitment to customer satisfaction and continuous improvement. 全面质量管理(TQM)是一种经营理念,强调致力于客户满意和持续改进。

TQM is committed to quality and excellence and to being the best in all functions. TQM 在所有功能中是最好的,它致力于质量和卓越。

Competitive Strength of a DMNC in Global Markets Competitive advantage potential is based on Using a related diversification strategy based on Resource-sharing and resource-transfer opportunities among businesses Economies of scope and brand name benefits Managing related businesses to capture important cross-business strategic fits Using cross-market or cross-business subsidizations paringly to secure foot holds in attractive country markets.

Competitive Power of a DMNC in Global MarketsA DMNC has a strategic arsenal capable ofdefeating both a domestic-only rival or asingle-business rival by competing inMultiple businesses and Multiple country markets.

Chapter 8 Strategic Evaluation and Control

Evaluation and control is the process by which corporate activities and performance results are monitored so that actual performance can be compared with desired performance. 评价和控制是监控企业活动的绩效结果的过程，有助于将实际绩效与预期绩效进行比较。

This process can be viewed as a five-step feedback model, as depicted in: determine what to measure; establish standards of performance; measure actual performance; compare actual performance with the standard; take corrective action. 这个过程被看作五个反馈的步骤，即确定衡量内容、建立绩效标准、衡量实际绩效表现、根据标准比较实际绩效表现、采取纠正措施。

8.1 Product Diversification as an Example of an Agency Problem

A corporate-level strategy to diversify the firm's product lines can enhance a firm's strategic competitiveness and increase its returns, both of which serve the interests of all stakeholders and certainly shareholders and top-level managers. However, product diversification can create two benefits for top-level managers that shareholders do not enjoy, meaning that they may prefer product diversification more than shareholders do.

The fact that product diversification usually increases the size of a firm and that size is positively related to executive compensation is the first of the two benefits of additional diversification that may accrue to top-level managers. Diversification also increases the complexity of managing a firm and its network of businesses, possibly requiring additional managerial pay because of this complexity for top-level managers to increase their compensation.

8.2 Ownership Concentration

Ownership concentration is defined by the number of large-block shareholders and the total percentage of the firm's shares they own. Large-block shareholders typically own at least 5 percent of a company's issued shares. Ownership concentration as a governance mechanism has received considerable interest because large-block shareholders are increasingly active in their demands that firms adopt effective governance mechanisms to control managerial decisions so that they will best represent owners' interests. In recent years, the number of individuals who are large-block shareholders has declined. Institutional owners have replaced individuals as large-block shareholders.

In general diffuse ownership produces weak monitoring of manager's decisions. One reason for this is that diffuse ownership makes it difficult for owners to effectively coordinate their actions. As noted earlier, diversification beyond the shareholders' optimum level can result from ineffective monitoring of managers' decisions. Higher levels of monitoring could encourage managers to avoid strategic decisions that harm shareholder value, such as too much diversification. Research evidence suggests that ownership concentration is associated with lower levels of firm product diversification. Thus, with high degrees of ownership concentration, the probability is greater that managers' decisions will be designed to maximize shareholder value.

As noted, ownership concentration influences decisions made about the strategies a firm will use and the value created by their use. In general, but not in every case, ownership concentration's influence on strategies and firm performance is positive. For example, when large-block shareholders have a high degree of wealth, they have power relative to minority shareholders to appropriate the firm's wealth; this is particularly the case when they are in managerial positions. Excessive appropriation at the expense of minority shareholders is somewhat common in countries such as Korea where minority shareholders rights are not as protected as they are in the United States. The importance of boards of directors to mitigate excessive appropriation of minority shareholder value has been found in firms with strong family ownership wherein family members have incentives to appropriate shareholder wealth, especially in the second generation after the founder has departed.

8.3 Enhancing the Effectiveness of the Board of Directors

Because of the importance of boards of directors in corporate governance and as a result of increased scrutiny from shareholders-in particular, large institutional investors investors-the performances of individual board members and of entire boards are being evaluated more formally and with greater intensity. The demand for greater accountability and improved performance is stimulating many boards to voluntarily make changes. Among these changes are (1) increases in the diversity of the backgrounds of board members(2) the strengthening of internal management and consistently using formal processes to evaluate the board's performance, (4) modifying the compensation of directors, especially reducing or elimination of directors, especially reducing or eliminating stock options as a part of their package, and(5) creating the "lead director" role that has strong that has strong power with regard to the board agenda and oversight of nonmanagement board member activities.

Corporate governance is an increasing important issue in economies around the world, including emerging economies. Globalization in trade, investments, and equity markets increases the potential value of firms throughout the world using similar mechanisms to govern corporate activities. Moreover, because of globalization, major companies want to attract foreign investment. For this to happen, foreign investors must be confident that adequate corporate governance mechanisms are in place to protect their investments.

Although globalization is stimulating an increase in the intensity of efforts to improve corporate governance and potentially to reduce the variation in regions and nations' governance systems, the reality remains that differences in various countries' governance systems as well as changes taking place within those systems improves the likelihood a firm will be able to compete successfully in the international markets it chooses to enter. Next, to highlight the general issues of differences and changes taking place in governance systems, we discuss corporate governance practices in two developed economies-Germany and Japan-and in china, a developing economy.

8.4 Evaluating the Strategy of Diversified Companies

Resource Fit Analysis Rank Business Units Based on Performance Decide on Resource Allocation Priorities and General Strategic Direction Crafting a Corporate Strategy Guidelines for Managing the Corporate Strategy Process.

Building Shareholder Value: Questions to Ask About a Diversified Company 1. How attractive is the group of businesses the company has diversified into? 2. How good is the firm's overall performance outlook in the years ahead with these businesses? 3. If previous two answers aren't satisfactory, what should the firm do to realign its business line up? Divest unattractive businesses? Strengthen positions of remaining ones? Acquire new businesses?

How to Evaluate a Diversified Company's Strategy Step 1: Identify present corporate strategy Step 2: Evaluate long-term attractiveness of each industry firm Step 3: Evaluate competitive strength of firm's business units Step 4: Apply strategic fit test Step 5: Apply resource fit test.

How to Evaluate a Diversified Company's Strategy. Step 6: Rank business units based on historical performance and future prospects. Step 7: Rank business units in terms of priority for resource allocation and decide on general strategic posture Step 8: Craft new strategic moves to improve overall company performance.

Identifying a Diversified Company's Strategy Corporate Strategy Narrow or broad-based diversification Approach to allocating investment capital and resources. Is diversification related, unrelated or a mix? Scope of geographic operations. Efforts to capture cross-business strategic fits Moves to divest weak business units. Moves to add new businesses. Moves to build positions in new industries.

Step 1: Identify Present Corporate Strategy Extent to which firm is diversified (broad versus narrow, % of sales contributed by each business) Is portfolio keyed to related or unrelated diversification or both? Is scope of operations mostly domestic, increasingly multinational, or global? Recent moves to add new businesses.

Step 1: Identify Present Corporate Strategy(continued) Recent moves to divest weak businesses. Actions to boost performance of key business units. Efforts to capture cross-business strategic fit benefits and exploit value chain relationships to create competitive advantage Percentage of capital expenditures allocated to each business unit.

Step 2: Evaluate Industry Attractiveness of each industry in portfolio Each industry's attractiveness relative to the others Attractiveness of all industries as a group.

Industry Attractiveness Factors Market size and projected growth Intensity of competition Emerging opportunities and threats cyclical factors. Resource requirements Cross-industry strategic fits and resource fits with present businesses Industry profitability Social, political, regulatory, and environmental factors Degree of risk and uncertainty.

Procedure: Rating the Relative Attractiveness of Each Industry Step 1: Select industry attractiveness factors Step 2: Assign weights to each factor(sum of weights=1. 0)Step 3: Rate each industry on each factor (use scale of 1 to 10)Step 4: Calculate weighted ratings; sum to get an overall industry attractiveness rating for each industry.

Attractiveness of Mix of Industries as a Whole How appealing is the whole group of industries in which the company is invested? Is the company in too many relatively unattractive industries? Does the portfolio of industries hold promise for attractive growth and profitability? Should some form of portfolio restructuring be considered?

Step 3: Evaluate Each Business Unit's Competitive Strength Objectives Determine how well each business is positioned in its industry relative to rivals. Evaluate whether it is or can be competitively strong enough to contend for market leadership!

Factors to Use in Evaluating Competitive Strength Relative market share Costs relative to competitors Ability to match/beat rivals on key product attributes. Ability to exercise bargaining leverage with key suppliers or customers Caliber of alliances and collaborative partnerships. Ability to benefit from strategic fits with sister businesses Technology and innovation capabilities. How well business's competencies match industry KSFs Brand name recognition and reputation. Profitability relative to competitors.

Procedure: Rating the Competitive Strength of Each Business Step 1: Select competitive strength factors. Step 2: Assign weights to each factor(sum of weights=1. 0) Step 3: Rate each business on each factor(use scale of 1 to 10) Step 4: Calculate weighted ratings; sum to get an overall strength rating for each business.

Using a Matrix to Display Industry Attractiveness and Competitive Strength Use quantitative measures of industry attractiveness and business strength to plot location of each business in matrix. Each business unit appears as a circle Area of circle is proportional to size of business as a percent of company revenues. Or area of circle can represent relative sizeof industry with pie slice showing the company's market share.

Industry Attractiveness-Competitive Strength Matrix Low High Medium Strong Average Weak6. 73. 310. 01. 06. 73. 31. High priority for investment Medium priority for investment Low priority for investment Business Unit Competitive Strength Idustry Attractvieness.

Strategy Implications of Attractiveness/Strength Matrix Businesses in upper left corner Accorded top investment priority Strategic prescription-grow and build Businesses in three diagonal cells Given medium investment priority. Invest to maintain position Businesses in lower right corner Candidates for harvesting or divestiture May, on occasion, be candidates for an overhaul and reposition strategy.

Appeal of the Attractiveness/Strength Matrix Incorporates a wide variety of strategically relevant variables. Stresses concentrating corporate resources in businesses that enjoy. High degree of industry attractiveness and High degree of competitive strength. The lesson here is emphasize businesses that are market leaders or that can contend for market leadership.

Step 4: Strategic Fit Analysis Objective Determine competitive advantage potential of value chain relationships and strategic fits among sister businesses. Examine strategic fit from two angles Whether one or more businesses shave valuable strategic fits with other businesses in portfolio. Whether each business meshes well with firm's long-term strategic direction.

Evaluate Portfolio for CompetitivelyValuable Cross-Business Strategic Fits Identify businesses which have value chain match-ups offering opportunities to Reduce costs. Purchasing E-commerce systems Manufacturing Distribution Transfer skills/technology/ intellectual capital Leverage use of a well-known and competitively powerful brand name Create valuable new competitive capabilities or to leverage existing resources.

Identify Cross-BusinessStrategic Fits Value Chain Activities Sales and Marketing Inbound Logistics Technology Operations Distribution Service Business A-Business B-Business C-Business D-Business E Opportunity to combine purchasing activities to gain more leverage with suppliers Opportunity to share technology, transfer technical skills, combine R&D Opportunity to combine sales&marketing activities, use common distribution channels, leverage use of a common brand name, and/or combine after-sale service No strategic fit opportunities.

Step 5: Assess Resource Fit Objective Determine how well firm's resources match business unit requirements Good resource fit exists when A business adds to a firm's resource strengths, either financially or strategically. Firm has resources to adequately support requirements of its businesses as a group.

Checking for Financial Resource Fit Determine cash flow and investment requirements of the business units Which are cash hogs and which are cash cows? Assessing cash flow of each business Highlights opportunities to shift financial resources between businesses Explains why priorities for resource allocation can differ from business to business Provides rationalization for both invest-and-expand strategies and divestiture.

Characteristics of Cash Hogs Internal cash flows are inadequate to fully fund needs for working capital and new capital investment Parent company has to continually pump incapital to "feed the hog" Strategic options Aggressively invest inattractive cash hogs Divest cash hogs lacking long-term potential.

Characteristics of Cash Cows Generate cash surpluses over and above what is needed to sustain present market position Such businesses are valuable because surplus cash can be used to Pay corporate dividends Finance new acquisitions Invest in promising cash hogs Strategic objectives Fortify and defend present market position Keep the business healthy.

Good vs. Poor Financial Fit Good financial fit exists when a business Contributes to achievement of corporate objectives Enhances shareholder value Poor financial fit exists when a business Soaks up disproportionate share of financial resources Is an inconsistent bottom-line contributor Is too small to make a sizable contribution to total corporate earnings. Experiences a profit downturn that could jeopardize entire company.

Checking for Competitive and Managerial Resource Fits Involves determining whether Resource strengths are well matched to KSFs of industries firm is in Ample resource depth exists to support resource requirements of all the businesses. Ability exists to transfer competitive capabilities from one business to another Company must invest in upgrading its resources/capabilities to stay ahead of efforts of rivals.

Notes of Caution: Why Diversification Efforts Can Fail Transferring resource capabilities to newbusinesses can be far more arduous and expensive than expected Trying to replicate a firm's success in one business and hitting a second home run in anew business is easier said than done Management can misjudge difficulty of overcoming resource strengths of rivals it will face in a new business.

Step 6: Rank Business Units Based on Financial Performance Yardsticks for comparing performance of different businesses Sales growth Profit growth Contribution to company earnings Return on capital employed in business Cash flow generation.

Step 7: Decide Resource Allocation Priorities and Strategic Direction Objective "Get the biggest bang for the buck" in allocating corporate resources Procedure Rank each business from highest to lowest priority for corporate resource support and new investment Decide on general strategic direction for each business.

Options: General Strategic Direction Invest and grow Aggressive expansion Fortify and defend Protect current position Overhaul and reposition Make major strategy changes. Harvest or divest Gradual market retreat. Spin off business as independent company Sell business will be.

Options for Allocating Financial Resources Strategic purposes Invest in ways to strengthen or expand existing businesses. Make acquisitions to establish positions in new industries Fund long-range R&D ventures Financial purposes. Pay off existing long-term debt Increase dividends Repurchase company's stock Stock certificate.

Step 8: Crafting a Corporate Strategy-Key Issues Are enough businesses in attractive industries? Is the number of mature or declining businesses so great corporate growth will be sluggish? Are businesses overly vulnerable to seasonal influences or recession? Are there too many average-to-weak businesses in the company's business make-up? Is there ample strategic fit among the businesses?

Step 8: Crafting a Corporate Strategy-Key Issues(continued) Is there ample resource fit among the businesses? Are there enough cash cows to finance those cash hogs with potential to be star performers? Do core businesses generate dependable profits and/or cash flow? Does makeup of business portfolio put firm in good future position?

The Performance Test Can the company's performance targets be reached with the current businesses? If yes, no major corporate strategy changes are indicated. If a performance gap is likely, actions can betaken to close the gap.

Options for Addressing a Performance Shortfall Alter strategic plans for some, or all, of businesses Add new businesses Divest weak-performing businesses Form cooperative alliances Upgrade firm's resource base Lower corporate performance objectives.

Identifying AdditionalDiversification OpportunitiesRelated Diversification Identify businesses whose value chain shave fits with value chains of present businesses. Identify businesses whose resource requirements are well-matched to firm's corporate resource capabilities Unrelated Diversification Find firms offering attractive financial returns regardless of industry.

8.5 How Corporate Strategies Form

In diversified companies corporate strategy tends to emerge incrementally As internal and external events unfold As managers Probe the future Experiment Gather more information Sense problems Build awareness of options Spot new opportunities. Develop ad hoc responses to unexpected crises. Acquire a feel for strategically relevant factors and their importance and interrelationships Develop consensus of how to proceed Our strategy will be.

Managing the Process of Crafting Corporate Strategy Not done all at once in comprehensive fashion Approached a step at a time, emerging gradually Begin with broad, intuitive concepts and then fine-tune and embellish them as More information is gathered Formal analysis confirms or modifies emerging judgments about situation Confidence and consensus build for the proposed strategic moves.

8.6 Building Core Competencies and Competitive Capabilities

Implementing and Executing Strategy Action-oriented, operations-driven activity revolving around managing people and business processes Tougher and more time-consuming than crafting strategy. Success depends on doing a good job of Leading Motivating Working with others Creating fits between requirements for good strategy execution and how organization conducts its business Implementation involves.

Why Implementing and Executing Strategy is a Tough Management Job Demanding variety of managerial activities that have to be performed Numerous ways to tackle each activity Requires good people management skills Requires launching and managing a variety of initiatives simultaneously Number of be deviling issues to be worked out Battling resistance to change. Hard to integrate efforts of many different work groups into a smoothly-functioning whole.

Implementing a Newly Chosen Strategy Requires Adept Leadership Implementing a new strategy takes adept leadership to Convincingly communicate reasons for the new strategy Overcome pockets of doubt Build consensus and enthusiasm Secure commitment of concerned parties Get all implementation pieces in place and coordinated.

Characteristics of the Strategy Implementation Process Every manager has an active role No 10-step checklists Few concrete guidelines Least charted, most open-ended part of strategic management Cuts across many aspects of"how to manage".

Characteristics of the Strategy Implementation Process (continued). Each implementation situation occurs in a different context, affected by differing Business practices and competitive situations Work environments and cultures Policies Compensation incentives Mix of personalities and firm histories. Approach to implementation has be customized to fit the situation People implement strategies-Not companies!

The Eight Components of Implementing and Executing Strategy Building a Capable Organization Allocating Resources Establishing Strategy-Supportive Policies Instituting Best Practices for Continuous Improvement Installing Support ying Rewards Systems to

Achievement of Key Strategic Targets Exercising Strategic Leadership Shaping Corporate Culture to Fit Strategy Strategy Implementer's Action Agenda.

8.7 What the Goals of the Strategy Implementing-Executing Process Are

Unite total organization behind strategy See that activities are done in a manner tightly matching first-rate strategy execution Generate commitment so an enthusiastic crusade emerges to carry out strategy. Fit how the organization conducts its operations to the requirements of strategy.

Who are the Strategy Implementers? Implementation involves a company's whole management team Every organization unit and all employees have a role in the strategy implementing and executing process CEO, senior executives, and heads of major departments must lead the process and orchestrate major initiatives. But they must rely on middle and lower-level managers to push things on the front line, seeing that strategy is well-executed on a daily basis.

Ways to Lead the Implementation and Execution Process Take active, visible role or low-key, behind the scenes role Make decisions authoritatively or based on consensus Delegate much or little Be personally involved in details or coach others to carry day-to-day burden Proceed swiftly to achieve results or move deliberately, content with gradual progress.

Factors Shaping How Managers Lead the Implementation Process Experience and knowledge of business New to job or seasoned? Network of personal relationships Diagnostic, administrative, interpersonal, and problem-solving skills. How much authority they have Leadership style most comfortable with How they view their role in gettingthings done The organization's situation.

The Components of Building a Capable Organization Staffing the Organization? Putting together a strong management team? Recruiting and retaining talented employee. Building Core Competencies and Competitive Capabilities? Developing a competence/capability portfolio suited to current strategy? Updating and reshaping the portfolio asexternal conditions and strategy change Structuring the Organization and the Work Effort.

Putting Together a Strong Management Team Determine kind of core management team needed to execute the strategy Find the right people to fill each slot Existing management team may be suitable Core executive group may need strengthening Promote from within Bring in skilled outsiders.

Selecting the Management Team: Key Considerations Determine mix of Backgrounds Experiences and know-how Beliefs and values Styles of managing and personalities

Personal chemistry must be right. Talent base needs to be appropriate Picking a solid management team needs to be acted on early in implementation process.

Recruiting and Retaining Talented Employees: Implementation Issues Assemble the needed human resources and knowledge base for effective strategy execution Biggest challenge facing companies building a future in the Internet Economy. How to recruit and retain the be stand brightest talent with strong skill sets and management potential Intellectual capital, not tangible assets, is increasingly being viewed as the most important investment Talented people are a prime source of competitive advantage.

Key Human Resource Practices to Attract and Retain Talented Employees Spend considerable effort in screening job applicants, selecting only those with Suitable skill sets Energy and initiative Judgment and aptitudes for learning. Ability to adapt to firm's workenvironment/culture Put employees through training programs throughout their careers Give employees challenging, interesting, and skills-stretching assignments.

Key Human Resource Practices to Attract and Retain Talented Employees(continued) Rotate employees through jobs with great content, spanning functional and geographic boundaries Encourage employees to. Be creative and innovative. Challenge existing ways of doing things and offer better ways Submit ideas for new products or businesses. Foster a stimulating and engaging work environment Exert efforts to retain high-potential, high performing employees with excellent salary and benefits.

Key Organization-Building Objectives Staff organizational units with the specialized talents, skills, and technical expertise needed to develop and build core competencies Build competitively valuable organizational capabilities.

Power of Unique Competencies and Capabilities When it is difficult to out-strategic rivals with a superior strategy. Best avenue to industry leadership is to out-compete rivals with superior strategy execution! Building competencies and capabilities rivals can't match is one of the best ways to out-compete them.

Strategically-Relevant Core or Distinctive Competencies Greater proficiency in product development Better manufacturing know-how Capability to provide better after-sale service. Faster response to changing customer needs Superior cost-cutting skills Capacity to speed new products to market Superior inventory management systems. Better marketing and merchandising skills Specialized depth in unique technologies Greater effectiveness in promoting union-management cooperation.

Strategic Management Principle Building core competencies, resource strengths, and organizational capabilities that rivals can't match is a sound foundation for sustainable competitive advantage!

8.8 Key Traits to Building Core Competencies

Rarely grounded in skills or know-how of a single department. Typically emerge from collaborative efforts of different work groups, requiring senior management oversight. Leveraging competencies into competitive advantage requires concentrating more effort and talent than rivals on strengthening competencies to create valuable organizational capabilities. Sustaining competitive advantage requires adaptingcompetencies to new conditions

Developing CompetitivelyValuable Competencies Involves Managing human skills, knowledge bases, and intellect Coordinating efforts of related work groups Collaborative networking among internal groups and with external partners. Achieving dominating depth Senior managers have to guide the process Ongoing challenge: Broaden, deepen, or modify competencies and capabilities in response to market changes.

Building Competencies: Keys to Success Selecting superior employees. Training Cultural influences Cooperation and collaboration Motivation Empowerment Attractive incentives Organizational flexibility Short deadlines Good databases.

The Most Valuable Organizational Capabilities Contribute heavily to better strategy execution. Provide a differentiating factor customers can see and value Difficult for rivals to match Time consuming to build Difficult to purchase Hard to replicate or imitate.

Process of BuildingOrganizational Capabilities. Develop ability to do something. Select people with relevant skills/experience Upgrade individual abilities as needed Mold work of employees into cooperative effort. As experience builds, ability can translate into a competence and/or capability. Capability becomes a distinctive competence, resulting in a potential competitive advantage

Process of BuildingOrganizational Capabilities: Step 1Develop ability to do something Select people with relevant skills/experience Broaden or deepen individual abilities as needed Mold efforts and work products of individuals into a cooperative group effort to create organizational ability.

Process of Building Organizational Capabilities: Step 2. As experience builds, such that the organization learns to accomplish the activity consistently well and at acceptable cost, the "ability" begins to translate into a competence and/or a capability Capabilities emerge from establishing and nurturing collaborative working relationships between individuals and groups in departments and between a company and its external allies.

Process of Building Organizational Capabilities: Step 3. If mastery is achieved to the point where the organization has the capability to perform the activity better than rivals, the "capability" becomes a distinctive competence and holds potential for competitive advantage The optimal outcome of the capability-building process!

Updating Competencies and Capabilities as Conditions Change Competencies and capabilities must continuously be modified and perhaps seven replaced with new ones due to. New strategic requirements Evolving market conditions Changing customer expectations Ongoing efforts to keep core competencies up-to-date can provide a basis for sustaining both Effective strategy execution and Competitive advantage.

Strategic Role of Employee Training Plays a critical role in implementation when a firm shifts to a strategy requiring different Skills-based competencies Competitive capabilities Managerial approaches Operating methods Types of training approaches Internal "universities" Orientation sessions for new employees Tuition reimbursement programs Online training courses.

Matching Organization Structure to Strategy Few hard and fast rules for organizing The One Big Rule: The role and purpose of the organization structure is to support and facilitate good strategy execution! Each firm's structure is idiosyncratic, reflecting Prior arrangements and internal politics. Executive judgments and preferences about how to arrange reporting relationships. How best to integrate and coordinate work effort of different work groups and departments Vice President Vice President Vice President CEO.

Structuring the Organization to Promote Successful Strategy Execution. Identify strategy-critical value chain activities Decide value chain activities to perform internally and those to outsource Make internally-performed strategy-critical value chain activities the main building blocks in the structure. Decide how much authority to centralize at the top and how much to delegate to managers and employees. Provide cross-unit coordination and collaboration to build/strengthen internal competencies and capabilities Provide the necessary collaboration and coordination with outsiders.

Step 1: Identify Strategy-Critical Activities Which activities are strategy-critical depends on Particulars of a firm's strategy Value-chain make-up Competitive requirements. External market conditions. Identify strategy-critical activities1. What business processes have to be performed extra well or in timely fashion to achieve competitive advantage? 2. In what value-chain activities would poor work performance impair strategic success Critical activities.

Step 2: Potential Advantages of Outsourcing Non-Critical Activities Decrease internal bureaucracies Flatten organization structure Speed decision-making. Provide firm with heightened strategic focus Improve a firm's innovative capacity. Increase competitive responsiveness Outsourcing makes strategic sense when outsiders can perform certain activities at a lower cost and/or with higher value-added.

Appeal of Outsourcing non-critical activities allows a firm to concentrate its energies and resources on those value-chain activities where it Can create unique value Can be best in the industry Needs strategic control to Build core competencies Achieve competitive advantage Manage key customer-supplier—distributor relationships.

Potential Advantages of Partnering By building, improving, and then leveraging partnerships, a firm enhances its overall capabilities and builds resource strengths that Deliver value to customers Rivals can't quite match. Consequently pave the way for competitive success Partnering makes strategic sense when the result is to enhance organizational capabilities.

Step 3: Make Strategy-Critical Activities the Main Building Blocks Assign managers of strategy-critical activities a visible, influential position Avoid fragmenting responsibility for strategy-critical activities across many departments. Provide coordinating linkages between related work groups Meld into a valuable competitive capability Assign managers key roles Primary activities Strategic relationships CoordinationValuable capability Support functions.

Strategic Management Principle Matching structure to strategy requires making strategy-critical activities and organizational units the main building blocks in the organization structure!

Why Structure Follows Strategy Changes in strategy typically require a new structure New strategy often involves different skills, different key activities, different staffing and organizational requirements Hence, a new strategy signals a need to reassess the organization structure How work is structured is a means to an end—not an end in itself!

Guard Against Functional Designs That Fragment Activities Scattering pieces of critical business processes across several specialized departments results in Many hand-offs which Lengthens completion time Increases coordination and overhead costs. Increases risk of details falling through the cracks Obsession with activity rather than result Solution Business process reengineering. Involves pulling strategy-critical processes from functional silos to create process-complete departments or cross- functional work groups.

Example: Fragmented Strategy-Critical Activities in a Functional Structure Filling customer orders Speeding new products to market Improving product quality Supply chain managemen tBuilding capability to conduct business via the Internet Obtaining feedback from customers, making product modifications to meet their needs,

Step 4: Determine How MuchAuthority to Delegate to WhomIn a centralized structureTop managers retain authority for most decisionsIn a decentralized structure Managers and employees are empowered to make decisions Trend in most companies Shift from authoritarian to decentralized structures stressing empowerment.

Advantages of Decentralized Decision-Making and Empowerment Fewer management layers Less bureaucracy Shorter response times More creativity and new ideas Better motivation of employees Greater employee involvement Increased organizational capability.

Principles Underlying the Global Trend Toward Decentralization and Empowerment. As the world economy moves into the Internet Age, traditional hierarchical structures must undergo radical surgery to capitalize on External market and Internal operating potential of e-commerce. Decisions are best made at the lowest organizational level capable to make timely, informed, competent decisions. Empowering employees to exercise judgment on job-related matters improves motivation and job performance.

Step 5: Reporting Relationships and Cross-Unit Coordination Classic method of coordinating activities-Have related units report to single manager Upper-level managers have clout to coordinate/unify efforts of their units. Support activities should be woven into structure in ways to Maximize performance of primary activities Contain costs of support activities Formal reporting relationships often need to be supplemented.

Options to Supplement the Basic Organization Structure Coordinating teams Cross-functional task forces Dual reporting relationships Informal networking Incentive compensation tied to group performance Teamwork and inter-departmental cooperation.

Step 6: Assign Responsibility for Collaboration With Outsiders Need multiple ties at multiple levels to ensure CommunicationCoordination and control Find ways to produce collaborative efforts to enhance firm's capabilities and resource strengths While collaborative relationships present opportunities, nothing valuable is realized until the relationship develops into an engine forbetter organizational performance.

Roles of Relationship Managers With Strategic Partners Get the right people together Promote good rapport See that plans for specific activities are developed and implemented. Help adjust internal procedures and communication systems Successfully link partners Iron out operating dissimilarities Nurture interpersonal ties.

Perspectives on Organizing All basic organization designs have strategy-related strengths and weaknesses. No ideal organization design exists To do a good job of matching structure to strategy Pick a basic design Modify as needed Supplement with appropriate coordinating, networking, and communication mechanisms to support effective execution of the strategy.

Organizational Structures of the Future: Overall Themes Revolutionary changes in how companies organize work have been triggered by New strategic priorities Rapidly shifting competitive conditions Tools of organizational design include Empowered managers and workers Reengineered work processes Self-directed work teams. Rapid incorporation of Internet technologies and cutting-edge e-commerce infrastructure Networking with outsiders.

Organizational Structures of the Future: Overall Themes Traditional, authoritarian structures have often proved to be a liability where Market conditions are fluid Customer preferences shift from standardized to customized products Product life-cycles grow shorter

Flexible manufacturing replaces mass production Customers want to be treated as individuals Pace of technological change accelerates.

Organizational Structures of the Future: Requirements for Success Decentralized structures with fewer managers Small-scale business units Reengineering to decrease fragmentation Development of stronger and newer capabilities Collaborative partnerships with outsiders Empowerment and self-directed work teams Lean staffing of corporate support functions Electronic information systems Accountability for results Use of e-commerce in daily operations.

Characteristics of Organizations of the Future The future structure will be. Change&Learning Fewer boundaries between Different vertical ranks Functions and disciplines Units in different geographic locations Firm and its suppliers, distributors, strategic allies, and customers Capacity for change and learning Collaborative efforts among people indifferent functions and geographic locations Extensive use of e-commerce technology and Internet business practices.

8.9 Instituting Best Practices and Installing Support Systems

Linking Budgets to Strategy Allocating resources in ways that support effective strategy execution involves Funding capital projects that can make a contribution to strategy implementation Funding efforts to strengthen competencies and capabilities or to create new ones Shifting resources—downsizing some areas, upsizing others, killing activities no longer justified, and funding new activities with a critical strategy role.

Strategic Management Principle Depriving strategy-critical groups of the funds needed to execute their pieces of the strategy can undermine the implementation process!

How Policies and Procedures Aid Strategy Implementation Provide top-down guidance regarding expected behaviors Help align internal actions with strategy, channeling efforts along the intended path. Enforce consistency in performance of activities in geographically scattered units Serve as powerful lever for changing corporate culture to produce stronger fit with a new strategy.

Creating Strategy-Supportive Policies and Procedures Role of new policies Channel behaviors and decisions to promote strategy execution Counteract tendencies of people to resist chosen strategy Too much policy can be as stifling as Wrong policy or as Chaotic as no policy. Often, the best policy is empowering employees and letting them operate between the white lines anyway they think best.

Instituting Best Practices and Continuous Improvement Searching out and adopting best practices is integral to effective implementation Benchmarking has spawned new approaches to improve strategy execution Reengineering TQM Continuous improvement programs.

Characteristics of Benchmarking Involves determining how well a firm performs particular activities and processes against "Best in industry" and/or "Best in world" performers Represents a solid methodology to identify options to improve Caution-Exact duplication of best practices of other firms is not feasible due to differences in implementation situations. Best approach-Best practices of other firms need to be modified or adapted to a firm's own specific situation Best Practices.

Information evaluation and control consist of performance data and activity reports. 信息评价和控制信息涉及性能数据和活动报告。

Information evaluation and control must be relevant to what is being monitored. 信息评价和控制必须与监测有关。

Evaluation and control is not an easy process. One of the obstacles to effective control is the difficulty in developing appropriate measures of important activities and outputs. 评价和控制并非那么容易的过程。原因之一是在重要的活动和表现中发展合适措施的有效控制是困难的。

Corporations are increasingly being evaluated on criteria other than economic. 目前越来越多的公司评估标准已经不仅仅是经济指标。

8.10 What Total Quality Management Is

TQM is a philosophy of managing a set of business practices that emphasizes Continuous improvement in all phases of operations, 100 percent accuracy in performing activities, Involvement and empowerment of employees a tall levels, Team-based work design, Benchmarking, and Fully satisfying customer expectations. Goals of Quality Improvement Programs Defect-free manufacture Superior product quality Superior customer service Total customer satisfaction.

Components of Popular TQM Approaches Deming's 14 Points1. Constancy of purpose2. Adopt the philosophy3. Don't rely on mass inspection4. Don't award business on price5. Constant improvement6. Training7. Leadership8. Drive out fear9. Break down barriers10. Eliminate slogans and exhortations11. Eliminate quotas12. Pride of workmanship13. Education and retraining14. Plan of action.

Components of Popular TQM Approaches The Juran Trilogy Quality Planning Quality Control Quality Improvement? Set goals? Identify customers and their needs? Develop products and processes? Evaluate performance? Compare to goal sand adapt? Establish infrastructure? Identify projects and teams? Provide resources and training? Establish controls.

Components of Popular TQM Approaches Crosby's Quality Steps. Management commitment. Quality improvement teams. Quality measurement. Cost of quality evaluation. Quality awareness. Corrective action. Zero-defects committee. Supervisor training. Zero-defects day. Goal-setting. Error cause removal. Recognition. Quality councils. Do it over again.

Components of Popular TQM Approaches 1992 Baldridge Award Criteria(1000 points)Quality1. Leadership(90 points)2. Information &analysis(80 points)3. Strategic quality planning(60 points) 4. Human resource development (150 points) 5. Management of process quality (140 points) 6. Quality&operation results (180 points) 7. Customer focus&satisfaction(300points).

Twelve Aspects Common to TQM and Continuous Improvement Programs1. Committed leadership2. Adoption and communication of TQM3. Closer customer relationships4. Closer supplierrelationships5. Benchmarking6. Increased training7. Open organization8. Employee empowerment9. Zero-defects mentality10. Flexible manufacturing11. Process improvement12. Measurement.

Implementing a Philosophy of Continuous Improvement In still enthusiasm to do things right throughout company Strive to achieve little steps forward each day, (what the Japanese call kaizen). Ignite creativity in employees to improve performance of value-chain activities. Preach there is no such thing as good enough Reform the corporate culture.

Characteristics of TQM/ContinuousImprovement Programs Valuable competitive asset in a company's resource portfolio Have hard-to-imitate aspects Require substantial investment of management time and effort Expensive in terms of training and meetings Seldom produce short-term results Long-term payoff—instilling a TQM culture

TQM vs. Process Reengineering Aims at quantum gains of 30 to 50%or more TQM Stresses incremental progress. Techniques are not mutually exclusive Reengineering-Used to produce a good basic design yielding dramatic improvements TQM-Used to perfect process, gradually improving efficiency and effectiveness.

Using Best Practice Programs as an Implementation Tool Select indicators of successful strategy execution Benchmark against best practice companies Reengineer business processes. Build a TQ culture Requires top management commitment Install TQ-supportive employee practices. Empower employees to do the right things Provide employees with quick access to required information Preach that performance can be improved.

Installing Support Systems Essential to promote successful strategy execution Types of support systems On-line data systems Internet and company intranets. Electronic mail E-commerce systems Mobilizing information and creating systems touse knowledge effectively can yield Competitive advantage.

Examples: Support Systems Airlines Computerized reservation system Federal

Express Computerized parcel-tracking system, leading-edge flight operations systems, and e-business tools.

Examples: Support Systems Otis Elevator Sophisticated maintenance support system Arthur Andersen Internet and digital technology (Knowledge Xchange system has data, voice, and video capabilities)links more than 70, 000 people in 382 offices in 81 countries.

Examples: Support Systems Domino's Pizza Computerized systems at each outlet facilitate ordering, inventory, payroll, cash flow, and work flow functions Mrs. Fields' Cookies System to monitor sales, at 15-minute intervals, to suggest product mix changes and to improve customer response.

Strategic Management Principle Innovative, state-of-the-art support systems can be a basis for competitive advantage if they give a firm capabilities that rivals can't match!

Formal Reporting of Strategy-Critical Information Accurate, timely information is essential to guide action Prompt feedback on implementation activities is needed before actions are fully completed Key strategic performance indicators must be tracked as often as practical Barometers of overall performance Statistical information Reports and meetings Personal contact.

8.11 What Areas Information Systems Should Address

Customer dataOperations data Employee dataSupplier/partner/collaborative ally dataFinancial performance data.

Exercising Adequate Contro lOver Empowered Employees Challenge How to ensure actions of employees stay within acceptable bounds Purpose of diagnostic control systems Relieve managers of burden of constant monitoring Control methods. Establish boundaries on what not to do, allowing freedom to act with limits Face-to-face meetings to assess performance.

Gaining Commitment: Components of an Effective Reward System Monetary Incentives Salary raises Performance bonuses Stock options Retirement packages Promotions Perks Non-monetary Incentives Praise Constructive criticism Special recognition More, or less, job security Interesting assignments More, or less, job responsibility.

Approaches: Motivating People to Execute the Strategy Well Inspire employees to do their best Get employees to buy into strategy Structure individual efforts in teamsto facilitate a supportive climate. Allow employees to participate in decisions about their jobs Make jobs interesting and satisfying Devise strategy-supportive motivational approaches.

Examples: Motivational Practices No Lay-Off Policies Japanese automobile producers, along with several U. S. based companies(Southwest Airlines, FedEx, Lands'End, and

Harley Davidson) have no lay-off policies, using employment security both as a positive motivator and a means of reinforcing good strategy execution.

Examples: Motivational Practices Stock Options More than 35 of the 58 publicly held companies on the 1999 list of the 100 Best Companies to Work for in America (includes Cisco Systems, Procter&Gamble, Merck, Charles Schwab, General Mills, Amgen, and Tellabs) provide stock options to all employees. Having employee-owners sharing in a company's success is widely viewed as a positive motivator.

Examples: Motivational Practices NordstromPay sales people higher than prevailing rates, plus commission. "Rule1: Use good judgment in all situations. There will be no additional rules." Cisco Systems Offers on-the-spot bonuses of up to $2, 000 for exceptional performance.

Examples: Motivational Practices MicrosoftTeam members enjoy working 60-80hours per week for a leading edge company, accompanied by attractive pay and lucrative stock options. Lincoln Electric Rewards productivity by paying for each piece produced (defects can be traced to worker causing them). Bonuses of 50 to 100% are common.

Balancing Positive vs. Negative Rewards Elements of both are necessary Challenge and competition are necessary for self-satisfaction Prevailing view Positive approaches work better than negative ones in terms of Enthusiasm Effort Creativity Initiative.

Linking the Reward System to Performance Outcomes Rewards are the single most powerful tool to win commitment to the strategy Objectives Generously reward those achieving objectives Deny rewards to those who don't Make strategic performance measures the dominant basis for designing incentives, evaluating efforts, and handing out rewards.

Strategic Management Principle A properly designed reward structure is management's most powerful tool for mobilizing organizational commitment to successful strategy execution!

8.12 Guidelines for Designing an Effective Compensation System

Strategic Management Principle The unwavering standard for judging whether individuals, teams, and organizational units have done a good job must be whether hey achieve performance targets consistent with effective strategy execution!

Key Considerations in Designing Reward Systems Create a results-oriented system Reward people for results, not for activity Define jobs in terms of what to achieve Incorporate several performance measures Tie incentive compensation to relevant outcomes. Top executives—Key measures of overall firm performance Department heads, teams, and individuals Incentives tied to achieving performance targets in their areas of responsibility.

Payoff must be a major, not minor, piece of total compensation package. Incentive plan should extend to all employees. Administer system with scrupulous fairness. Link incentives to achieving only the performance targets in strategic plan. Targets each person is expected to achieve must involve outcomes that can be personally affected. Keep time between performance review and payment short Make liberal use of non-monetary rewards. Avoid ways of rewarding non-performers.

后　　记

新经济时代中,现代企业的发展和生存环境都发生了巨大的变化,许多管理理念和方法在不断地被实践所扬弃。为了更为准确地把握新经济发展的脉搏,企业管理者有必要针对动态变化的环境对自身进行准确的战略规划、战略制订、战略实施和战略控制。因此,战略管理即成为工商管理专业的核心教学模块之一。

在本书中,编者们已经竭尽所能将战略管理学科的方法、工具和思路展示给读者。但是当这本书稿完成时,依然深感不安,因为离我们的目标还有很大差距,尤其是新经济环境下战略管理运行和实施的新理念和方法在企业经营活动中灵活应用的模式问题。

本书的完成得到了许多方面的帮助。首先要感谢湖南工学院分管教学工作的张平校长,经济管理学院杨凤鸣院长,赵少平副院长,是他们为本书的撰写创造了非常好的学习和工作条件;其次要感谢经济管理学院的学术先行者陈国生教授;最后还要感谢管理教研室的同事袁鹏老师、黄飞老师、刘秋英老师、祁德军老师、蒋晓林老师、肖晓峰老师、张桂华老师、王长富老师、唐跃文老师、范文峰老师、陈杰老师、陈晓亮老师、罗白璐老师、唐婧老师、陆利军老师、廖珊老师、刘锦志老师等。

谨以本书作为我们近几年课堂教学和教研教改工作的一个阶段性总结,同时也作为以后继续研究的一个起点。

本书所有编者

2015 年 12 月于湖南工学院